THE ARTIST'S PATH IN 500 WALKS

Thunder Bay Press
An imprint of Printers Row Publishing Group
9717 Pacific Heights Blvd, San Diego, CA 92121
www.thunderbaybooks.com • mail@thunderbaybooks.com

Printers Row Publishing Group is a division of Readerlink Distribution Services, LLC. Thunder Bay Press is a registered trademark of Readerlink Distribution Services, LLC.

Correspondence regarding the content of this book should be sent to Thunder Bay Press, Editorial Department, at the above address. Author, illustration, and rights inquiries should be addressed to The Bright Press at the address below.

This book was conceived, designed, and produced by
The Bright Press, an imprint of The Quarto Group
Ovest House, 58 West Street, Brighton, BN1 2RA, UK.
www.quartoknows.com

Thunder Bay Press
Publisher: Peter Norton
Associate Publisher: Ana Parker
Acquisitions Editor: Kathryn Chipinka Dalby
Editor: Angela Garcia

The Bright Press
Editor: Kath Stathers
Senior Editor: Caroline Elliker
Managing Editor: Jacqui Sayers
Editorial Director: Isheeta Mustafi
Editorial Assistant: Chloe Porter
Designer: Tony Seddon
Illustrator: La Shuks
Cover Illustration: Lynn Hatzius
Picture Researcher: Susannah Jayes
Art Director: Katherine Radcliffe
Publisher: James Evans

Library of Congress Control Number: 2020933073
ISBN: 978-1-64517-245-1

Printed in Malaysia

25 24 23 22 21   2 3 4 5 6

THE ARTIST'S PATH IN
500
WALKS

Follow the
inspired footsteps of
William Shakespeare,
Frida Kahlo,
Otis Redding,
and more

EDITED BY
KATH STATHERS

THUNDER BAY
P · R · E · S · S

San Diego, California

CONTENTS

INTRODUCTION

Walking can be both a pleasure and a necessity. We can walk for no reason other than to clear our minds and enjoy the surroundings, or we can walk to the local shop because we need a pint of milk. Yet every journey can be an inspiration.

For every jaw-dropping view that has inspired the composition of a masterpiece, there is also the smaller, everyday joy in the overheard conversation, or the peculiarity of a street name.

This book celebrates many different types of walks, from epic pilgrimages across several countries, to small meanders around a particular neighborhood. Each, though, is inspired in some way by a writer, artist, or musician.

In some cases this means walking in the places that inspired great works—such as in the Mourne Mountains in northern Ireland where C. S. Lewis found his Narnia, and where you can see the very stone that Aslan's stone table was based on; while for others, it can mean discovering the place where your hero or heroine lived, the hotel where they met their lover, and the café they sat in while they wrote their novel, as with Anaïs Nin in her bohemian corner of Paris.

The walks are long and short, rural and urban, known trails and those created especially for this book.

One of my favorites is in Washington State, in the U.S.A., a stunning trek in the North Cascades National Park from Ross Lake up to Desolation Peak. It is inspired by Jack Kerouac who took a job as a fire ranger on the mountain because he wanted to escape the frenetic hedonism of his life and thought it might feed into his writing. In retracing his steps, we know we are in the same place where Kerouac was, experiencing the same views; we can see the hut he lived in; we can breathe the same air. For many of us, these surroundings would be enlightening and uplifting. Kerouac, though, found it futile and dull. The fact that he hated it, tells us as much about him as had he loved it—probably more.

The real joy in working on this book has been discovering the stories, such as this one, behind the inspirational figures. For example, Ernest Hemingway is deeply linked to Key West, Florida, which he loved, but he initially only spent time in the town because of a late delivery of a car that meant he was stranded there for longer than he intended. Or Dorothy Wordsworth, who wrote a beautiful letter about climbing Scafell Pike, in England, but her words were published by her brother, the poet William Wordsworth, with no acknowledgement that he hadn't made the climb and written the descriptions himself. She only became known as a talented writer and poet after her death.

The stories behind the walks bring us closer to the personalities just as the walks themselves do. When we consciously follow in another's footsteps, hunt out the views they painted, and visit the houses they lived in, we do so with them in our thoughts—and in doing so, we might hope to share a small window into their minds.

Walking and discovering are two of life's great pleasures. It has been inspirational to bring them together in this book with a surrounding cast of the greats from the world of art, music, and literature.

There are walks that you might turn to if you're visiting an area, and walks that you might travel the world to make. Even without taking a single step, there are some that might inspire a walk of the mind, as you discover writers, artists, and musicians in here whose work you are driven to seek out.

Inspiration comes in many forms. I hope you find some within the pages of this book.

HOW TO USE THIS BOOK

This book is organized by areas of the world, and within each chapter you will find entries organized under individual countries—or in the case of North and Central America by state, province, and territory. The entries are also color coded, as shown below, to indicate with which area of the arts they are closely associated. This will allow you to select walks based on the kind of experience that suits your interests.

▮ LITERATURE

▮ ART

▮ MUSIC

NORTH AND CENTRAL AMERICA

Put yourself in an Albert Bierstadt painting in the Rocky Mountains, trace the walks of Anne of Green Gables on Prince Edward Island, and find Frida Kahlo's inspiration in Mexico City, in this most diverse of continents.

1

EXPLORE THE OLD GROWTH FORESTS OF EMILY CARR'S VANCOUVER ISLAND

The West Coast Trail, Vancouver Island, Canada

Walk with: Emily Carr (1871–1945)

Route: Bamfield to Port Renfrew

Length: 47 miles

Essential viewing: *Forest, British Columbia* (1931–1932)

At the turn of the twentieth century a single woman traveling to remote Pacific Northwest outposts to paint totems and trees was considered, at best, unorthodox, but Emily Carr loved to defy convention. She studied art in San Francisco, Paris, and London, but always returned to her beloved Vancouver Island: "The underlying spirit, all it stands for, the mood, the vastness, the wildness, the Western breath of go-to-the-devil-if-you-don't-like-it, the eternal big spaceness of it. Oh the West! I'm of it and I love it."

Today, the wilderness of Vancouver Island and its colossal old growth forests are best explored on the remote West Coast Trail, which forges a week-long route through the traditional territories of the Huu-ay-aht, Ditidaht, and Pacheedaht First Nations. Trailheads can be accessed at Pachena Beach (near Bamfield), Gordon River (near Port Renfrew), or at Nitinaht Narrows at the mouth of Nitinaht Lake, the midway point that has to be crossed by boat—this is the place to join the trail if you don't want to walk the full six to eight days.

In her journals, Carr writes of a dream she had of a typical Vancouver Island landscape: "The beach is sandy and covered with drift-wood, and all the steep bank above is covered with arbutus trees, monstrous ones with orange-scarlet boles twisting grandly in a regular, beautiful direction that sings, slow powerful twists all turning together, shifting angle and turning again." As you can see, she also painted with words.

ABOVE: The Emily Carr statue in Victoria, Vancouver Island.

RIGHT: Tsusiat Falls on the West Coast Trail falls onto the wild kind of beach that Carr so loved.

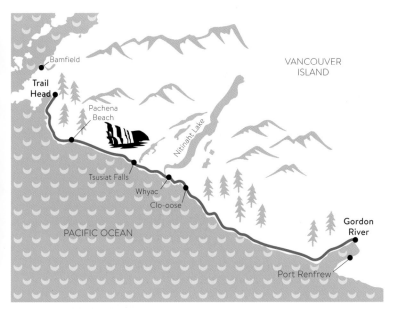

2

ALONG THE NOOTKA TRAIL
Nootka Island, Canada

The thirty-five-mile-long Nootka Trail meanders along the isolated west coastline of Nootka Island from Louie Bay to Yuquot (Friendly Cove) where, in 1929, Emily Carr was inspired to paint *Church at Yuquot Village* (originally known as *Indian Church*). The island is the territory of Mowachaht/Muchalaht First Nation and the white church building that stands today is now a cultural center and museum.

3

JOIN DOUGLAS COUPLAND IN THE HOMETOWN HE LOVES

Coal Harbour Seawall, Vancouver, Canada

Walk with: Douglas Coupland (1961–)

Route: Coal Harbour seawall walk

Length: 3.5 miles

Essential reading: *City of Glass* (2000)

RIGHT: A walk along the seawall in Vancouver offers the perfect way to explore the city.

The man who wrote *Generation X* (1991), and added words like "McJob" to the Western vernacular, grew up in Vancouver but "spent his twenties scouring the globe thinking there had to be a better city out there, until it dawned on [him] that Vancouver is the best one going." *City of Glass* is Coupland's literary love letter to Vancouver.

On the water's edge of Burrard Inlet, Coal Harbour is a downtown neighborhood that epitomizes the laidback city of Vancouver. Skyscrapers dominate the skyline. The Coal Harbour seawall walk is a good place for a first-time visitor to start their explorations—the 3.5-mile loop begins and ends on Canada Place, once heavily industrialized, but now the hub of economic and tourist activity in Vancouver. The trail starts out heading west toward Jack Poole Plaza and the Canada Convention Centre, where Coupland's 2009 pixel art sculpture *Digital Orca* is installed. Continue along the waterfront—with its superb marina, Stanley Park, and North Shore views—before turning inland at Denman Street and left at the commercial thoroughfare of Robson Street. Turn left once again at Burrard Street, dominated by the 62 story-high Shangri-La building and with historic buildings including the Art Deco Marine Building, Gothic Revival Christ Church Cathedral, and the resplendent Hotel Vancouver.

For another Coupland insight into Vancouver, continue along the seawall as it traces Stanley Park, until you reach Lions Gate Bridge. Coupland calls this soaring bridge across Burrard Inlet "a thing of delicate beauty" in the book's extended essay, which was originally published in *Vancouver Magazine* under the title "This Bridge is Ours."

VANCOUVER'S DARKER SIDE
Vancouver, Canada

Alice Munro's (1931–)
Vancouver isn't always
immediately recognizable.
The short stories she wrote
there were often bleak
reflections of her own
dissatisfaction with her life
in the city. But real-life
locations pepper the Nobel
Prize-winning writer's short
stories. From Kitsilano
Beach, on a street of "high
wooden houses crammed
with people living tight,"
Munro moved first to North
Vancouver, then to the
Dundarave neighborhood of
West Vancouver. Following a
similar route across the city
passes significant spots from
both the writer's personal
history and her fiction.

HAIDA IN THE CITY
Stanley Park, Vancouver, Canada

Stanley Park, the green lungs
of Vancouver, is home to
several artworks by Bill Reid
(1920–1998), son of an
American father and Haida
mother. In the mid-1960s,
Reid carved a replica of a
Haida mortuary pole (see
p. 16) that was originally
raised in Skedans in
Haida Gwaii—today, this
monumental totem pole
stands among eight others
at Brockton Point, in the
east of Stanley Park. A short
loop of this eastern section
of the park also takes in
Reid's eighteen-feet bronze
Killer Whale sculpture outside
the Vancouver Aquarium.

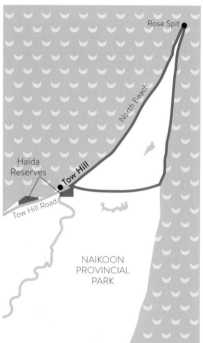

6

LET BILL REID LEAD YOU TO THE BEACH OF THE HAIDA CREATION LEGEND

Haida Gwaii, Canada

Walk with: Bill Reid
(1920–1998)

Route: Tow Hill Trail

Length: 1.8 miles

Essential viewing: *Raven and the First Men* sculpture (1980)

TOP LEFT: Bill Reid's totem poles brought Haida First Nation art to a wider audience.

LEFT: North Beach in Naikoon Provincial Park.

Artist Bill Reid is credited with bringing Northwest Coast art to the mainstream in Canada. It wasn't until his twenties, and a visit to Haida Gwaii, that Reid began to explore his maternal First Nations cultural heritage.

Haida Gwaii is a remote Pacific Northwest archipelago reached by an eight-hour ferry ride from Prince Rupert, or a propeller plane from Vancouver, and the traditional territory of the Haida First Nation. The isolation of these islands has helped the wildlife thrive—it's known as the Canadian Galapagos, and native species include black bears, river otters, horned puffins, and bald eagles. Orcas are often spotted in the Juan Perez Sound. Haida myths and legends are bound together with the animals, birds, and sea creatures of the archipelago, and to the Haida, the raven is both creator and trickster.

One of Reid's greatest achievements is his *Raven and the First Men* yellow cedar sculpture, on display at Vancouver's Museum of Anthropology at the University of British Columbia. The Haida story goes that after a great flood, the Raven found a giant clamshell on a beach, from where he coaxed out the first humans. North Beach, on the northern border of Haida Gwaii's Naikoon Provincial Park, is said to be the setting for the creation myth, and this wild beach—with its volcanic bedrock and pounding surf—is surely the stuff of legend. An unbeatable view of North Beach stretches out beneath 360 feet-high basalt-black Tow Hill, the summit of which is accessed by a short boardwalk trail through coastal forest.

A MEANDER THROUGH CAROL SHIELDS' "STONE CITY"

GABRIELLE ROY IN WINNIPEG

Winnipeg, Manitoba, Canada

Pulitzer Prize-winning author Carol Shields (1935–2003) spent much of her life in Winnipeg, and this "stone city rising up out of our soft prairie loam" is a prominent setting for several of her books. This eight-mile walk starts at the neoclassical Manitoba Legislative Building, which features in *The Stone Diaries* (1993). It then crosses the Assiniboine River to Osborne Village, a neighborhood that pops up in *The Republic of Love* (1992). The trail winds south to the University of Manitoba, where Shields taught, and finishes in King's Park at the Carol Shields Memorial Labyrinth, a tribute to the author and one of the recurring themes in her work.

Winnipeg, Manitoba, Canada

Gabrielle Roy (1909–1983) was one of Canada's leading Francophone writers and thinkers. The back of a Canadian $20 has her quote: "Could we ever know each other in the slightest without the arts?" Her hometown of Winnipeg is deeply proud of the author whose works include *The Tin Flute* (1945) and *Street of Riches* (1955). The latter short story collection features Roy's childhood home, 375 Rue Deschambault, and you can wander past the old frame house as part of an official Gabrielle Roy Route, which is 1.6 miles long. Head through the east quarter of St. Boniface and then along the Seine River Greenway, which is brimming with plant and bird life, and you can feel why Roy treasured her childhood growing up here—and wrote so emotively about it.

ABOVE: Winnipeg's charming Assiniboine River.

RIGHT: The surreal sight of the city behind Sunnyside "Echo" Beach in Toronto.

9
DISCOVER ECHO BEACH SOME DAY

Lake Ontario, Toronto, Canada

"Echo Beach" (1979) was the third song that Mark Gane, guitarist in Martha and the Muffins, ever wrote. Although the song is supposed to be a symbol of perfection and not a real place, the inspiration was Sunnyside Beach on the shore of Lake Ontario in Toronto. "The lake and beach could have been in the middle of nowhere," said Gane, "while the city behind became a surrealistic sight." To share Gane's vision, take a 1.25-mile walk starting from the Art Deco Palais Royale and head west along the boardwalk, passing the angular Freedom for Hungary monument and on to the 1990s' Humber Bay Arch Bridge.

10
EXPLORE MUNRO COUNTY

Huron County, Ontario, Canada

"I am intoxicated by this particular landscape," Alice Munro (1931–) said of Huron County, her home in southwestern Ontario. So deep is the writer's connection with the county of her birth, where she returned after ending her first marriage and leaving Vancouver, that it is often called Munro County. Hike the Maitland Valley trails for a glimpse of Munro County at its finest, and for the towns and landscapes that the writer treasured so dearly. Munro's birthplace, Wingham, is recognizable as the inspiration for many of her fictional small towns.

11
HOME OF THE HOCKEY SWEATER

Sainte Justine, Canada

French-Canadian author Roch Carrier (1937–) has dabbled in politics and been the National Librarian of Canada. However, he is first and foremost a writer, most notably of short stories. His most famous of these is *The Hockey Sweater* (1979)—the tale of Carrier's humiliation as a boy, when his mother made him wear the jersey of a rival team to a hockey game. Set in his hometown of Sainte Justine, the sports center where Carrier suffered his shame, still stands at 106 Rue Kirouac. From there, walk in to the center of the village, which becomes "Bralington" in many of his novels, containing, as Carrier once said, "all those forces which were in the French Canadian."

12
MAN OF STEEL

Cape Breton, Nova Scotia, Canada

Cape Breton is one of Canada's favorite hiking destinations, and part-time home of one of America's greatest sculptors, Richard Serra (1938–). Serra's brutalist, minimalist works have delighted and caused controversy in equal measure—while selling for millions of dollars—and visitors to the rough and rugged areas overlooking the Northumberland Strait, where he lives, will soon understand his inspiration. There are many great walks in the area—the most famous and evocative is probably the Skyline Trail, a six-mile loop with spectacular views over the west coast. Start at the Highlands National Park—it's a well-marked and popular route.

13
LEONARD COHEN'S MONTREAL

Montreal, Canada

As a poet and songwriter, Leonard Cohen (1934–2016) was beloved around the world, but his heart was always in Montreal—as were his roots. Cohen worked at his grandfather's clothing factory in the Sommer Building, on Mayor Street, while studying—and becoming a poet—at nearby McGill University. A walk from the university to Cohen's home will take you past The Main Deli, at 3864 Saint-Laurent Boulevard, which Cohen described as a great place to eat "because it's open all night." Continuing along this road is another Cohen haunt of Moishes Steakhouse (3961 Saint-Laurent Boulevard) and a huge mural of the great man (Cooper Building, 3981 Saint-Laurent Boulevard) painted by Kevin Ledo. Cohen lived farther up the boulevard at 28 Rue Vallières.

14
RIOPELLE'S NATURE

Île-aux-Oies, Canada

One of Canada's greatest artists, Jean-Paul Riopelle (1923–2002) lived on the Île-aux-Oies between the mid 1970s and his death in 2002. He was wildly inspired by the Pointe aux Pins area of the island, which is around 50 miles east of Quebec City—an exceptional forest ecosystem teeming with rare wetland species. To recognize his cultural contribution to the area, the reserve, acquired by the Nature Conservancy of Canada in 2007, was named in his honor. A circular, 1.5-mile, easy-to-follow trail through the woodlands has been created for walkers. Start on the escarpment trail and visit the old cabin on the 300-year-old maple sugar stand before returning to your starting point.

LEFT: Look out for the sky-high mural of Leonard Cohen in Montreal.

15

WALK THROUGH THE LANDSCAPES OF L. M. MONTGOMERY

Prince Edward Island, Canada

Walk with: L. M. Montgomery (1874–1942)

Route: Balsam Hollow Trail

Length: 1 mile

Essential reading: *Anne of Green Gables* (1908)

ABOVE: L. M. Montgomery.

TOP RIGHT: The house which became Green Gables.

RIGHT: It's possible to wander down Lover's Lane and into the Haunted Woods of "Avonlea."

While Anne Shirley takes center stage in the titles of L. M. Montgomery's *Anne of Green Gables* books, the novels are as much about the location in which they're set as they are the eponymous heroine. Barely a page goes by without some luscious description of the natural world and Anne's delight in it. When she first wakes up at Green Gables in the village of Avonlea (Cavendish on Prince Edward Island in real life), Montgomery writes of "Anne's beauty-loving eyes… taking everything greedily in."

Although Montgomery always claimed that the books weren't based on anyone she knew, it is difficult not to draw parallels between the author herself and the character of Anne. Montgomery grew up on Prince Edward Island, raised by her grandparents after her mother's death.

Montgomery suffered from depression and it was the beauty she saw around her, and finding the right words to write about it, that helped her keep the dark days at bay. Through Anne, Montgomery often reveals the joy she found in nature: "I can hear the brook laughing all the way up here. Have you ever noticed what cheerful things brooks are? They're always laughing."

The house which Montgomery based Green Gables on (in reality the home of two of her elderly cousins) is now a heritage center with two well-marked trails in its grounds. Both are about one mile long. One leads you into the Haunted Woods of the book and along to Montgomery's grave, and the other goes down Lover's Lane and across that cheerful brook and into woodlands.

The
Old Lane

As I walked up it I would
see the kitchen light shining
through the trees. I would
pass under the birches...
and then around the curve,
The old house would be
before me.

L.M.M.

16

AT HOME WITH
PAUL THEROUX

Kaena Point, Hawaii, U.S.A.

The westernmost point of Oahu is a bewitching lava shoreline. It's said in Hawaiian mythology that this is where the ancient ancestors jumped into the spirit world, and with remarkable views of the Pacific, you can see why it was deemed a special place. You can only get to it by walking—a trailhead runs from the north side, or, from the south, start at the end of Farrington Highway, which takes in Yokohama beach. Travel writer Paul Theroux (1941–)—who has been almost everywhere—lives in Oahu, and can often be seen paddling his kayak. He calls it, "a paradise pinned like a bouquet to the middle of the Pacific, fragrant, sniffable and easy of access."

17

REFLECT ON THE LIFE AND
LYRICS OF KURT COBAIN

Aberdeen, Washington, U.S.A.

"Underneath the bridge; The tarp has sprung a leak; And the animals I've trapped; Have all become my pets." The bridge that vocalist and guitarist Kurt Cobain (1967–1994) is referring to in "Something in the Way," from Nirvana's 1991 album *Nevermind*, is Young Street Bridge that spans the Wishkah River in Cobain's native town of Aberdeen, Washington State. It won't take long to walk around the tiny Kurt Cobain Memorial Park next to the bridge, where there is a thirteen feet-tall statue of the rock star's guitar and a shrine of Nirvana-related graffiti.

18

JOHN LUTHER
ADAMS' ALASKA

College, Alaska, U.S.A.

John Luther Adams (1953–) has come a long way from his time as a teenage drummer in Mississippi rock bands. Composing for anything from a solo harp to a full orchestra, he has won a Grammy and a Pulitzer Prize over a 45-year career. For much of that (1978–2014) he lived in Alaska: "I took the passion I felt for Alaska together with my hopes for changing the world, and put them into my art." One such piece is *The Place Where You Go To Listen*, a bespoke sound-and-light installation driven by the realtime positions of the sun and moon, seismic activity, and the aurora. It's at the University of Alaska's Museum of the North, just north of which are several trails ranging from half a mile to ten miles.

LEFT: Hawaii: "A paradise pinned like a bouquet to the middle of the Pacific."

19

BE INSPIRED BY KEROUAC'S DESOLATION PEAK HIDEAWAY

Washington, U.S.A.

Walk with: Jack Kerouac, American writer (1922–1969)

Route: Desolation Trailhead, Ross Lake to Desolation Peak

Length: 4.5 miles one way

Essential reading: *Desolation Angels* (1965)

RIGHT: The view from Desolation Peak where Kerouac found futility and boredom.

"I needed solitude... I just wanted to lie in the grass and look at the clouds." In the summer of 1956, Jack Kerouac decided to take some time out. The writer, then aged 34, was struggling to find a publisher for the novel he'd been working on since the 1940s, *On The Road*. (The Beat classic was finally published the following year, 1957.) His Buddhist poet friend, Gary Snyder, had introduced him to hiking and the mountains; Kerouac hoped a few months spent removed from other people and intoxicating substances might clear his head, help his muse, and reveal existential truths.

So Kerouac hitchhiked from San Francisco into the North Cascades Mountains, those "twisted rock and snow-covered immensities, enough to make you gulp." He took the boat across Ross Lake and, with a mule, a ranger, and $45 worth of groceries, he ascended Desolation Peak, where he spent sixty-three days as a U.S. Forest Service fire lookout, holed up in a one-room cabin.

It was a semisuccessful self-exile. Kerouac wrote little while here, only a few poems and journal entries. Rather than finding enlightenment in the wilderness, he found futility and boredom. But the experience eventually inspired large parts of later works, written in his spontaneous, jazz-like style: *Desolation Angels*, *The Dharma Bums* (1958), and *Lonesome Traveler* (1960).

Today, many Kerouac devotees make a pilgrimage up the peak. From the trailhead (three hours' drive from Seattle), it's a long hike around, or short boat trip across, Ross Lake to the mountain's base. The path up is steep, leaving the lakeside to climb into cool forests and out into open wildflower meadows to the stark, exposed summit. And there is the lonely cabin, where Kerouac didn't quite find the fantasy of freedom he was seeking, but found something nonetheless: "Farewell, Desolation, thou hast seen me well."

Desolation Peak

Ross Lake

NORTH CASCADES NATIONAL PARK

Ross Lake Cabins

Route 20

20

RECREATE ARMISTEAD MAUPIN'S
TALES OF SAN FRANCISCO

San Francisco, California, U.S.A.

Walk with: Armistead Maupin, writer (1944–)

Route: Hyde Street to Coolbrith Park

Length: 1 mile, with considerable hills

Essential reading: *Tales of the City* (1978–2014)

LEFT: Maupin chose San Francisco's charming Macondray Lane as the basis for the books' Barbary Lane.

Armistead Jones Maupin, Jr. came from grand old East Coast stock: his great-great-grandfather was a Congressman and a Civil War general, and his father founded one of North Carolina's largest law firms. Maupin began his adulthood as a Nixonian, virginal Vietnam volunteer, but rose to prominence in a very different way.

Moving to San Francisco and embracing his homosexuality, Maupin wrote a warm, witty serial called *Tales Of The City*. The stories introduced a rainbow of very San Franciscan personalities to a wide public.

The *Tales* begin at the Buena Vista bar (2765 Hyde St), where Mary Ann Singleton decides to move to the city. Eight blocks south of the Buena Vista—and so around 600 vertical feet up and over Russian Hill (if the weather is harsh, cable cars are a tempting alternative)—is the corner of Hyde and Union Streets, around which cluster several *Tales* locations: Zarzuela restaurant (aka Marcel et Henri, 2000 Hyde St), Swensen's Ice Cream (1999 Hyde), Searchlight Market (1964 Hyde), and the former Green Plant Store (1898 Hyde).

Two blocks east—past Maupin's old rooftop "pentshack" apartment at 1138½ Union, and a short but steep half-block up Jones St—is the arboreal, pedestrian-only Macondray Lane. This was the inspiration for 28 Barbary Lane, where the *Tales*' transgender matriarch Anna Madrigal presides over a "logical family" of misfit tenants. Macondray Lane emerges 300 feet later onto the wooden steps, used in the *Tales* miniseries, down to Taylor St.

As Maupin wrote, "The worst of times in San Francisco was still better than the best of times anywhere else. There was beauty here and conspicuous bravery."

21
FRIDA KAHLO'S
SAN FRANCISCO

San Francisco, U.S.A.

From November 1930 to June 1931, Mexican artist Frida Kahlo (1907–1954) lived in San Francisco with her husband, the artist Diego Rivera. Dressed in traditional Mexican costume, Kahlo explored the city streets. "The city and bay are overwhelming…What is especially fantastic is Chinatown…" She painted *Frida and Diego Rivera* while here and held the first public exhibition of her work. The couple stayed with friends at 716 Montgomery Street, the artistic hub of the city. From here, head to China Town to retrace Kahlo's walks, and then on to Mission Street for the Mexican Museum, and 151 Third Street for the San Francisco Museum of Modern Art, which contains works by Kahlo and Rivera.

22
ANDY GOLDSWORTHY'S
ART OUT OF NATURE

Presidio, San Francisco, U.S.A.

The artwork of Andy Goldsworthy (1956–) captures the nature of a place and imbues it with a sense of time. Here he explores trees' relationship with the built environment around Presidio in San Francisco. A 2.7-mile loop takes in three of his artworks. Start at *Tree Fall*—a tree covered in clay—in the Powder Magazine building (open on the weekends), then head into the woods to *Spire*, constructed from the trunks of thirty-seven Monterey cypress trees formed to resemble a church tower, and on to the majestic *Wood Line* of eucalyptus logs laid in a zigzag through a eucalyptus grove, then loop back to where you started.

23
JACK KEROUAC'S
CITY STREETS

San Francisco, U.S.A.

Jack Kerouac (1922–1969) was born in Massachusetts, and died in Florida, but the author of *On The Road* (1957), is strongly associated with what that book described as "the fabulous white city of San Francisco on her eleven mystic hills with the blue Pacific and its advancing wall of potato-patch fog beyond, and smoke and goldenness of the late afternoon of time." Begin this Kerouac route at the alley named after him off Columbus Avenue. Kerouac, who wrote "everything belongs to me because I am poor," never owned a place in the city but stayed in the attic of Neal and Carolyn Cassady's house on 29 Russell Street. Walking nearby one night, he stumbled upon the filming of the movie *Sudden Fear* at 1201 Greenwich Street and promptly included the account in the book.

24
A GOLDEN GATE
JAUNT WITH JANIS

San Francisco, U.S.A.

The raw blues of Janis Joplin's (1943–1970) voice expressed her untameable spirit. At twenty, she left Texas for San Francisco and spent much of her remaining seven years there. As she rose to fame during the 1967 Summer Of Love, she shared a one-bedroom apartment at 122 Lyon St, right by the Golden Gate Park's Panhandle. In the Golden Gate Park, the counterculture still congregates on Hippie Hill. At the hill's edge is the bent-trunked Janis Joplin tree, under which she sat and played her acoustic guitar and dreamed of a better time: "I knew I had a good voice and I could always get a couple of beers off of it. All of a sudden someone threw me in this rock 'n' roll band…"

RIGHT: Andy Goldsworthy's *Wood Line.*

25

SOAK UP REALITY IN JOHN STEINBECK'S MONTEREY

Monterey, California, U.S.A.

Walk with: John Steinbeck (1902–1968)

Route: Monterey Bay Coastal Trail

Length: 18 miles

Essential reading: *Cannery Row* (1945)

ABOVE: John Steinbeck, who set his 1945-novel *Cannery Row* in California's Monterey.

RIGHT: The Monterey beachfront.

The capital of Alta California under Spain and Mexico, Monterey was the setting for John Steinbeck's *Cannery Row*, set around the city's sardine-tinning factories during the Depression. The novel's opening sentence displays Steinbeck's ambivalent admiration: "Cannery Row in Monterey in California is a poem, a stink, a grating noise, a quality of light, a tone, a habit, a nostalgia, a dream." Later in life, he revisited and revised his opinion: "They fish for tourists now, not pilchards. And that species they are not likely to wipe out."

Frequently hugging the waterside, this walk uses the Monterey Bay Coastal Trail, most of which follows the route of the old Southern Pacific Railway tracks that serviced Cannery Row during the sardine era. The walk starts at Municipal Beach and passes the adjacent Fisherman's Wharf—the seas are still farmed, although not on the previous scale when Monterey's twenty-four canneries processed a billion sardines per year—before snaking past Custom House, where, in 1846, Commodore John D. Sloat claimed California for the U.S.A.

After Sister City Park, the trail hits Cannery Row by San Carlos Beach Park. The area has now transformed from a dangerous industrial zone to an idealized heritage park. Note the author perched atop the seafront Cannery Row Monument, on Steinbeck Plaza.

Farther along, before the Lovers Point Mural, 11th Street runs inland: Steinbeck lived with his first wife at number 147, a red cottage now privately owned; the cross street is Doc Ricketts Row, named after a Cannery character.

JOHN STEINBECK'S BIRTHPLACE

Salinas, California, U.S.A.

The Grapes Of Wrath (1939) author, John Steinbeck, had a complicated relationship with his central Californian birthplace, Salinas, which he described as "spreading like crabgrass toward the foothills." When the local newspaper celebrated him in 1963, he wrote to say: "No town celebrates a writer before he's dead." The city certainly celebrates him now. Steinbeck's name and image are everywhere. Start your walk at the mural at 123 W. Alisal Street, behind the John Steinbeck Library (350 Lincoln Avenue). Make your way from here to the National Steinbeck Center, which is just a couple of blocks from the author's childhood home at 132 Central Avenue.

27

CAPTURE THE MAJESTY
OF YOSEMITE

Yosemite National Park, California, U.S.A.

Walk with: Ansel Adams
(1902–1984)

Route: North Dome Trail,
Yosemite National Park

Length: 10.4 miles

Essential viewing: *Yosemite
and the High Sierra* (1994)

RIGHT: The stunning Yosemite
National Park.

There are few artists as closely linked to one particular place as Ansel Adams is to Yosemite National Park. The spectacular landscape captured Adams' heart when he was just fourteen years old, exploring the area with his Box Brownie, a gift from his parents.

As an only child who was taught at home, Adams led a fairly solitary existence and spent his time taking long walks in the wild areas around the Golden Gate, developing a love of nature. When this passion took him to Yosemite, it changed his life.

Originally he was pursuing a career as a classical pianist, but photography became an ever greater passion. His first pictures were published in 1922, and he became the official photographer for many of the adventurous Sierra Club's month-long hiking expeditions.

It was in 1927, after hiking 4,000 feet uphill through snow to photograph Half Dome, that Adams used filters to create his technique of "visualization"—the ability to see the finished photo as he took it, rather than to create effects in the darkroom.

Adams took hundreds of photos of Half Dome over his lifetime, saying: "It is never the same Half Dome, never the same light or the same mood."

To hike up high above Yosemite and find the views that show its scale, as Adams used to do, start at the Porcupine Creek trailhead off the Tioga Pass and follow the signposts to North Dome. The trail winds through forest, across Porcupine Creek, through a grassy meadow, and along Indian Ridge, before bringing you to the base of North Dome. Climb to the summit for a magnificent view of Yosemite Valley, Half Dome, and El Capitan.

28
RAISE A GLASS TO JACK LONDON

Oakland, California, U.S.A.

Enjoy a stroll on the Oakland waterfront, taking in the sounds and sights that inspired author Jack London's (1876–1918) novels *Call of the Wild* (1903) and *The Sea Wolf* (1904). Oakland is where London studied at the nearby University of California in Berkeley. The tuition fees were supposedly lent to London by John M. Heinold, the owner of the First and Last Chance Saloon on the waterfront, where London met intoxicated sailors and adventurers who later influenced his writing.

29
HUNTER S. THOMPSON'S LAS VEGAS

Las Vegas, Nevada, U.S.A.

"We're looking for the American dream, and we were told it was somewhere in this area," says Dr. Gonzo, the deranged co-protagonist of Hunter S. Thompson's (1937–2005) best-known work, *Fear and Loathing in Las Vegas* (1971). In a wild, drug-and-booze fueled narrative, Gonzo and his colleague, Duke, thunder around Sin City, finding an America that has replaced the peace and idealism of the 1960s with repression and cynicism. Their journey can never really be replicated—but a stagger along the Strip, with a detour into the casino Circus Circus ("what the whole hep world would be doing on Saturday night if the Nazis had won the war") can still provide an idea of what Thompson was getting at.

LEFT: A stagger along the Las Vegas strip is all you need to feel Hunter S. Thompson's inspiration.

30
HUNTER S. THOMPSON'S COLORADO

Woody Creek, Colorado, U.S.A.

For a price, it's now possible to—almost literally—walk in Hunter S. Thompson's (1937–2005) shoes. The Gonzo writer's legendary cabin at Woody Creek, Colorado, (Thompson referred to it as a "fortified compound") is now accessible, thanks to the fact that his widow, Anita, is renting it out. Packed with memorabilia from the writer's crazy adventures, visitors can even sit and write some tales of their own on his I.B.M. typewriter. While there, a walk is a must: follow the trail up to the top of the hill, where Thompson's ashes were fired into the sky from a 153-feet tower, then take a stroll around the compound—guided by Anita herself.

31
CREATE YOUR PERFECT ALBUM-COVER PHOTO

The Joshua Tree National Park, California, U.S.A.

The title of U2's fifth album, released in March 1987, came from the Joshua trees in the California Mojave Desert. It was while taking photos here that photographer Anton Corbijn told lead singer Bono about the trees—twisted desert plants with stretching branches, named by early settlers after the Old Testament prophet, Joshua. The next day, Bono declared that the album should be called *The Joshua Tree* and an iconic destination was born. To see the trees at their best, walk the Hi-View or Cap Rock trails.

32
ROCK 'N' ROLL IN LAUREL CANYON

Los Angeles, California, U.S.A.

Snaking up into the Hollywood Hills behind Sunset Boulevard, Laurel Canyon was (and is) perfectly placed to house the beautiful people. As Joni Mitchell (1943–) said: "Ask anyone in Hollywood where the craziest people live and they'll say Laurel Canyon." The stars would visit the Canyon Country Store at 2108 Laurel Canyon Boulevard to stock up and have jam sessions. Start your walk here before heading next door to 8021 Rothdell Trail, where The Doors' Jim Morrison wrote *Love Street*. Farther along Lauren Canyon Boulevard, Frank Zappa lived in The Log Cabin on the corner with Lookout Mountain—its burned-out ruins are still visible. As for Mitchell, she lived at 8217 Lookout Mountain Avenue: "My dining room looked out over Frank Zappa's duck pond. Once when my mother was visiting, three naked girls were floating around on a raft."

33
MUSIC IN THE MOUNTAINS WITH OLIVIER MESSIAEN

Bryce Canyon, Utah, U.S.A.

The enticing scenery of Bryce Canyon National Park, Utah, makes it a regular destination for hikers. A twisting trail of gold and orange awaits. French composer Olivier Messiaen (1908–1992) was so inspired by the birds and colors he saw in Bryce Canyon that he wrote *Des Canyons aux Étoiles* (*From the Canyons to the Stars*), a twelve-movement orchestral work dreamed up thanks to Messiaen's sound-color synesthesia. For the most impactful walk, full of spectacular formations and viewpoints, follow The Queen's Garden Loop.

EXPLORE KATHARINE LEE BATES' GREAT AMERICAN LANDSCAPE

Scale Pikes Peak, Colorado Rocky Mountains, U.S.A.

Walk with: Katharine Lee Bates (1859–1929)

Route: Barr Trail from Manitou Springs

Length: 26 miles (there and back)

Essential listening: "America the Beautiful," performed by Ray Charles

RIGHT: Climb to the top of Pikes Peak, for the view which inspired "America the Beautiful."

Scholar, poet, and writer Katharine Lee Bates wrote her rousing poem "America the Beautiful" after scaling the 14,115-feet summit of Pikes Peak, in Colorado's Rocky Mountains. She wrote:

O beautiful for spacious skies,
For amber waves of grain,
For purple mountain majesties
Above the fruited plain!
America! America!

First published on July 4, 1895, her words were almost immediately set to the tune of various folk songs (including "Auld Lang Syne"), but today it's Samuel A. Ward's melody of "Materna" that people around the world know so well and which has been performed by singers including Ray Charles, Aretha Franklin, Willie Nelson, and Mariah Carey.

In the summer of 1893, Bates reached the summit by way of horse-drawn wagon and the back of a mule, and today shuttles take tourists to the summit on the winding nineteen-mile Pikes Peak Highway. But in the 1900s, local man Fred Barr blazed a walking trail—Barr Trail—and it's still the only way to get to the summit on foot. The popular trail of mostly packed dirt is clearly laid out, but it's a grueling six to ten hours from the trailhead at Manitou Springs to the high-altitude summit.

The red-rock summit, with its big skies and breathtaking views across the Rocky Mountains and the Great Plains, does truly have a feeling of "America the Beautiful." Bates said later that "all the wonder of America seemed to be displayed there."

ROCKY MOUNTAINS

Manitou
Incline

**Manitou
Springs**

Barrs Camp

Pikes Peak Railway Depot

Pikes Peak
Summit

Colorado Springs

35

ROBERT SMITHSON'S SPIRAL JETTY

Great Salt Lake, Box Elder County, Utah, U.S.A.

In 1970, the monumental earthwork Spiral Jetty emerged like a floating, swirling abstract on Utah's Great Salt Lake. Located at Rozel Point, Gunnison Bay, on the lake's northeastern shoreline, American sculptor and artist Robert Smithson's (1938–1973) man-made installation interacted with the pinkish waters of the lake. Smithson used 6,000 tons of local black basalt rock and earth to create a walkway 15 feet wide and 1,500 feet long that curved in a spiral. The lake level varies year by year, so Spiral Jetty may at times be submerged but with the right footwear is always a fun walk.

36

ELMORE LEONARD IN MOTOR CITY

Detroit, Michigan, U.S.A.

Known as the "Dickens of Detroit," Elmore Leonard (1925–2013) put his hometown on the literary map with his crime-fiction portrayals of its characters and their gritty dialogue. About a third of Leonard's published novels are set in the Motor City, where he lived for most of his life and where he was buried in 2013. Spot landmarks from his books on a walk from Fox Theatre on Woodward Avenue, past the famed art deco Guardian Building in the Financial District, before looping northeast up into Greektown and 1300 Beaubien Street, the former police headquarters where Leonard hung out to learn the lingo in the late 1970s.

37

WELCOME TO STEPHEN KING'S OVERLOOK HOTEL

The Stanley Hotel, Colorado, U.S.A.

Spend a night at the hotel that inspired American horror novelist Stephen King (1947–) before undertaking a hike to the Rocky Mountain National Park. The Stanley Hotel, Colorado, was the inspiration for the infamous Overlook Hotel in King's 1977 bestselling novel *The Shining* (and where the TV mini-series was filmed in 1997). King and his wife, Tabitha, spent a night in room 217 while on vacation in 1974, and upon arrival discovered they were the only guests.

38

HIKE JIM HARRISON'S WILD COUNTRY

Patagonia, Arizona, U.S.A.

Patagonia, Arizona—population 880—is as sparsely inhabited as most of Jim Harrison's (1937–2016) literary locations. The writer fell in love with the town in the 1960s, and wintered there every year for the rest of his life. "This feels like the right place," he once quipped to an interviewer. "There's so much wild country, and I have my ideal neighbors. No one." Patagonia is an official Gateway for the Arizona National Scenic Trail, which traverses south to north from the U.S./Mexico border to the northern edge of the state—the perfect place to witness some of the "wild country" up close.

LEFT: Walk on water on Robert Smithson's Spiral Jetty in Utah.

LET LAURA INGALLS WILDER LEAD YOU TO THE *LITTLE HOUSE IN THE BIG WOODS*

Great River Road, Pepin, Wisconsin, U.S.A.

Walk with : Laura Ingalls Wilder (1867–1957)

Route: Pepin to Wayside

Length: 7.5 miles (one way)

Essential Reading: *Little House* series; *Pioneer Girl: The Annotated Autobiography*, ed. Pamela Smith Hill (2014)

ABOVE: Laura Ingalls Wilder, author of the *Little House on the Prairie* books.

RIGHT: A replica of the log cabin where Ingalls Wilder was born and spent her first two years.

Situated on the shores of Lake Pepin, the village of Pepin, Wisconsin, is a good place to begin the search for childhood locations recalled so vividly in Laura Ingalls Wilder's *Little House* book series, the third of which is *Little House on the Prairie* (1935). The village became the official starting point of the Laura Ingalls Wilder Historic Highway in 1996, linking her homes across the Upper Midwest.

About seven miles north from the village, at Wayside, walkers can visit a replica of the Ingalls' log cabin, the "little house." Step inside and go back in time to when Laura was born in 1867, and where she lived for the first two years of her life. The place that began her memoirs is less-wooded now, due to agricultural changes, but it draws like a magnet the many readers of her books, who want to see the exact spot where "Ma" and "Pa" farmed.

In this walk, one replicates "Pa" Ingalls' seven-mile journey to Pepin, a walk that now takes visitors along the County Road, crisscrossing Lost Creek River, from Pepin to Wayside, through agricultural farmlands. Pepin, where "Pa" did business, and the family bought their provisions, is the location of the Laura Ingalls Wilder Museum, where there is a mock-up of a schoolroom and a covered wagon, as well as displays of furniture and objects from the period.

Little House
Wayside Cabin

Route 35

WISCONSIN
MINNESOTA

Lost Creek River

Mississippi River

Chippewa River

Laura Ingalls
Wilder Museum

Pepin

40

INGALLS WILDER'S SOUTH DAKOTA

De Smet, South Dakota, U.S.A.

Laura Ingalls Wilder's childhood was shaped by crop failures, drought, grasshopper plagues, and harsh winters, which caused the family to move many times. By the age of twelve, Wilder had lived in Wisconsin (twice), Missouri, Kansas (on Indian Territory Lands), Minnesota, Iowa, and South Dakota. The family's final move was to the new settlement of De Smet, where the last four *Little House* books take place. There is a replica of the family's first De Smet home, the Surveyor's House. From here, it's a short walk to their later, more permanent home, built by Charles Ingalls in the 1880s, and on past The Loftus Store (opened 1879) at 205 Calumet Avenue SW, which is the shop mentioned in *The Long Winter* (1940). Continue to Silver Lake, the original location of the Surveyor's House.

41

FREE YOUR INNER LANDSCAPE ARTIST WITH ALBERT BIERSTADT

Yosemite National Park, California, U.S.A.

After his first trip to the American West in 1859, German-American painter Albert Bierstadt (1830–1902) produced a sequence of landscape paintings based on Yosemite Valley in central California. The valley is filled with waterfalls, glacier points, and large lakes, which can all be accessed via various hikes. Bierstadt spent several weeks doing *en plein air* studies of the natural landscape as part of his transcontinental journey by train, stagecoach, and horseback.

42

JOIN ALBERT BIERSTADT IN THE AMERICAN WEST

Lander's Peak, The Rocky Mountains, U.S.A.

From the same journey to Western America, Bierstadt sketched the early forms for his later oil painting *The Rocky Mountains, Lander's Peak*. Traveling alongside explorer Frederick W. Lander and the Honey Road Survey Party, Bierstadt was captivated by the serene nature of the landscape. Following the death of General Lander during the Civil War in 1862, Bierstadt named the peak Lander's Peak. Hike in Estes Park for many similarly stunning Bierstadt views.

RIGHT: The landscape of Estes Park in the Rocky Mountains inspired Albert Bierstadt.

43

GEORGIA O'KEEFFE IN NEW MEXICO

Abiquiú, New Mexico, U.S.A.

Walk with: Georgia O'Keeffe (1887–1986)

Route: To Cerro Pedernal and back

Length: 8 miles

Essential viewing: *My Front Yard, Summer* (1941); *Ranchos Church* (1930)

American artist Georgia O'Keeffe's life spanned nearly a century. Her remarkable still-life paintings mix emotional sensitivity with sensual connotation. O'Keeffe's landscape paintings explored many locations, from the skyscrapers in New York, to her summer home in the Adirondack Mountains, to the arid landscapes of New Mexico, and tropical forests of Hawaii.

From 1929, O'Keeffe chose to spend most of her summers in New Mexico. The panoramic scenery and local architecture, such as the rocky forms of Ranchos Church at Taos, near Santa Fe, became the focus of her work. In 1934, she stayed at Ghost Ranch, a 21,000-acre ranch near Abiquiú. O'Keeffe rented a room, creating a studio there, and eventually buying her own property.

From the junction of FR100 and FR160, it is possible to hike to Cerro Pedernal, the table-top mountain, which she painted many times, as in *My Front Yard, Summer*. She could see it from her studio at Ghost Ranch and felt a strong empathy with it: "It's my private mountain. It belongs to me. God told me if I painted it enough, I could have it," she said. Her ashes were scattered there.

ABOVE: Georgia O'Keeffe, whose inspirational life lasted almost a century.

RIGHT: O'Keeffe had a strong affection for Cerro Pedernal in New Mexico.

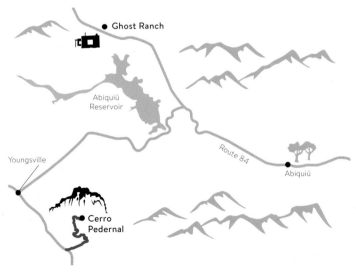

44
O'KEEFFE IN HAWAII
Island of Maui, Hawaii, U.S.A.

From late January until mid-April 1939, Georgia O'Keeffe traveled through the Hawaiian islands on a trip paid for by the Dole Hawaiian Pineapple Company to create two artworks for an advertising campaign. O'Keeffe created over twenty paintings during her stay, of which *Pineapple Bud* and *Crab's Claw Ginger* were used in the 1940 campaign. Walking the coastline from Kahului to the bijou town of Hana in east Maui, take in the spectacular black lava rock landscape captured in O'Keeffe paintings, such as *Black Lava Bridge, Hana Coast, no.1.*

45

LOSE YOURSELF UNDER WILLA CATHER'S ENDLESS SKY

Nebraska, U.S.A.

Possibly America's finest writer about frontier life on the Great Plains, Willa Cather (1873–1947) moved to Nebraska in 1883, when she was just nine years old. In her 1918 novel, *My Antonia*, she wrote: "there was nothing but land: not a country at all, but the materials out of which countries were made." Many of Cather's novels explore the harsh realities immigrant families faced as they forged lives on the broad, flat landscapes of the Nebraska prairie. The Willa Cather Memorial Prairie, located five miles south of Cather's hometown, Red Cloud, is a 610-acre site dedicated to returning the land to its nineteenth century conditions, and features over two miles of hiking trails for those wanting to lose themselves under the vast, seemingly endless skies.

46

VISIT D. H. LAWRENCE'S "OUTSIDE WORLD"

Mabel Dodge Luhan House, Taos, New Mexico, U.S.A.

Mabel Dodge Luhan was a woman of many talents, and irresistible persuasiveness was certainly one of them. In 1918, she built the "Big House" on the outskirts of Taos, and within a few years she had created an artistic salon to which she drew the biggest artists, writers, and musicians of the day. Most famous among her guests, perhaps, was D. H. Lawrence (1885–1930), who she lured to Taos with letters describing it as "like the dawn of the world." Hike the trails around Taos, as Lawrence once did, and witness the New Mexico that had such a profound influence on him that he called it "the greatest experience I ever had from the outside world."

47

PARTY LIKE YOU'RE F. SCOTT FITZGERALD

Saint Paul, Minnesota, U.S.A.

Though he is synonymous with East Coast excess, F. Scott Fitzgerald (1896–1940) spent much of his first twenty-five years in Saint Paul, atop Summit Hill. His novel *The Great Gatsby* (1925) mentions, "a city where the dwellings are still called through the decades by a family's name," but the Fitzgeralds were peripatetic. He was born at 481 Laurel Avenue, and before World War I the family had lived at 499, 509, and 514 Holly Avenue. Two blocks west is the Saint Paul Academy, where Fitzgerald was schooled; around the corner at 593 and 599 Summit Avenue, he wrote his debut novel *This Side of Paradise* (1920). Later, he and his wife, Zelda, liked to party at the University Club while living at the Commodore Hotel, a brief stumble away.

48

HIKE BACK IN TIME WITH LOUISE ERDRICH

Minneapolis, Minnesota, U.S.A.

Louise Erdrich's (1954–) series of novels explore the interrelated lives of families living on an Indian reservation near the fictional town of Argus, North Dakota. Erdrich, herself, is part Chippewa Native American, and while she lives in Minneapolis—and owns a bookstore there—she has also run writing workshops on Turtle Mountain Indian Reservation, her ancestral land. Old Oak Trail, North Dakota's first nationally recognized trail, is a three-mile moderate forest hike through the rolling terrain of the scenic Turtle Mountains.

RIGHT: The Mabel Dodge Luhan house with its views on "the dawn of the world."

REFLECT ON THE LEGACY OF RACHEL CARSON'S *SILENT SPRING*

Rachel Carson Trail, Pennsylvania, U.S.A.

Walk with: Rachel Carson
(1907–1964)

Route: Rachel Carson Trail

Length: 45 miles

Essential reading: *Silent Spring*
(1962)

In 1962, alarmed by the effect chemical pesticide spraying was having on wildlife, Rachel Carson wrote *Silent Spring*. In doing so, she has been credited with kickstarting the environmental movement in the U.S.A., influencing the direction of U.S. policy with everything from the Clean Air Act in 1963, to the establishing of the Environmental Protection Agency in 1970, and was named by *Time* magazine as one of the twenty-five most powerful women of the past century.

Carson knew that people would only protect what they loved, and alongside the scientific evidence, her book is full of the wonder of nature.

In honor of Carson's achievements, in 1972, the American Youth Hostel Association established the Rachel Carson Trail that runs through Allegheny County where Carson grew up. It passes close by her family home (which is open to the public) in the town of Springdale.

As hikers walk this suburban trail now (as day walks, there are no places to stay), through fields and woodlands, past farms and housing developments, they can listen to birdsong or spot a grasshopper and wonder if, without Rachel Carson, they would be walking through a silent spring instead.

ABOVE: Rachel Carson, who had an immeasurable effect on environmental protection.

RIGHT: The Rachel Carson Trail winds through Allegheny County where Carson grew up.

50

CONJURE UP JOHN DENVER'S ALMOST-MYTHICAL WEST VIRGINIA

Appalachian Trail, Jefferson County, West Virginia, U.S.A.

Walk with: John Denver (1943–1997)

Route: Appalachian Trail

Length: 1 mile

Essential listening: "Take Me Home, Country Roads"

TOP RIGHT: The Appalachian Trail ends in Maine.

RIGHT: Looking down at Harpers Ferry from Maryland Heights.

Mention West Virginia to outsiders and they'll probably start singing John Denver's "Take Me Home, Country Roads," with its evocative lyrics mentioning the Blue Ridge Mountains and Shenandoah River. Thing is, those mountains are barely in the state, and the Shenandoah is only in it for ten of its fifty-five miles. Denver wasn't a local, nor were his cowriters, husband-and-wife team Taffy Nivert and Bill Danoff, who had originally written the song about Maryland and considered using Massachusetts in the lyrics. However, the song was quickly adopted locally as well as globally.

If you stick as literally as possible to the lyrics, there is only one part of West Virginia that ticks the boxes for containing both the Blue Ridge Mountains and Shenandoah River, and that's Jefferson County, right at the northeast tip.

This walk starts, rather prosaically, at the parking lot off Shenandoah Street, where it picks up the Appalachian Trail. As the town of Harpers Ferry looms above it to the north (with the Shenandoah's Staircase Rapids often audible to the south), the trail heads east past Jefferson Rock and the ruins of St. John Episcopal Church. Past John Brown's Fort is the confluence of the Potomac and the Shenandoah, and the trail crosses the Potomac via the old railway trestle bridge into Maryland. From here, after a short detour for the view from Maryland Heights, hikers can follow the river east to continue the Appalachian Trail all the way to Maine. Already it has left West Virginia. But perhaps West Virginia is a state of mind, an idealized escape into a rural retreat—the sort that makes for a perfect John Denver song.

51
ROCKY MOUNTAIN SINGALONG

Williams Lake, Colorado, U.S.A.

Singer/songwriter John Denver wrote classic folk rock song "Rocky Mountain High" after a summer camping in his beloved Colorado Rockies. The song—said to be about getting high from nature—has inspired generations to get out into the wilderness at Williams Lake in the Maroon Bells-Snowmass Wilderness Area. The Williams Lake Trail is 3.8 miles long and accessed from the Hell Roaring Trailhead (a 4WD is needed to get there). The summer meteor showers here inspired Denver's famous words: "I've seen it rainin' fire in the sky."

52

SURVIVE THE APOCALYPSE WITH EMILY ST. JOHN MANDEL

Petoskey, Michigan, U.S.A.

"This is my soul and the world unwinding, this is my heart in the still winter air. Finally whispering the same two words over and over: Keep walking. Keep walking. Keep walking." So writes Emily St. John Mandel (1979–) in her post-apocalyptic novel *Station Eleven* (2014), which follows a troupe of nomadic actors in the Great Lakes region following a devastating swine flu pandemic. The town in the book, St. Deborah by the Water, is fictional, but Mandel visited Petoskey during an earlier book tour before choosing the area as the backdrop for her novel. Along the hilly Skyline Trail, southeast of the town, a short (1.5 mile) climb is rewarded at an observation deck with panoramic views.

53

JOHN JAMES AUDUBON'S BIRDLAND PARADISE

Mill Grove, Audubon, Pennsylvania, U.S.A.

John James Audubon (1785–1851) was creator of the ornothological masterpiece *Birds of America* (published 1827–1838), containing 435 life-size illustrations of birds. Audubon was born in the French colony of Saint Domingue (Haiti) but lived on a 284-acre farm, Mill Grove, in Pennsylvania (now the John James Audubon Center). Raised and educated in Nantes, France, he entered the U.S.A. aged eighteen in 1803, to avoid conscription into the Napoleonic wars. Mill Grove now has five miles of nature trails, from which you can spot 175 species of birds.

54

RANDY NEWMAN AND R.E.M. VISIT CUYAHOGA

Cleveland, Ohio, U.S.A.

A week before humankind landed on the moon, Cleveland's Cuyahoga River burned. Industrial pollutants meant this was common, but coverage in *Time* magazine sparked outrage. In 1972, Randy Newman referenced the fire in the song "Burn On," and in 1986, R.E.M.'s "Cuyahoga" combined the theme with the mistreatment of Native Americans. Thankfully, the Cuyahoga ("crooked river" in the Mohawk language) is now much cleaner, and walkers can enjoy the 87-mile Towpath Trail along its route. It starts (or finishes) in downtown Cleveland, before heading upstream toward Akron via the beautiful Cuyahoga Valley National Park.

55

HOLE UP WITH MARTHA GELLHORN

Sun Valley, Idaho, U.S.A.

When Ernest Hemingway (1899–1961) invited esteemed war correspondent and novelist Martha Gellhorn (1908–1998) to rendezvous with him in Sun Valley Resort, Idaho, in 1939, it cemented both the demise of his third marriage and the start of what would become his fourth. Gellhorn and Hemingway became long-stay visitors in Suite 206 of the newly opened Swiss-inspired resort (where Hemingway would write *For Whom The Bell Tolls*, 1940). Visitors today can stay in this celebrity suite, enjoying the same mountain views plus miles of hiking trails.

56
INDUSTRIAL REHABILITATION WITH BILLY JOEL

Allentown, Pennsylvania, U.S.A.

Billy Joel (1949–) accidentally alighted upon Allentown as the setting for his 1982 song about industrial decline in the Rust Belt. He originally wrote the song about Levittown, near his Long Island childhood home, but relocated the story to Pennsylvania. The Hoover-Mason Trestle is a fine way to key into the industrial history. Completed in 1907, it connected the ore yards to the blast furnaces to make the iron and steel that built America's skyscrapers; now it has been repurposed as an elevated park and walkway, in the style of New York's High Line.

57
EARLY FEMINISM WITH KATE CHOPIN

Grand Isle, Louisiana, U.S.A.

Kate Chopin (1850–1904) based her short stories and novels in Louisiana—with her best known being 1899's *The Awakening*, set on the barrier island of Grand Isle. With themes including marital infidelity, the novel was heavily criticized before being rediscovered and reprinted in the 1970s, gaining popularity as an early example of feminist fiction. The Grand Isle of Chopin's day was a popular holiday resort for the well heeled of nearby New Orleans. Today, the long sandy beaches (about which Chopin wrote, "The voice of the sea speaks to the soul.") and thirteen miles of easy shoreline trail can be readily enjoyed as part of the Grand Isle State Park.

LEFT: Sun Valley was home for a while to Martha Gellhorn and Ernest Hemingway.

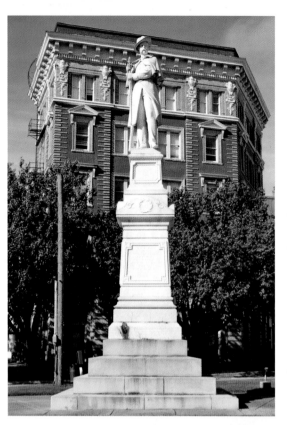

58

TRY A LITTLE TENDERNESS WITH OTIS REDDING: "THE MADMAN FROM MACON"

Macon, Georgia, U.S.A.

Walk with: Otis Redding (1941–1967)

Route: Around Macon

Length: 1 mile

Essential listening: *Otis Blue*; *The Soul Album*

TOP FAR LEFT: An anonymous Confederate soldier overlooks the Otis Redding Foundation and Museum.

TOP LEFT: Otis Redding sits with his guitar by the Ocmulgee River.

LEFT: Inside Macon's Grand Opera House.

Otis Ray Redding, Jr. was born in Dawson, Georgia, but the family soon moved one hundred miles northeast to the much more sizeable Macon, "the Heart of Georgia." It became the soul legend's home, even after making it big: "I own a 400-acre farm in Macon, Georgia. I raise cattle and hogs. I own horses, too. I love horses as much as singing."

And oh, how he loved singing. Otis Redding, Sr. preached in local churches, including the Vineville Baptist Church (2591 Vineville Ave), where young Otis joined the choir and later a gospel quartet. Attending Ballard Hudson Senior High (1070 Anthony Rd), he was a drummer in the school band—and already earning money through his glorious voice, singing gospel songs every Sunday for Macon radio station WIBB.

But the downtown Douglass Theater (355 MLK Blvd) is where Redding's career really started. At the Douglass, Redding regularly entered a teen talent show. "I won fifteen Sunday nights straight," he recalled. "I showed up the sixteenth night, and they wouldn't let me go on any more." (He also met his future wife, Zelma Atwood, there.)

A few blocks behind the theater, down Cherry Street, is Cotton Avenue, and at 330 is the Otis Redding Foundation and Museum. This is where Otis and his partner, Phil Walden, relocated their music promotion business RedWal; it had started a few blocks northwest at 830 Mulberry Street, now the Robert E. Lee Building, but earlier the headquarters of the radio station of Redding's youth, WIBB.

Back down Mulberry Street, past the Grand Opera House, a walk through several streets takes you to the Charles H. Jones Gateway Park. Here, a lifesize bronze statue of a guitar-playing Otis sits by the river (spanned by the Otis Redding Memorial Bridge).

59

JOIN BOB DYLAN AT THE BEGINNING OF HIS JOURNEY

Duluth, Minnesota, U.S.A.

Walk with: Bob Dylan (1941–)

Route: Bob Dylan Way

Length: 1.8 miles

Essential listening: *Bob Dylan*; *Highway 61 Revisited*

TOP RIGHT: Bob Dylan Way runs through downtown Duluth, the town of the singer's birth.

RIGHT: Fitger's on Superior Street, Duluth, was once a brewery but is now a hotel and shopping mall.

As a port at the westernmost tip of the Great Lakes, the Minnesota city of Duluth was built on exports. But one of its most world-changing exports has proved to be a young Jewish boy named Robert Allen Zimmerman, who we know as Bob Dylan. Born in Duluth, he was brought up seventy miles northwest in Hibbing, but when he discovered music, his heart yearned to travel in the opposite direction—south to New Orleans, at the other end of Highway 61.

"Highway 61, the main thoroughfare of the country blues, begins about where I began," Dylan wrote. "I always felt like I'd started on it, always had been on it, and could go anywhere."

As New Orleans is 1,300 miles south of Duluth, this walk remains in Dylan's birthplace. A 1.8-mile section of downtown has been rebranded Bob Dylan Way; marked by a Dylan manhole cover, it starts near the front of the Lake Superior Railroad Museum (506 W. Michigan St). A few blocks along the way is 1st Ave E.; at this avenue's intersection with 6th Street is the former Nettleton Elementary School, where a young Dylan attended kindergarten. The Zimmerman family home was a block away at 519 North 3rd Ave E.

Back down on Bob Dylan Way, there's an exhibit (and another musical manhole) in front of Fitger's (600 E. Superior Street). Two-thirds of a mile northeast is the Armory Arts & Music Center (1626 London Rd), a former National Guard drill hall where, in January 1959, Dylan had a formative experience: "When I was about 16 or 17 years old, I went to hear Buddy Holly play at the Duluth National Guard Armory, and I was three feet away from him, and he looked at me…" Within three days Holly would be dead, but Dylan was just starting on his own long road.

60

HEAD TO WILLIAM FAULKNER'S HOME TOWN

Oxford, Mississippi, U.S.A.

It's estimated that around 25,000 "literary pilgrims" visit Oxford, Mississippi, every year to walk in the footsteps of William Faulkner (1897–1962). Oxford was the template for most of his deeply evocative tales of the south—a "postage stamp of native soil." Connecting with his world is easy in Oxford: coming into town, the courthouse in Oxford Square bares a plaque with a passage from his work; the Confederate soldier statue is also featured in *The Sound and The Fury* (1929). From here, you can walk to his mother Maude Faulkner's home—one block south, on Lamar, and then around the block to tour Rowan Oak, Faulkner's former home and now a museum dedicated to his life.

61

THE AMERICAN SIDE OF *THE SECRET GARDEN*

Knoxville, Tennessee, U.S.A.

Although Frances Hodgson Burnett's (1849–1924) most famous books are very English in setting and feel (think *Little Lord Fauntleroy* (1886) or *The Secret Garden* (1911)), she and her family had left England and moved to Tennessee when Burnett was sixteen. They lived in Knoxville, at one point in an isolated house at the top of a hill to which Burnett gave the address of Noah's Ark, Mt Ararat. Start this walk at the Burnett family resting place, in Knoxville's Old Gray Cemetery (Burnett herself was buried in England). From here, head south toward the river, past Market Square, where a young Burnett sold grapes to raise money to post her work to publishers, and onto the Bijou Theatre, once a hotel where she would dance the night away at masquerade balls. Finish up on the river, along which Burnett and her family lived, the spot now marked with a stone memorial.

62

NASHVILLE'S MUSICAL MAGIC

Nashville, Tennessee, U.S.A.

You don't have to walk far in Nashville to discover why it is known as "Music City." The city's heritage as the birthplace of country music is apparent with almost every step, as you pass concert venues, live music bars, radio stations, and offices of recording companies. Start a walk on the Music City Walk of Fame—a stretch of star-studded pavement that honors names such as Dolly Parton, Johnny Cash, Little Richard, Jack White, and Kings of Leon. From there, it's a block to the Honky Tonk Highway, which is packed with bars offering live music every single day—and night—of the year. Head down Fifth Avenue North to the Ryman Auditorium—former home of the Grand Ole Opry, the live radio show that launched many a country career.

63

LISTEN OUT FOR MOCKING BIRDS

Monroeville, Alabama, U.S.A.

Wander anywhere in Monroeville, Alabama—the hometown of Harper Lee (1926–2016) and inspiration for her fictional "tired old town" of Maycomb—and Lee's seminal work *To Kill A Mockingbird* (1960) will not be far from mind. South Alabama Avenue now hosts an ice cream parlor where Lee's house once stood, next door to the home of childhood friend Truman Capote. Walk north to find the courthouse and the jail, where Atticus Finch defended Tom Robinson first as his lawyer and then from a lynch mob (a mural depicting this scene stands off the road opposite). The courthouse is now a museum dedicated to Lee and Capote. Half a mile farther along Pineville Road, is the family burial plot, where Lee was laid to rest in 2016.

64

DISCOVER THE MAGICAL LAND OF PASAQUAN

Buena Vista, Georgia, U.S.A.

During his life, Eddie Martin (1908–1986) worked as a street hustler, bartender, gambler, drag queen, and fortune-teller, but it was when he returned to his mother's old farmhouse in the rural hills of Georgia in 1957, that he began work on his visionary art environment, Pasaquan. He changed his name to St. EOM (pronounced om) and over the next thirty years created a world full of color that brought together elements of many cultures and religions, where, as St. EOM said, "I can have my own spirits and my own thoughts." The seven-acre site is now owned by Columbus State University and visitors can wander in the grounds, drinking in the art and the spirituality.

65

FLANNERY O'CONNOR'S GOTHIC INFLUENCES

Savannah, Georgia, U.S.A.

It is difficult to imagine how the childhood home of Mary Flannery O'Connor (1925–1964) in any way inspired the gothic novels and short stories for which she is famed. This simple Georgian-style classical building in East Charlton Street, now a museum dedicated to the author, sits, however, opposite 330 Abercorn St, which has all the features one would expect from her *oeuvre*. This gothic mansion faces Lafayette Square, at the opposite corner of which is the neo-gothic edifice of the Roman Catholic Cathedral of St. John the Baptist, which dominates the space. Behind the church is the Colonial Park Cemetery, a popular location for ghost tours.

BELOW: The visionary art environment of Pasaquan in Georgia.

EXPLORING TENNESSEE WILLIAMS'
VIEUX CARRÉ

New Orleans, Louisiana, U.S.A.

Walk with: Tennessee Williams
(1911–1983)

Route: Around New Orleans'
French Quarter

Length: 1.2 miles

Essential Reading: *Vieux Carré*
(1977); *A Streetcar Named
Desire* (1947)

RIGHT: Tennessee Williams lived
in the old French Quarter of
New Orleans.

In 1977, Tennessee Williams wrote his semiautobiographical play *Vieux Carré*, based on his time living in New Orleans' old French Quarter. He had begun writing it in the late 1930s, shortly after he moved here, although he would not complete it for almost another forty years. It tells the story of a young writer newly arrived from St. Louis and living at a boarding house at 722 Toulouse Street—just as Williams himself had done. He referred to the property as a "poetic evocation of all the cheap rooming houses of the world." While the writer in the play is nameless, Williams was far from it—it was while living at this address that Thomas Lanier Williams experimented with many pen names, finally settling on Tennessee Williams (his father had hailed from Tennessee).

Toulouse Street is just round the corner from Bourbon Street—New Orleans' party district. At number 209, a six-minute walk from William's old home, is Galatoire's, immortalized in *A Streetcar Named Desire* with Stanley Kowalski's outcry of "I'm not going to no Galatoire's!" The menu here has not changed much in almost a century, since the days when Williams would take his favorite seat in the window to people-watch.

After Galatoire's, find Hotel Monteleone on Royal Street, which features in his play *The Rose Tattoo*. Another left after this, and you are back on Bourbon Street. Head north to visit another of Williams' haunts, Café Lafitte in Exile, the oldest gay bar in the country. The café corners Dumaine Street, where, at number 1014, Williams lived from 1962 until his death in 1983.

67

CROSS TINKER CREEK WITH ANNIE DILLARD

Appalachians, U.S.A.

"I live by Tinker Creek, in a valley in Virginia's Blue Ridge." So writes Annie Dillard (1945–) in the opening chapter of her Pulitzer Prize-winning work of nonfiction, *Pilgrim at Tinker Creek* (1974). The novel is a work of poetic observation and contemplation on nature and life, based on the author's journals. A little northwest of Roanoke, Virginia, the Appalachian Trail crosses Tinker Creek. A popular twenty-mile stretch of it takes hikers from here across the creek, up Tinker Mountain and over its ridgeline to the overhang at McAfee's Knob—which must be the most photographed spot along the Appalachian Trail.

68

ERNEST HEMINGWAY'S KEY WEST

Key West, Florida, U.S.A.

Ernest Hemingway (1899–1961) only meant to stop off in Key West to pick up a car on his way home from Paris with his second wife, Pauline Pfeiffer. However, the car was delayed and Hemingway fell in love with this laid-back corner of Florida. The couple bought a Spanish colonial house on Whitehead St—now the Ernest Hemingway Home and Museum. From here, pop by Blue Heaven on the corner of Thomas and Petronia St; although now a restaurant, it was a boxing gym where Hemingway both boxed and refereed. Then on to either Sloppy Joe's on Duval St or Captain Tony's Saloon on Greene St—there is a dispute over which was the original Sloppy Joe's bar. End your walk at Mallory Square, where there is a bust of Hemingway.

69

WALK AMONG ANNE TYLER'S BALTIMOREANS

Baltimore, Maryland, U.S.A.

Baltimore feels like a living Anne Tyler (1941–) novel. The author lives in the city, transferring its people and personalities to the pages of her books, capturing both Baltimore and Baltimoreans. Begin in Penn Station, the iconic setting of *A Patchwork Planet* (1998). Make your way up through Charles Village, an eclectic neighborhood of crumbling nineteenth-century Baltimore row houses, home for many of Tyler's characters. Continue to the affluent suburb of Roland Park, where "everybody... has a last name for a first name." Visit Eddie's grocery store, where the opening scene of *Ladder of Years* (1996) takes place in the fresh produce aisle.

70

FEEL THE ISOLATION WITH CARSON McCULLERS

Charlotte, North Carolina, U.S.A.

When she moved to Charlotte, North Carolina, as a newlywed at the age of twenty, Carson McCullers (1917–1967) would wander the streets looking for inspiration for her first novel—which would become the best-selling *The Heart Is A Lonely Hunter* (1940). McCullers lived first at 311 East Boulevard, where she began writing—you can now eat at the restaurant there, which pays homage to the spot—before moving to 806 Central Avenue. The 90-minute walk between her two homes in Charlotte explores the streets McCullers trod, as she pondered the themes of isolation and outcasts that would make up her Southern gothic fiction.

LEFT: Colorful row houses in Charles Village, Baltimore, where Anne Tyler sets her novels.

71
FRANK SINATRA—HOBOKEN'S "GIFT TO THE WORLD"

Hoboken, New Jersey, U.S.A.

American crooner Francis Albert Sinatra (1915–1998) was known simply as Frankie when growing up in Hoboken, the suburban town on the shores of the River Hudson. He was born in a tenement building, 415 Monroe Street, to doting Italian immigrant parents. His mother became a politician, his father owned a tavern at 333 Jefferson St where Sinatra sang. Follow Jefferson north, and you'll arrive at St. Ann's Church, where it's said Sinatra made his debut, singing at a St. Ann's "ravioli dinner." Round the corner on Adams St is Tutty's bar, where Sinatra would hang out with friends singing a capella, while eight blocks south is the Union Club, where Ole Blue Eyes earned $40 a week singing in 1935. From here it's a short walk to the Frank Sinatra Memorial Park, created the year he died, "in memory of Francis Albert Sinatra, Hoboken's gift to the world."

72
MAKE BRUCE SPRINGSTEEN'S ASBURY PARK ALL YOURS

Asbury Park, New Jersey, U.S.A.

Few musical acts can be as strongly associated with a place as The Boss is with New Jersey. Although born just up the coast in Long Branch, Bruce Springsteen (1949–) called his debut album *Greetings From Asbury Park* after a postcard he saw in a shop on the boardwalk: "I said, 'Yeah, greetings from Asbury Park. That's New Jersey. Who's from New Jersey? Nobody. It's all mine.'" Springsteen first met his longterm collaborator Clarence Clemons at The Student Prince (911 Kingsley St) in 1971. Just a block away is the Stone Pony (900–978 Ocean Avenue), where Springsteen has played more than any other venue. Farther up the boardwalk is the booth of fortune-teller Madam Marie, namechecked in the song *4th Of July, Asbury Park (Sandy)*, and a little farther on is the Asbury Park Convention Hall, where Springsteen's band rehearse before touring.

73
LITERARY LANDMARKS IN PHILIP ROTH'S HOMETOWN

Newark, New Jersey, U.S.A.

"Sitting there in the park, I felt a deep knowledge of Newark, an attachment so rooted that it could not help but branch out into affection," wrote Philip Roth (1933–2018) in his first work *Goodbye, Columbus* (1959). Roth's birthplace would become intrinsic to so many of his novels. In the same story, he wrote of, "the Newark Museum… two oriental vases in front like spittoons for a rajah," and it is a good place to start a walking tour. The Italian Renaissance-inspired public library farther up the same street, and the elegantly columned Essex County Courthouse a short stroll southeast, also feature in his work. Southward again, on Clinton Avenue, spot the Riviera Hotel and Temple B'nai Abraham, from *Plot Against America* (2004).

TOP RIGHT: The Stone Pony, where Bruce Springsteen has played more than anywhere else.

RIGHT: Asbury Park Convention Hall serves as Springsteen's band's rehearsal rooms.

BREATHE THE SAME AIR THAT INSPIRED MARK TWAIN

Hannibal, Missouri, U.S.A.

Walk with: Mark Twain (1835–1910)

Route: Around Hannibal, Missouri

Length: 2.5 miles (with steps)

Essential reading: *The Adventures of Tom Sawyer* (1876); *Adventures of Huckleberry Finn* (1884)

ABOVE: The author Mark Twain.

RIGHT: The famous fence from *The Adventures of Tom Sawyer.*

"All modern American literature comes from one book by Mark Twain called *Huckleberry Finn*. There was nothing before. There has been nothing as good since." So said Ernest Hemingway in 1935, and there are many who would agree.

Twain's novel was not only one of the first to confront slavery, and the internal battle between doing right in the eyes of the law or respecting your own moral conscience, but it was also one of the first to be written in the first person and from the point of view of a young uneducated boy.

Place plays a hugely important factor in Twain's novels. Think of the dark and confusing cave system where Tom and his "betrothed" Becky Thatcher get lost; or the graveyard where Tom and Huck go to cure warts with a dead cat, and end up witnessing a crime. All these are real places around the town of Hannibal in Missouri (renamed St. Petersburg for the novels).

Start at the Mark Twain Cave, southeast of town, where you can experience the atmosphere deep underground, albeit with far more lighting and built-up footways than Tom and Becky enjoyed, then head down to the river, "the magnificent Mississippi, rolling its mile-wide tide," and turn left to walk into town. Wander along Main Street, which will lead you to the Mark Twain Boyhood Home and Museum, and then round to Rock Street, which meanders up Cardiff Hill—the site of many of Tom and Huck's adventures—to the Mark Twain Memorial Lighthouse up 244 steps at the top. The lighthouse was built to commemorate Twain's 100th birthday. Breathe deep, and imagine those mischievous boys and their escapades in the woods below.

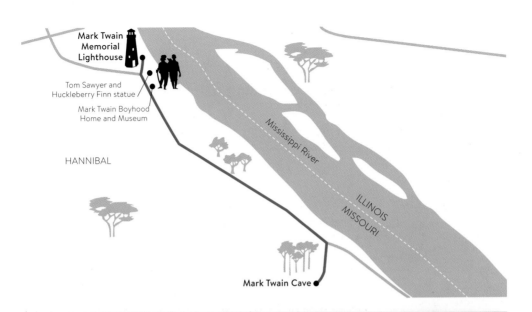

Mark Twain
Memorial
Lighthouse

Tom Sawyer and
Huckleberry Finn statue

Mark Twain Boyhood
Home and Museum

HANNIBAL

Mississippi River

ILLINOIS

MISSOURI

Mark Twain Cave

TOM SAWYER'S FENCE
HERE STOOD THE BOARD
FENCE WHICH TOM SAWYER
PERSUADED HIS GANG TO
PAY HIM FOR THE PRIVILEGE
OF WHITEWASHING. TOM
SAT BY AND SAW THAT IT
WAS WELL DONE

BECOME A WALKER IN THE CITY WITH ALFRED KAZIN

New York City, New York, U.S.A.

Walk with: Alfred Kazin (1915–1998)

Route: Brownsville, Brooklyn to Central Park, Manhattan

Length: 10.8 miles

Essential reading: *A Walker in the City* (1951)

TOP RIGHT: Alfred Kazin found Central Park "an oases to stop in the beyond."

RIGHT: Kazin's journey begins across the Brooklyn Bridge, in Brownsville.

Alfred Kazin's lyrical memoir *A Walker in the City* reads as a personal history of New York. Although Kazin traverses seemingly all of the city, symbolically showing through his walks how he left behind Brooklyn and poverty and moved to "the city," the prose centers around his childhood neighborhood. The poor son of two immigrants, Kazin grew up in Brownsville, where, he writes, "we were of the city, but somehow not in it."

The city—in fact everything outside of Brownsville—was "Beyond." Manhattan itself seemed like a foreign country to the child Kazin, for whom the "eternity of the subway ride" made Brownsville feel like it was at "the end of the world."

To follow in Kazin's footsteps, one could circle only within the confines of Brownsville, a place that had seemed oppressive and hopeless to the writer in his youth, but which incessantly drew him back. Better still, copy the meandering route of the book and walk from Brownsville, across the Brooklyn Bridge, into Manhattan. End in Central Park, one of the places the young Kazin had seen as "oases to stop in the beyond."

At its core, the tale of a second-generation immigrant seeking a way out of poverty, a way to immerse himself in the dream of "Americana," is a familiar one. In following Kazin across the water to "the city," a walker in New York will simultaneously be tracing the hopeful route of a long history of immigrants.

76
YAYOI KUSAMA'S WALK

New York City, New York, U.S.A.

Yayoi Kusama, born 1929 in Matsumato, Japan, moved to New York in 1958 to, in her own words, "… conquer New York City, make my name in the art world… create a new history of art in the U.S.A." She came to notice for her art "happenings." Her solo performance *Walking Piece* (1966), was documented in twenty-five slides. Carrying a florally-decorated umbrella and dressed in a bright pink floral kimono, her "walk" traversed New York's abandoned industrial sites, neglected sidestreets, and bridges. Observing locations and individuals, Kusama subjectively mapped bleaker, alienated areas of the city.

77
REVEL IN JOHN LENNON'S FOREIGNESS

New York City, New York, U.S.A.

John Lennon (1940–1980) came from Liverpool, but he chose to live in New York: "Everybody's a foreigner... I just dig it." He and Yoko Ono initially lived at 105 Bank St in Greenwich Village. A mile up 8th Avenue is Madison Square Garden, where Lennon performed several times, but his first NYC show was with The Beatles at the Ed Sullivan Theater (1697 Broadway), another mile up 8th Avenue. Round the corner at 353 W. 48th St is the (sixth-floor) site of The Hit Factory, where Lennon and Ono recorded their final album; on December 8, 1980, they were mixing at the Record Plant (four blocks south at 321 W. 44th St) before going home to the Dakota building (1 W. 72nd St), where Lennon was shot dead. There is a memorial at Strawberry Fields in nearby Central Park.

78
JOIN LEONARD COHEN AT THE CHELSEA HOTEL

New York City, New York, U.S.A.

New York's redbrick Chelsea Hotel is twelve stories tall, but the stories don't end there. Residents have included Mark Twain, Charles Bukowski, Arthur Miller (who said it had: "No vacuum cleaners, no rules, no shame"), Arthur C. Clarke (who wrote *2001: A Space Odyssey* there), and Jack Kerouac (*On The Road*). Dylan Thomas slipped into his fatal coma there. And Leonard Cohen used its name to title a song about a night spent there with Janis Joplin. Retrace Cohen's steps that night—*sans* Janis—by starting from the writers' watering hole, the White Horse Tavern at 567 Hudson Street, then heading north up 8th Avenue. The hotel itself is at 22 West 23rd Street.

79
SALUTE SUBURBIA WHICH SPAWNED THE RAMONES

Queens, New York, U.S.A.

Clad in leather jackets, The Ramones played ferocious rock songs that became the template for punk rock and inspired countless bands. But their subjects, such as glue-sniffing, murder, and suicide, were a long way from their roots in the middle-class suburb of Queens in New York. The four original Ramones met at Forest Hills High School on 110th St; the section in front of the school is now renamed after them—no small accolade considering previous alumni include Burt Bacharach and Simon & Garfunkel. Lead singer Jeffrey Hyman (later Joey Ramone) lived at Birchwood Towers apartment complex at 102-10 66th Road. While John Cummings (later Johnny Ramone) lived a block southeast of school at 67-38 108th Street.

80
PATTI SMITH AND ROBERT MAPPLETHORPE

Manhattan, New York, U.S.A.

Patti Smith's (1946–) memoir *Just Kids* (2010) is wonderfully evocative, not just of the life of the artist before she made it, and of her impassioned relationship with Robert Mapplethorpe, but also of New York City itself. Start where they met at Tompkins Square Park and wander past the site of the former Fillmore East. Mapplethorpe worked there as an usher and it's where Smith saw a performance by The Doors, which inspired her to put her poetry to music. From here, it's a half-hour walk to the Chelsea Hotel on West 23rd Street, where the pair lived for a while, trading their art for rent before moving to an apartment nearby at number 206.

RIGHT: New York's legendary Chelsea Hotel inspired a song by Leonard Cohen.

81

WALK HARLEM'S HISTORIC STREETS, HOME TO LEGENDARY WRITERS

Harlem, New York, U.S.A.

Walk with: Langston Hughes (1902–1967) et al.

Route: West 135th St to Edgecombe Avenue

Length: 2.3 miles

Essential reading: *The New Negro* (1925) by Alain Locke; *Home to Harlem* (1928) by Claude McKay; *The Big Sea: An Autobiography* (1940) by Langston Hughes

ABOVE: Langston Hughes, part of the Harlem Renaissance.

RIGHT: The Harlem YMCA was a base for many new arrivals to the area.

"Harlem was like a great magnet for the Negro intellectual, pulling him from everywhere. Or perhaps the magnet was New York, but once in New York, he had to live in Harlem," said Langston Hughes in *The Big Sea*.

The first Harlem Renaissance (1918–1929) developed after the First World War, when many African-Americans relocated to Harlem. In 1914, 50,000 were living in the area; by 1923, it was 150,000. The boom was called the "New Negro Movement" after an anthology of poems by Alain Locke.

This walk begins at 135th St subway station, for Langston Hughes, aged twenty, emerging from the platform, it was his first sight of Harlem. "Hundreds of colored people. I wanted to shake hands with them. Speak to them…" (*The Big Sea*). Walk southeast along West 135th St. At 180, between 7th and Lenox Avenue, is the YMCA, a Harlem base to Hughes, Claude McKay, and Ralph Ellison, among others. At 103 is the Schomburg Center for Black Culture, New York Public Library, founded in 1925. Walk northeast on Lenox Avenue/Malcolm X Boulevard. The streets between West 136th St and West 139th St were overflowing with meeting places—cafés, restaurants, nightclubs, and speakeasies—at the height of the era. Number 104 West 136th St was the home of A'Lelia Walker Robinson, famed for her parties frequented by writers, poets, and artists. West 138th St, between Seventh and Eighth Avenue, is Strivers' Row, an architectural landmark and home to Harlem writers, including composer Noble Sissle and writer Eric Walrond. At St. Nicholas Avenue, turn northward to 940, which was the residence of Countee Cullen, author of *Color*. From here, turn south, taking a left at West 157th St, and on to Edgecombe Avenue. At 409, the tall apartment block was where many famed residents, including Aaron Douglas, WEB Dubois, Jessie Redmon Fauset, Regina M. Anderson, and Rudolph Fisher lived.

82

ALLEN GINSBERG'S NEW YORK

Greenwich Village and Lower East Side, New York, U.S.A.

Allen Ginsberg (1926–1997) was a central figure in the Beat movement—downtown may be more gentrified these days, but squint and you can still imagine their version of the Big Apple. Start in Washington Square Park, where Ginsberg gave poetry readings (referenced in his poem *Howl* (1956)), then head a couple of blocks over to 150 Bleeker Street, where he lived. From here, traverse over to 114 MacDougal Street—where the poet used to hang out with Andy Warhol—before ending up at Cafe Wha?, the site of Bob Dylan's first NYC performance, beloved by the Beats, and still a popular music spot.

83

WALT WHITMAN'S BROOKLYN

Brooklyn, New York, U.S.A.

"A great city is that which has the greatest men and women / If it be a few ragged huts it is still the greatest city in the whole world," wrote Walt Whitman (1819–1892) about New York City. Much of his life was spent in Brooklyn, where there is now a Walt Whitman Park. A few blocks north at 28 Old Fulton Street is the entrance to what was the *Brooklyn Daily Eagle*, which Whitman edited in the 1840s. Old Fulton Street draws you down to the East River Ferry, where the railings carry quotes from Whitman's "Crossing Brooklyn Ferry."

84

FIND PEACE ON A WALK WITH PAUL AUSTER

New York, U.S.A.

"Each time he took a walk, he felt as though he were leaving himself behind, and by giving himself up to the movement of the streets, he was able to escape the obligation to think, and this, more than anything else, brought him a measure of peace." So wrote Paul Auster (1947–) in his remarkable book *City of Glass* (1985). The protagonist, Quinn, tells the tale of losing himself through aimless meandering, and he eventually follows another character, Stillman, whose strolls are also without purpose, but "bounded on the north by 110th Street, on the south by 72nd Street." In keeping with this spirit, a random stroll in the Upper East and West sides is prescribed.

85

EDGAR ALLAN POE'S FAVORED BRIDGE

Fordham, New York, U.S.A.

There is a famous lithograph of gothic writer Edgar Allan Poe (1809–1849) crossing New York's recently constructed High Bridge in the late 1840s, with his dark cloak billowing out behind him. Poe was an avid walker, and when he moved to the village of Fordham, now part of the Bronx, the three-mile walk between his cottage and the Harlem River crossing was a favored route, day or night. In 2015, the bridge, New York's oldest, reopened to pedestrians after forty-five years. From his cottage at Poe Park at 2640 Grand Concourse (the lithograph is on view here), head southeast to reach it.

86

BLACK, FEMALE, AND GAY IN GREENWICH VILLAGE

Greenwich Village, New York, U.S.A.

Audre Lorde (1934–1992) was born in New York City to immigrant Caribbean parents. Her first book of poetry, *First Cities,* was published in 1968. In Greenwich Village, walk through the streets to reimagine her life as a pioneer activist in the lesbian community here. One hangout was the Bagatelle, known as "the bag," a lesbian bar at 86 University Place. "To be Black, female, gay, and out of the closet in a white environment, even to the extent of dancing in the Bagatelle, was considered by many Black lesbians to be simply suicidal." From here, walk southwest on University Place toward East 11th Street. Turn right into Washington Square North. Cross the square, turning right onto West 4th Street, to what was the Pony Stable Inn, at 150, a lesbian bar from 1945–1970.

87

DISCOVER NEW YORK'S LOST "AGE OF INNOCENCE"

Flatiron District to Greenwich Village, New York, U.S.A.

Edith Wharton (1862–1937) was born Edith Jones during New York's Gilded Age, to a socially prominent family which was said to inspire the phrase "keeping up with the Joneses." She captured the times with precise cynicism in *The Age of Innocence* (1920), the novel that made her the first woman to win the Pulitzer Prize for Literature in 1921. Walking from Wharton's childhood home—now a Starbucks—around the corner from the Flatiron Building to Greenwich Village, one can still spot a few of the mansions that were ubiquitous in the author's youth. Grace Church, where Wharton was baptized, and where May Welland and Newland Archer marry in the novel, stands among them on Broadway.

RIGHT: New York's High Bridge, a staple of Edgar Allan Poe's walks, day or night.

88
TEJU COLE'S MODERN NYC
New York, U.S.A.

"And so when I began to go on evening walks last Fall, I found Morningside Heights an easy place from which to set out into the city," begins Teju Cole's (1975–) book about post-9/11 New York. The narrator, Julius, wanders in Lower Manhattan, reflecting on the sights. Start on Pearl Street, walk up to United States Custom House, then along Broadway to 60 Wall Street (the grandeur of which Julius contemplates at length). Then head back down to Ground Zero, of which Cole writes: "I remembered a tourist who once asked me how he could get to 9/11: not the site of the events but to 9/11 itself, the date petrified into broken stones."

89
THE ROARING TWENTIES
Long Island, New York, U.S.A.

Travel to the Roaring Twenties with a *Great Gatsby*-inspired tour of Long Island, "that slender riotous island which extends itself due east of New York." F. Scott Fitzgerald (1896–1940) and his wife, Zelda, spent a few summers of recklessness here between 1922 and 1924. Places of note include the decadent twelve-story Willard Hotel, where the couple first stayed in 1920, and the areas of Kings Point and Sands Point, which became the fictional townships of West Egg and East Egg in the novel.

90

SEEKING HARLEM IN
TONI MORRISON'S *JAZZ*

Harlem, New York, U.S.A.

Toni Morrison's (1931–2019) novel *Jazz* (1992) features an African-American couple from Virginia who move to live in New York, specifically around Lenox Avenue in Harlem—which is now also called Malcolm X Boulevard. Life in Harlem is the historical and cultural base for its three main characters—the husband, Joe, has a passionate affair. "I'm passionate about this city," he says. The narrative takes place in the birthplace of jazz in the mid 1920s, and compares to its musical structure. A wander down Lenox Avenue can reveal some of the sights, and certainly sounds, from this time.

91

RELIVE *SOPHIE'S CHOICE*

Prospect Park, Brooklyn, New York, U.S.A.

Like his character Stingo, from his 1979 novel *Sophie's Choice*, William Styron (1925–2006) arrived in Flatbush, Brooklyn, looking for cheap digs. He landed on a boarding house overlooking Prospect Park, immortalized as the Pink Palace in his novel, from where Stingo was struck by the "placid and agreeable view." He wrote: "Old sycamore trees and maples shaded the sidewalks at the edge of the park, and the dappled sunlight aglow on the gently sloping meadow of the Parade Grounds gave the setting a serene, almost pastoral quality." A full loop of the park today is just over three miles, with plenty of places to enjoy a picnic, just as Sophie did in the eponymous novel.

92

JOIN FEDERICO GARCÍA LORCA
AT COLUMBIA

Columbia University, New York, U.S.A.

In 1929, poet Federico García Lorca (1898–1936) left his native Spain to study English at Columbia University, New York. He never took the final exam but the city inspired him to write some of his best work—on the back of university stationery. Living in Columbia's John Jay Hall, Lorca would sit and compose by the College Walk sundial. He was a regular at Casa Hispánica, now at 612 West 116th Street with the piano he used to play and a plaque to him over the fireplace. Around the corner is Riverside Drive, where Lorca used to wander; his family later lived at number 448, but by then he was gone, murdered back home in Spain by Franco's troops during the Civil War.

93

WANDER THROUGH
WASHINGTON SQUARE

Greenwich Village, New York, U.S.A.

Despite spending most of his life in England, Henry James (1843–1916) was continually influenced by his roots in the U.S.A. Particularly by Greenwich Village, where the author grew up. For James, New York consisted of the small neighborhood stretching from Washington Square to his brownstone home on 14th Street, the center of fashionable New York at the time. This is the setting for one of James' best-loved works, *Washington Square* (1880). The New York captured in its pages was already unrecognizable by the time the book was published, and today can only be seen in tantalizing glimpses on a walk from James' birthplace on Washington Place, through Washington Square Park, to 14th Street.

LEFT: Wander down Lenox Avenue in Harlem to feel the mood of Toni Morrison's *Jazz*.

94

KEITH HARING'S NEW YORK

Manhattan, New York, U.S.A.

Walk with: Keith Haring
(1958–1990)

Route: Harlem to Midtown,
New York

Length: 10.7 miles

Essential Reading: *Keith Haring
Journals* (1987)

TOP RIGHT: The Carmine
Swimming Pool boasts a Keith
Haring mural as its backdrop.

RIGHT: Haring's *Crack is Wack*
mural is painted on the wall of a
handball court next to a freeway.

Pennsylvania-born artist Keith Haring was a legend of New York's counterculture art movement in the 1980s. From 1978–1980, on a scholarship, Haring attended New York's School of Visual Art, 209 East 23rd Street. A member of the East Village art scene, he came to the public's attention through his "studio" of subway stations across New York City. Haring used empty matte-black advertising panels, to draw characters in white chalk.

The success of his subway art attracted contemporary art collectors and curators. As he moved into the gallery and museum world, he continued working in public spaces. In New York, some public and semipublic wall murals are still in place. *Crack is Wack* is on E. 128 Street, created to highlight and discourage cocaine use. Start your walk here and then head to the Ascension School at 220 W. 108 St (viewed by appointment). It's probably worth a little walk cheat here, with a bus ride down to *Once Upon a Time* inside the LGBT center, from where it's a short walk to Clarkson St and the Carmine Swimming Pool mural. In 1986, experiencing global recognition, Haring opened a commercial Pop Shop in New York, at 292 Lafayette Street, Soho, as an extension of his art (now closed). He painted the walls and ceiling with murals for an immersive art experience. He explained: "I wanted to continue this same sort of communication as with the subway drawings. I wanted to attract the same wide range of people, and I wanted it to be a place where, yes, not only collectors could come, but also kids from the Bronx…"

Haring used his art to support many causes, campaigning against racism, homelessness, and poverty. He created artworks to raise awareness of the AIDS/HIV epidemic spreading across America. Haring contracted AIDS in 1988, and died aged thirty-one on February 16, 1990.

95
ANDY WARHOL'S FACTORY
Manhattan, New York, U.S.A.

Andy Warhol (1928–1987) was at the center of Manhattan's bohemians in the 1960s, many of whom dropped into his studio, The Factory. Initially, he lived on Lexington Avenue with his mother and their cats; it's a short walk from there to 33 Union Square, one of the sites of The Factory.

96
LOUISE BOURGEOIS
New York, U.S.A.

One of the great American artists of the twentieth century, Louise Bourgeois (1911–2010) has over thirty pieces of her work at the Whitney Museum in New York. A fifteen-minute walk northeast along 9th Avenue takes you to the artist's residence at 347 West 20th Street, an unassuming brown-stone row house.

97
A STROLL WITH EDWARD HOPPER
Greenwich Village, New York, U.S.A.

The realist painter Edward Hopper (1882–1967) lived at 3 Washington Square North for over fifty years. It was his home and his studio. His theatrical paintings reflect life around the area. From Washington Square Park (*Roofs of Washington Square*), walk to 233–237 Bleecker Street (*Early Sunday Morning*), to Greenwich Avenue and West 11th Street intersection (*Nighthawks*).

98

SPEND A RURAL HOUR WITH THE FENIMORE COOPERS

Cooperstown, New York, U.S.A.

Walk with: Susan Fenimore Cooper (1813–1894)

Route: Sleeping Lion Trail, Glimmerglass State Park

Length: 2 miles

Essential reading: *Rural Hours* (1850) by Susan Fenimore Cooper; *Deerslayer* (1841) by James Fenimore Cooper

TOP LEFT: Hyde Hall near the start of this walk.

TOP RIGHT: Statue of James Fenimore Cooper.

RIGHT: The covered bridge at Hyde Hall.

William Cooper founded Cooperstown, New York, in 1786. His son, writer James Fenimore Cooper, set three of his novels in the town and on nearby Otsego Lake. And, in turn, James' daughter, Susan Fenimore Cooper, wrote *Rural Hours*, based on her daily journals of her life here.

Publishing under the anonymity of "by a lady," Fenimore Cooper was an early example of nineteenth-century naturalist writing, and her work was an explicit call to preserve the forests (four years before Henry David Thoreau would publish *Walden*). "The old trees which bordered this fine field in past years are fast falling before the axe," she wrote of walking in the Great Meadow. "A few summers back, this was one of the most beautiful meadows in the valley… shut out from the world by a belt of wood sweeping round it in a wide circle… There are few such colonnades left in our neighborhood."

Near Cooperstown, the two-mile Sleeping Lion Trail at Glimmerglass State Park is a beautiful forest walk through majestic white pines, hemlocks, and hardwoods, which starts near Hyde Hall and loops around on Mount Wellington, partially overlooking Otsego Lake, or Glimmerglass, as it was named in James Fenimore Cooper's *Leatherstocking Tales* (published 1823–1841). Susan was her father's assistant and secretary, and recalls how they were riding in his wagon one day and came upon the lake. "I must write one more book, dearie, about our little lake!" he exclaimed—and promptly started work on what would become his *Deerslayer* novel.

Mount Wellington

Hyde Hall

Glimmerglass State Park

Hyde Bay

OTSEGO LAKE

Cooperstown

84 NORTH AND CENTRAL AMERICA

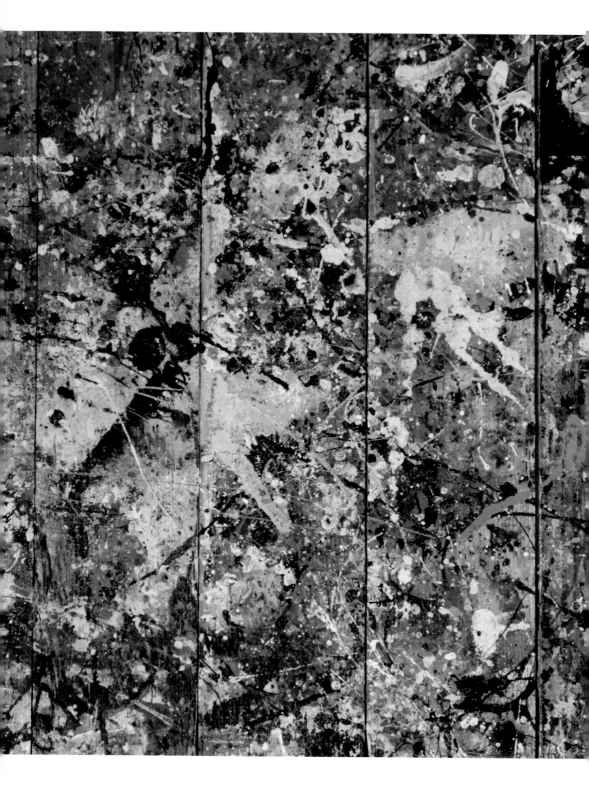

99
WALK ON JACKSON POLLOCK'S LEFTOVER PAINT

Springs, East Hampton, New York, U.S.A.

The walking Jackson Pollock (1912–1956) was most famous for was around his own huge canvases, spread out on the floor of his studio barn so he could work from all four sides using his famous paint-pouring technique. Pollock moved to East Hampton in 1945, and by the 1950s it had become a hub for the abstract expressionism art movement. Walk on the same studio floor—speckled with the very paint from his masterpieces—at 830 Springs Fireplace Rd.

100
GET BACK TO NATURE WITH HENRY DAVID THOREAU

Walden Pond, Concord, Massachusetts, U.S.A.

Walden Pond, a lake in Concord, Massachusetts, on the shores of which Henry David Thoreau (1817–1862) spent two years living in a cabin, is protected as part of a larger state park. This means visitors can step back in time and experience the lake and its surrounds much as it would have been when it inspired Thoreau to write his seminal work on simple living in nature, *Walden; Or, Life In The Woods* (1854). A 1.7-mile path circuits the lake, allowing visitors to wander among the oaks and pines, connect with nature, and visit a replica of the cabin Thoreau lived in.

101
WASHINGTON IRVING'S SPOOKY SLEEPY HOLLOW

Sleepy Hollow, Massachusetts, U.S.A.

Early nineteenth-century New York writer Washington Irving (1783–1859) wrote several books, but his best-known is probably *The Legend of Sleepy Hollow* (1820), a spooky short story that introduced the world to the "headless horseman" (now a popular Halloween outfit). The Massachusetts town immortalized in the tale is considered one of the most haunted places in the world, and tours are regularly run around Sleepy Hollow cemetery—including some at night. If you don't want an official tour, enter via Broadway and seek out the graves of Andrew Carnegie, Samuel Gompers, William Rockefeller, and Irving himself.

102
MARVEL AT THE MARSHES WITH MARTIN JOHNSON HEADE

Rhode Island, U.S.A.

America's smallest state, Rhode Island, has many varied landscapes that have inspired some well-known works of art across the years. The marshes of the East Coast were a major source of inspiration to American artist Martin Johnson Heade (1819–1904), known mostly for his salt-marsh landscapes and seascapes. Captivated by their delicate beauty which changed with the light, Heade studied the Rhode Island marshes in all weather conditions before finally depicting a luminous sky in his well-known piece *The Marshes at Rhode Island*, painted in 1866. There are many, many walking trails in the salt marshes that can lead you to views such as those Heade found.

LEFT: Visitors can walk on the paint on Jackson Pollock's studio floor.

103

UNCOVER THOMAS COLE'S VIEWS OF CATSKILL

Catskill, New York State, U.S.A.

Walk with: Thomas Cole (1801–1848)

Route: Thomas Cole National Historic Site to Olana

Length: 3 miles

Essential viewing: *The Falls of Kaaterskill* (1826)

RIGHT: The Kaaterskill Falls, painted by Thomas Cole, are the highest in New York State.

English-born American painter Thomas Cole (he moved to the U.S.A. with his family in his late teens) was known for his landscape paintings, many of which were inspired by Catskill, a town in the southeast part of Greene County, New York State. Founder of the Hudson River School of American painting, America's first major art movement, Cole had a house and studio here from 1833 until his death in 1848.

To discover the vistas that inspired Cole and many of the Hudson River School students, visitors can walk the Hudson River Art Trail. The trail starts at Cole's former home and studio, Cedar Grove, now the Thomas Cole National Historic Site.

From here, head to Olana, the home of one of Cole's students, Frederic Church. It is a walk of just under three miles via the Hudson River Skywalk. At Olana, from the top of the hill, you can see the splendor of the Catskill landscape laid out below you.

Cole painted numerous scenes of the landscape around Cedar Grove in paintings such as *Lake with Dead Trees* (1825) and *View on the Catskill—Early Autumn* (1836–1837). Another nice walk is from Kaaterskill Clove to the Kaaterskill Falls, one mile along the path.

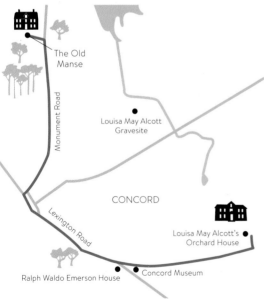

The Old Manse

Monument Road

Louisa May Alcott
Gravesite

CONCORD

Lexington Road

Louisa May Alcott's
Orchard House

Ralph Waldo Emerson House

Concord Museum

104

JOIN THE TRANSCENDENTALISTS ON A WALKING TOUR

Concord, Massachusetts, U.S.A.

Walk with: Ralph Waldo Emerson, Louisa M. Alcott, Nathaniel Hawthorne, and Henry David Thoreau

Route: The Old Manse to Orchard House

Length: 1.3 miles

Essential reading: *Little Women* (1868) by Louisa M. Alcott; Ralph Waldo Emerson's essay "Nature" (1836)

TOP LEFT: Concord, Massachusetts, where transcendentalism was born.

LEFT: The Concord Museum has furniture and artifacts from Henry David Thoreau's experiment in simple living.

Aside from its seminal role in the American Revolutionary War, Concord has a rich nineteenth-century literary history centered round Ralph Waldo Emerson and his circle. Located on the site of the 1775 battle is the Old Manse, the onetime home of Emerson's grandparents, and where he wrote his seminal essay "Nature," which laid the foundation of his philosophy of transcendentalism: "Nature is something that is experienced by humans and grows with human emotion."

Nathaniel Hawthorne, part of Emerson's circle, who wrote *Mosses from an Old Manse* (1854), a collection of short tales, also lived in this house.

Walk south for about half a mile along Monument Road until reaching Concord Monument Square. Turn left onto Lexington Road and walk to the Emerson House, a magnificent colonial home set in two acres of grounds. Emerson's study is where the transcendentalist group met.

A short distance away is the Concord Museum, which houses the Henry David Thoreau collection, that includes the furniture and other artifacts taken from his self-built wooden cottage (now demolished) near Walden Pond, about half a mile south of the museum (see page 87).

Farther along Lexington Rd is Orchard House, the home of the Alcott family, most notably the daughter, Louisa May Alcott, another member of Emerson's circle. The house and its residents were the inspiration for her most famous book, *Little Women*.

105
REFLECT AT A
BENCH BY THE ROAD

Bench by the Road, Lincoln, Massachusetts, U.S.A.

Toni Morrison's (1931–2019) Bench By The Road memorial project was born in 2006, after the author spoke out about the lack of memorials honoring those who were brought to the U.S.A. as slaves. Since then, benches have been placed at historical locations around the country. One of the benches is at Walden Woods, as celebrated by Henry David Thoreau—take a book, a short walk, and take a moment to remember.

106
FOLLOW MARGARET ATWOOD
ON A TRAIL TO A TALE

Cambridge, Massachusetts, U.S.A.

Margaret Atwood's (1939–) dystopian *Handmaid's Tale* (1985) is set in New England, with all the clues pointing to it being Cambridge and Harvard University, where Atwood once studied. In the novel, however, this incarnation has transformed from a place of knowledge and truth to one of torture and oppression. Nearby, at 3 Church Street, is a small church which, in the novel, "isn't used any more, except as a museum." Onward north, 45 Quincy Street is "ornate late Victorian, with stained glass. It used to be called Memorial Hall." Backtrack south to the river, of which the character Offred reminisced: "I wish I could go that far, to where the wide banks are, where we used to lie in the sun."

107
LOOK FOR THE POEMS
BEHIND THE FLOWERS

Holyoke Range, Massachusetts, U.S.A.

Reclusive poet Emily Dickinson (1830–1886) spent her life on the family homestead in Amherst, Massachusetts —now a museum—where she was better known for her way with flowers than with words. When she would send friends posies with her verse attached, it was her blooms which were most admired. It was only after her death that her poetry on themes of death and immortality would be found and widely acclaimed. Her poem "The Mountains Stood in Haze" (1945) is about Mount Holyoke near her home. The 215-mile New England National Scenic Trail runs along the spine of the range, offering miles of hiking routes with panoramic views across the valleys.

108
FIND PEACE WITH
MARY OLIVER

Provincetown, Massachusetts, U.S.A.

Pulitzer Prize-winning poet Mary Oliver (1935–2019) had a great affinity with the natural world. Most of her poetry was set in Provincetown, after she moved there in the 1960s. Her poems are filled with imagery from her daily—often pre-dawn—walks near her home on Commercial Street. An absolute must-walk is the Breakwater Causeway—a thirty to forty-five minute careful step along the uneven narrow rocks crossing the harbor at low tide to reach the very top of Cape Cod and the peaceful Long Point Beach.

RIGHT: Walk along the Breakwater Causeway in Provincetown.

109
FEEL AT HOME WITH EDITH WHARTON

Lenox, Massachusetts, U.S.A.

Edith Wharton (1862–1937) was the first woman to win the Pulitzer Prize. Born in 1862 into a wealthy society family, Wharton wrote about what she knew: upper-class society. She also found time to design her house and country estate—The Mount, in Lenox, Massachusetts—and wrote many of her novels there. Wander the glorious grounds—the sunken Italian garden, the formal flower garden, and the tree-lined Lime Walk that links the two—and then enjoy a longer, three-hour hike to Laurel Lake and back.

110
THANK-YOU NOTES BY ELIZABETH BISHOP

Duxbury, Massachusetts, U.S.A.

Opening her poem, "The End of March," Elizabeth Bishop (1911–1979) writes: "It was cold and windy, scarcely the day/to take a walk on that long beach." She is referring to Duxbury, Massachusetts, where Bishop stayed with friends in 1974 (she later said she wrote the poem as a thank-you note). Duxbury is a beautiful, unspoiled bay, great for bird spotting, and with seven and a half miles of sand and shingle—or fifteen if you are happy to walk back again.

TAKE A HOPPER-EYE VIEW OF CAPE COD

Cape Cod, U.S.A.

Walk with: Edward Hopper (1882–1967)

Route: From Highland Light lighthouse to Coast Guard Beach, Truro

Length: 1 mile

Essential viewing: *Cape Cod Evening* (1939); *Cape Cod Morning* (1950)

RIGHT: The Highland Lighthouse, which Edward Hopper painted in 1930.

BELOW: The wild beaches, big skies, and natural light have drawn many artists to Cape Cod.

Known for his paintings depicting urban isolation, Edward Hopper created some of his most-loved work in Cape Cod, where he found a different sort of isolation—lone roofs standing out against bright skies, buildings with a backdrop of the sea. He first visited the area in 1930, after which he spent every summer in the rural town of Truro, where he and his wife Josephine Nivison, also an artist, built their own house. He created hundreds of works here such as *Cape Cod Sunset, Corn Hill,* and *South Truro*.

Hopper used to paint from his car, but this walk leaves the road behind and takes the shore route from the Highland Light lighthouse in North Truro along the Cape Cod National Seashore to Coast Guard Beach. Hopper painted *Highland Light, North Truro* at the lighthouse in 1930, since then it has moved inland a little due to coastal erosion but is still recognizable from his work. Other views were never really there or have been lost over time, but the light remains as clear and compelling as it was in Hopper's day.

112

PAUL THEROUX'S HAPPINESS

Cape Cod, Massachusetts, U.S.A.

Novelist and travel writer Paul Theroux (1941–) has traveled the globe but he knows where he loves: "The Cape [Cod] is the scene of my childhood happiness. I remember the sunshine, the beaches, the smell of the salt marshes." Theroux advises visitors to paddle a kayak along Nantucket Sound, but as a walking alternative, stick to the shore and take the peninsular path from Long Point Lighthouse, which overlooks a delightfully deserted beach, back round to Herring Cove Beach.

113

MOBY DICK LAND

Nantucket, Massachusetts, U.S.A.

When he wrote his whaling classic *Moby Dick* (1851), native New Yorker Herman Melville (1819–1891) had been to England, Jerusalem, Tahiti, and Hawaii, but never Nantucket, off Cape Cod, where the novel is set. Melville did visit Nantucket the year after he published *Moby Dick*, staying at 29 Broad St. Captain Pollard, whose doomed whaleship the *Essex* inspired the book, lived just yards away at 46 Centre St. The author relied upon a book by historian Thomas Macy, whose house, half a mile away at 99 Main St, is now a museum.

114

DISCOVER WINSLOW HOMER'S TEN POUND ISLAND

Gloucester Harbor, Massachusetts, U.S.A.

On a visit to Gloucester, Massachusetts, in 1880, American-born artist Winslow Homer (1836–1910) lived on Ten Pound Island in Gloucester Harbor bay. The island is only reachable by boat. Here, Homer created over fifty marine artworks. The closest views of Ten Pound Island are from Rocky Creek peninsula and Fork Point. On a walk that circles the inner harbor from Rocky Creek on the eastern mainland, follow E. Main Street northward, into Main Street, circle Inner Harbor, then head to Fork Point for superb views.

115

ABSTRACT CLIMATES WITH HELEN FRANKENTHALER

Provincetown, Massachusetts, U.S.A.

Right at the tip of Cape Cod is Provincetown, a small town where artist Helen Frankenthaler (1928–2011) spent her summers, and which had a profound influence on her work. It wasn't just the watery seascapes outside her studio that inspired her creation of the soak-stain technique, but also the larger size of her studio here on Commercial Street allowed her to create larger canvases, such as *Provincetown I* (1964). There is a pleasant walk from Commercial Street out to the beach at Herring Cove—apt, as *Beach* (1958) was the title of the first painting of Frankenthaler's that got her noticed by the art world.

116

FEED ROBERT McCLOSKEY'S DUCKLINGS

Boston Public Gardens, Boston, Massachusetts, U.S.A.

The Boston Public Gardens is renowned for being the first public botanical gardens in America. It was also the inspiration for Robert McCloskey's (1914–2003) children's picture book *Make Way for Ducklings* (1941). The book tells the story of a pair of mallards who decide to raise their family on an island in the lagoon in the gardens. While attending the Vesper George Art School in the early 1930s, McCloskey would spend time in four acres of park, feeding the ducks and later painting. It is a pleasant Sunday stroll—especially for families.

117

REFLECT ON THE WRITINGS OF PHILLIS WHEATLEY

Boston, Massachusetts, U.S.A.

At the corner of Beach Street and Tyler Street in Boston, a young girl from West Africa (among many others) was auctioned as a slave in 1761. She would become Phillis Wheatley (*c.*1753–1784)—named Phillis after the boat on which she arrived there, and Wheatley for the family who purchased her and who would go on to encourage her to read and write. In 1773, Wheatley became the first African American to publish a book of poetry. Head east through the Theater District to Boston Women's Memorial, a 2003 sculpture on Commonwealth Avenue that commemorates Wheatley, among other great Boston women.

RIGHT: Provincetown had a profound influence on Helen Frankenthaler's work.

118

FOLLOW THE FREEDOM TRAIL

Boston, Massachusetts, U.S.A.

"If the British march/By land or sea from the town to-night,/Hang a lantern aloft in the belfry arch/Of the North Church tower as a signal light," wrote Henry Wadsworth Longfellow (1807–1882) in his poem *Paul Revere's Ride*. The 2.5-mile Boston Freedom Trail is a self-guided walk that passes this church and fifteen other historically significant sites in the city, stretching from Boston Common to the Bunker Hill Monument in Charlestown. Incidentally, the route also passes by Omni Parker House, where, at 3 p.m. on the last Saturday of the month, Longfellow would join his fellow nineteenth-century writers, including Charles Dickens, who gave his first American reading of *A Christmas Carol* here.

119

FIND FROST IN THE WOODS

Green Mountains, Vermont, U.S.A.

The Robert Frost Interpretive Trail near Ripton in Vermont's Green Mountains is a charming woodland walk, peppered with verse from New England's quintessential poet. Read "Mowing" (1913) next to the open field and "Birches" (1916) by—you guessed it— birch trees, during this one-mile circular walk.

WALKING THE ROAD NOT TAKEN

Hampshire and Vermont Woods, U.S.A.

Walk with: Robert Frost
(1874–1963)

Route: Robert Frost
Poetry Trail, Marsh-Billings-
Rockefeller National
Historical Park

Length: 1–2 miles

Essential reading: *The
Collected Poems* (1930)

LEFT: Fall is a spectacular time
to visit Robert Frost country.

BELOW: Nestled in the hills
of the Marsh-Billings-Rockefeller
National Historical Park is a
man-made pond, The Pogue.

The Marsh-Billings-Rockefeller National Historical Park, just outside of Woodstock, became the first national park in Vermont when it opened in 1998. There are thirty-three trails in the grounds, and one not to miss is the Robert Frost Poetry Trail. Robert Frost moved to Vermont from New Hampshire in the 1920s, and lived there for his remaining forty years, becoming the state's first national poet laureate. His commemorative trail winds through a mixture of trees and meadows, the same backdrop to the New England landscape that was his inspiration.

Thirteen of Frost's poems are posted along the hour or so walk, which begins by the mansion in the park, passing the formal garden and carriage house and heading into the wooded grounds. Featuring poems such as "The Sound of the Trees" and "Leaves Compared With Flowers"—his language of landscape can be very literally experienced here.

Frost won four Pulitzer Prizes, and maintained his down-to-earth command of colloquial speech until the end—his gravestone, in Old Bennington Cemetery, etched directly with a single line from his poem "The Lesson For Today," reads: "I had a quarrel with the world."

ON THE TRAIL OF MURDER IN VERMONT

Bennington, Vermont, U.S.A.

Walk with: Donna Tartt (1963–)

Route: Around South Vermont College Campus

Length: 2.5 miles

Essential reading: *The Secret History* (1992)

Donna Tartt's *The Secret History* opens with a confession of murder: "The snow in the mountains was melting and Bunny had been dead for several weeks before we came to understand the gravity of our situation." It transpires that Bunny, one of six cliquey classics students at an elite Vermont college, has discovered a secret the group are prepared to go to any lengths to keep covered up. So they decide to murder him——pushing him down a ravine during one of his regular walks, to make it look like a hiking accident.

The fictional Hampden College is based on Bennington College, where Tartt had been a student. The green, leafy region of Bennington does have a beautiful network of easily accessible trails that make it clear to see where Tartt got her plot inspiration from (choose your hiking companions carefully!).

Starting at Carriage Road, walk along the old cobblestoned access road to Everett Mansion, the historic building on South Vermont College's campus, which has great views over the valley. The trails here are the original logging roads. From here, move onto the Halloween Trail, north of the mansion, following the red signs on a two-mile hike named after the eerie maple tree en route. As Richard narrates in the novel of his arrival in Hampden: "The sun was rising over the mountains, and birches, and impossibly green meadows… it was like a country from a dream."

ABOVE: Donna Tartt whose novel *The Secret History* is about a murder on a walk.

RIGHT: The fabulous surroundings of Bennington College are full of walking trails.

THE VIEW THAT STARTED IT ALL FOR EDNA ST. VINCENT MILLAY

Mount Battie, Camden, Maine, U.S.A.

"All I could see from where I stood,
Was three long mountains and a wood;
I turned and looked another way,
And saw three islands in a bay."

The opening lines of Edna St. Vincent Millay's (1892–1950) poem "Renascence" (1912) succinctly describe the view from the top of Mount Battie in her hometown of Camden, Maine. Set off from Whitehall Inn, where Millay first read the poem aloud, she impressed arts patron Caroline B. Dow so much that she paid for the young poet's education at Vassar College. A few blocks from the inn, is the Mount Battie trail, a short but strenuous hike rewarding visitors with the same exceptional view that inspired Millay.

SCARE YOURSELF IN STEPHEN KING'S HOMETOWN

Bangor, Maine, U.S.A.

Horror master Stephen King (1947–) is based in Maine, and so are most of his stories. Derry, setting for several stories including *It* (1986), is based on Bangor, where King has lived since 1980 at 47 West Broadway—the wrought-iron fencing features spiders and bats. Just half a mile north of King's house, where Thomas Hill Road twists through Summit Park, is the Thomas Hill Standpipe. Since 1897, this has been crucial to Bangor's water supply; since 1986, it has been renowned as the model for the Standpipe in *It*, where Stan first encounters evil clown Pennywise. Another half mile north is the Kenduskeag Stream Park, aka the Barrens meeting place of Stan and his fellow Losers' Club members.

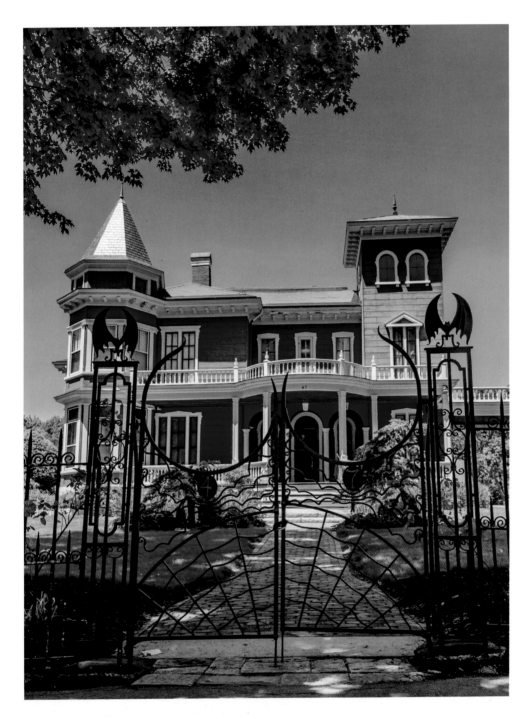

LEFT: A view from Summit Park, near Stephen King's house.

ABOVE: The fence of King's house is decorated with spiders and bats.

FRIDA KAHLO'S MEXICO CITY

La Casa Azul, Mexico City, Mexico

Walk with: Frida Kahlo (1907–1954)

Route: La Casa Azul to The Leon Trotsky House Museum

Length: 3 miles

Essential viewing: *Self-Portrait dedicated to Leon Trotsky* (1937); *Frieda and Diego Rivera* (1931)

The boundary-defying artist Frida Kahlo lived in the residential neighborhood of Coyoacán, Mexico City. She called home a cobalt-blue house named La Casa Azul (the Blue House) and this should be the starting point for this walk. The home and its contents were donated as a museum to the world by Kahlo's husband, artist Diego Rivera, in 1958.

The leafy residential neighborhood of Coyoacán has plenty to see, including museums, cafés, bookstores, and markets. Kahlo and Rivera liked to knock back the tequilas at Cantina La Guadalupana, which you can still see today, albeit without the drink.

Make your way to The Coyoacán Market, a vibrant two-story marketplace in operation since 1921, before heading to The Leon Trotsky House Museum, home of Leon Trotsky, the communist leader who had a big influence in the life of Kahlo and Rivera. Kahlo painted a self-portrait for Trotsky in which the paper she is holding dedicates the portrait to Leon.

Finish your walk with a visit farther afield to the Anahuacalli Museum in San Pablo Tepetlapa. Designed by Rivera, the building contains almost 60,000 pre-Hispanic pieces that both him and Kahlo collected, thanks to their own deep interest in Mexican culture.

ABOVE: Artist Frida Kahlo, who lived a passionate existence in Mexico City.

TOP RIGHT: It's easy to picture Kahlo at work inside her studio.

RIGHT: Kahlo's Casa Azul, now open as a museum, says plenty about the painter's passion.

A WOMAN WITH TALENT
San Juan de los Lagos, Mexico

"It is a crime to be born a woman and have talent," María Izquierdo (1902–1955) once declared. That didn't stop her rising to fame as Diego Rivera's star pupil, or being the first Mexican woman to have her art exhibited in the U.S.A. Although she died in poverty and nearly forgotten, today Izquierdo is remembered as having helped pave the way for female artists in Mexico. In her birthplace of San Juan de los Lagos, a street has been named in her honor, as has the town's Casa de la Cultura. Walking from Calle Maria Izquierdo to the town's historic center offers a glimpse of the vibrant colors for which Izquierdo's paintings were known.

126

ROBERTO BOLAÑO IN MEXICO'S CAPITAL

Mexico City, Mexico

The late Chilean author Roberto Bolaño (1953–2003), moved to Mexico City as a teenager and, though he later left for Spain, the city is a recurring setting in his books, including in *The Savage Detectives* (1998) and *2666* (2004). This four-mile route starts at his former home at Calle Samuel 27 in the Guadalupe Tepeyac neighborhood. It then heads south through the historic center before branching west to Café La Habana at Avenida Morelos 62. This old-school joint was one of Bolaño's popular haunts (he renamed it Café Quito in *The Savage Detectives*) and, as a plaque on the wall notes, has also played host to the likes of Gabriel García Márquez, Fidel Castro, and Che Guevara.

127

WHAT CAN YOU COLLECT ON A WALK?

Mexico City, Mexico

Belgian-born, Mexico City-based creative marvel Francis Alÿs (1959–) has turned walking into an artform. He calls his works *paseos*—walks that apparently "resist the subjection of common space and reconfigures time to the speed of a stroll." His most famous performance was perhaps "The Collector"— during which Alÿs dragged a small, magnetic dog-like toy through Mexico City, attracting debris to it, "until it is completely covered by its trophies." Alÿs went all over town during the work's creation—including the Centro Historico.

RIGHT: For a look at what others have collected in Mexico City, finish your Francis Alÿs-inspired walk at the Museo de la Ciudad.

128

CLIMB THE MOUNTAIN THAT SILENCED THE VIOLINS

Mount Pelée, Martinique

You won't find the titular setting of Patrick Leigh Fermor's (1915–2011) *Violins of Saint Jacque* (1953) on any atlas. The island, which "hung like a bead on the sixty-first meridian," exists only in the imagination of the writer. However, it is loosely based on the Caribbean island of Martinique and the eruption of Mount Pelée in 1902, which destroyed the decadent Mardi Gras ball captured so evocatively in Fermor's writing. A hike to the 4,583-feet pinnacle of Mt. Pelée passes through a lush tropical landscape that is technically the youngest part of the island, growing from the ashes of the last eruption in 1932.

129

TUNE IN TO BOB MARLEY

Nine Mile, Jamaica

Bob Marley (1945–1981) was born and grew up in Nine Mile, a little village in the mountains of St. Ann, Jamaica. It's a popular pilgrimage for devotees of the reggae pioneer and a great place to wander around, soaking up the atmosphere that inspired him. Start at Marley's childhood home, now a museum, where you can learn about his roots and witness the Rasta-colored rock on which he used to sit and write hits. It's also home to the singer's mausoleum, situated in a small, Ethiopian-style church. From there, a walk in any direction takes you into stunning rural Jamaican countryside.

130

BAR-HOPPING THROUGH HEMINGWAY'S HAVANA

Havana, Cuba

A warren of pastel-hued colonial buildings, the city of Havana still looks almost exactly as it would have when Ernest Hemingway (1899–1961) called it home; especially at the Ambos Mundos hotel, where Room 511 is still furnished with Hemingway's belongings and typewriter. From the hotel, the Hemingway trail winds through Havana's UNESCO-listed old quarter, leading—inevitably—to several bars. "My mojito in La Bodeguita, my daiquiri in El Floridita." The author's famous endorsement is framed on the wall of La Bodeguita del Medio, a cramped bar filled with cigar smoke and curios. From there, it's a short walk to El Floridita, where his statue still sits at the bar and his daquiri—the Papa Doble—is still on the menu.

131

WANDER THROUGH HAVANA'S LIVING ART

Fusterlandia, Jaimanitas, Cuba

At first glance, Jaimanitas is a seemingly ordinary neighborhood in the west of Havana. But within its suburban streets, a whimsical world of Naïve art awaits. Follow the murals north toward the sea, to Taller-Estudio José Fuster. Begun in 1975 by locally born artist José Rodríguez Fuster (1946–), who returned home from Europe hungry to create something similar to Antoni Gaudí's *Park Güell*, the neighborhood is an ongoing project of kaleidoscopic color. Fuster's unique restoration of his own home inspired his neighbors. Over the years, the murals, mosaics, and sculptures have spilled out into the barrio, transforming the streets into a living art project.

LEFT: The crumbling grandeur of Havana.

SOUTH AMERICA

Walk into the pages of *One Hundred Years of Solitude* in Colombia, sing protest songs with Violeta Parra in Chile, and imagine the final days of Che Guevara in Bolivia, in this colorful and passionate continent.

JOURNEY INTO THE MAGICAL REAL WORLD OF GABRIEL GARCÍA MÁRQUEZ

Aracataca, Colombia

Walk with: Gabriel García Márquez (1927–2014)

Route: Around Aracataca

Length: 3 miles

Essential reading: *One Hundred Years of Solitude* (1967)

RIGHT: The real town of Aracataca which inspired Gabriel García Márquez's Macondo.

Until the age of eight, Gabriel García Márquez lived beneath the tin roof of his grandparents' home in Aracataca—a small, sleepy village in the foothills of Colombia's Sierra Nevada, built on the banks of a river whose bed of polished stones "were white and enormous, like prehistoric eggs."

Aracataca is also Macondo: the fictional village of Gabo's magical-realism novel, *One Hundred Years of Solitude*.

Approaching the town from Santa Marta will draw visitors through endless swamps and verdant banana plantations. In town, a train station still stands along the tracks, but the railroad is no longer in use. A visit to the station calls to mind the fictional Banana Company, whose railroad brought modernity to Macondo.

Aracataca/Macondo is small enough for a self-guided walking tour. Start at the Casa Museo Gabriel García Márquez, the author's renovated childhood home, where fans of the novel may recognize many of the rooms and details. Pay your respects at Melquiades' tombstone, erected in honor of a crucial character. Finish with a stroll along the tranquil river, which laces through the landscape of both fact and fiction.

"The truth is that there's not a single line in all my work that does not have a basis in reality," García Márquez once told *The Paris Review*. "The problem is that Caribbean reality resembles the wildest imagination."

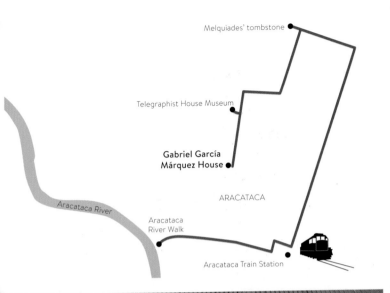

Melquiades' tombstone

Telegraphist House Museum

Gabriel García
Márquez House

ARACATACA

Aracataca River

Aracataca
River Walk

Aracataca Train Station

133
THE RIVER WALK
Barranquilla, Colombia

Gabriel García Márquez spent his formative writing years in Barranquilla, a bustling port city. He worked at the local paper *El Heraldo* and lived above a brothel while writing *One Hundred Years of Solitude*. He'd read chapters to his friends—local writers and journalists who met to drink and discuss literature. One of their haunts, La Cueva, can still be visited today, and forms an ideal starting point for a walk through the city and along the Magdalena River to its mouth. As a boy, Gabo journeyed by steamboat to the capital, Bogotá, and was enthralled by the river, which has a notable presence in his works.

134
GABO'S SPIRITUAL HOME
Cartagena, Colombia

"All of my books have loose threads of Cartagena in them." The candy-yellow city has both real-life ties to Gabriel García Márquez—he lived and worked here—and its cobbled streets are also full of the ghosts of Gabo's magical realism. Start at the "twisted tower" of Santo Domingo, and weave your way through the colonial streets to the almond trees of Plaza Fernández de Madrid, or "Park of the Evangels," as it became in *Love in the Time of Cholera* (1985).

135

STEP INTO FERNANDO BOTERO'S WORLD

Medellín, Colombia

Known for his exaggeratedly plump imagery, painter and sculptor Fernando Botero (1932–) was born in Medellín. This one-mile stroll starts at the Plaza Botero (also known as the Plaza de la Esculturas), home to twenty-three of the artist's sculptures. It then winds through the nearby Museo de Antioquia, which has the world's biggest collection of Botero artworks. The final stop is the Parque de San Antonio, which has a pair of bronze doves in the classical Botero style. One is damaged, the result of a 1995 terrorist bomb aimed as a warning for Botero's son, who was Colombia's defense minister. Botero's elegant response was to create another "Bird of Peace" and place it alongside the first.

136

FIND ARTHUR CONAN DOYLE'S LOST WORLD

Mount Roraima, Venezuela

Described as an island in the sky, and one of the most mystical rock formations in the world, Mount Roraima is a popular trekking spot. Located on the border of Brazil, Venezuela, and Guyana, this giant flat-topped mountain appears as if carved from a single rock and is home to many weird and wonderful flora and fauna. British writer Arthur Conan Doyle (1859–1930) used Roraima as the inspiration for his novel *The Lost World* (1912). Start your trek to the summit at Paratepui, a small Indigenous village in the Gran Sabana where you can find a guide to show you the way.

137

FOLLOW CHARLES DARWIN TO TAGUS COVE

Galápagos Islands, Ecuador

"The archipelago is a little world within itself," wrote Charles Darwin (1809–1882) of the Galápagos in *The Voyage of the Beagle* (1839). His visit to the islands lasted only five weeks but had a profound impact on the world. Today tourism is tightly controlled on the Galápagos and visitors can't explore with the freedom that Darwin enjoyed. But there are still places where it is possible to follow in his footsteps, such as Tagus Cove on Isabela island, where Darwin landed on October 1, 1835. A 1.1-mile trail leads through scrubland to the emerald-green Darwin Lake and then to the lava fields of Darwin Volcano. Darwin's finches, penguins, flightless cormorants, and sea lions are among the wildlife that can be spotted.

138

AROUND MIRAFLORES WITH MARIO VARGAS LLOSA

Lima, Peru

Nobel prize-winning author Mario Vargas Llosa (1936–) has had an interesting life and has written about much of it in his novels. His time at a military academy is *The Time of the Hero* (1963), his elopement with his aunt became *Aunt Julia and the Scriptwriter* (1977), and his failed presidential candidacy fueled the memoir, *A Fish in the Water* (1993). In the Miraflores district of Lima, where Llosa grew up, there is a 2.5-mile walking tour that starts in the Parque Central, a location that figures in *Conversation in the Cathedral* (1969). From here, it heads south and onto the former home—now a cultural center—of Llosa's influential teacher, Raúl Porras Barrenechea, before moving down Pasaje Champagnat, which has a plaque dedicated to the author.

LEFT: Plaza Botero in Medellín has twenty-three sculptures by Fernando Botero.

DISCOVER THE MAGIC OF BAHIA WITH JORGE AMADO

Salvador, Bahia, Brazil

Walk with: Jorge Amado (1912–2001)

Route: Pelourinho to Rio Vermelho

Length: 3 miles

Essential reading: *Dona Flor and Her Two Husbands* (1966)

RIGHT: The teenage Jorge Amado lived on the plaza of Largo do Pelourinho.

"The world… is incomprehensible and full of surprises," wrote Jorge Amado in his novel *Gabriela, Clove and Cinnamon* (1958). His words seem equally appropriate for the city with which he is most closely associated: Salvador de Bahia.

Amado—one of the finest Brazilian authors of the twentieth century— lived in Salvador da Bahia and used the city prominently in many of his books, including *Dona Flor and Her Two Husbands*, *Captains of the Sands* (1937), and *Tereza Batista: Home From the Wars* (1972). He was so closely linked with Salvador da Bahia that he was nicknamed its "emperor."

This three-mile walk starts in the historic neighborhood of Pelourinho. As a teenager, Amado lived in a house on the Largo do Pelourinho, a beautiful cobble-stone plaza. Nearby is the Fundação Casa de Jorge Amado, an interesting museum that explores the author's life and works. The route continues south through Pelourinho to the Museu Afro-Brasil, a museum that provides a wonderful insight into Brazil's African heritage, including the *Candomblé* religion, of which Amado—once an atheist— became an *obá* (honorary priest) in later life.

The walk continues in the neighborhood of Rio Vermelho (visitors are advised to take a taxi as it is not considered safe to walk directly here from Pelourinho). After a stroll around this bohemian area, finish at Rua Alagoinhas 33, where Amado was living at the time of his death in 2001; the house is open to the public. His ashes were scattered beneath a mango tree in the garden.

140
ACROSS THE CIUDAD VIEJA WITH EDUARDO GALEANO

Montevideo, Uruguay

"We are all mortal until the first kiss and the second glass of wine," according to journalist and author Eduardo Galeano (1940–2015). Café Brasilero, one of his hangouts, is a good place to test out the notion and start a 1.6-mile stroll through the Ciudad Vieja of Montevideo. Nearby is the Librería Linardi y Risso, a gorgeous bookshop frequented by the author of *The Open Veins of Latin America* (1971). Detour to the offices of *Brecha*, a newspaper Galeano cofounded, before heading to La Rambla Gran Bretaña, which overlooks the River Plate and was one of his favorite streets.

141
EXPLORE INHOTIM'S ART-FILLED GARDENS

Brumadinho, Minas Gerais, Brazil

Southwest of the city of Belo Horizonte is Inhotim, a vast open-air gallery containing works by leading contemporary Brazilian and international artists. It was created in 2004 for a local mining magnate's personal art collection, but has since been opened to the public. Visitors can walk through the beautifully maintained botanical gardens on a series of interlinked trails. As they do so, they will wander past and around sculptures and installations by the likes of Hélio Oiticica, Edgard de Souza, Anish Kapoor, and Matthew Barney.

142
THE VALLEY THAT INSPIRED GABRIELA MISTRAL

Elqui Valley, Chile

The Elqui Valley is a "heroic slash in the mass of mountains, but so brief that it is nothing but a torrent through two green banks," wrote poet Gabriela Mistral (1889–1957), the first Latin American to win the Nobel Prize for Literature. She was born in this lush region, just east of the city of La Serena, and it strongly influenced her lyrical, emotive poetry. This 0.6-mile stroll through the pretty village of Montegrande starts at the old school, now a museum; Mistral lived here with her sister, a teacher. It moves onto the main square, opposite which the poet's profile is marked out with white stones, and ends at her tomb, on a tranquil hillside south of Montegrande.

LEFT: Gabriela Mistral described the Elqui Valley as a "heroic slash in the mass of mountains."

ABOVE: A statue of Nobel Prize-winner Mistral stands in her hometown, the tiny village of Montegrande.

143

HEAR THE ECHOES OF NUEVA CANCIÓN CHILENA IN SANTIAGO

Santiago, Chile

Walk with: Violeta Parra (1917–1967) and Víctor Jara (1932–1973)

Route: Parque Quinta Normal to the Cementerio General de Santiago

Length: 6.5 miles

Essential listening: *Manifiesto* (Jara); "Me Gustan los Estudiantes" (Parra)

TOP RIGHT: The cemetery in Santiago where these two musical greats lie.

RIGHT: Santiago's La Moneda palace was heavily bombed during Pinochet's coup of 1973.

Pioneered by Violeta Parra, energized by Víctor Jara, and closely associated with the rise of Salvador Allende in the 1960s and early 1970s, Nueva Canción Chilena (New Chilean Song) was a powerful, political, and influential folk-music movement.

The multitalented Parra—she was also an accomplished artist and the first Chilean to have an exhibition at the Louvre in Paris—committed suicide in 1967. Jara was murdered by General Pinochet's forces in 1973. Despite their untimely deaths, the pair remain icons of progressive politics and their songs continue to ring out whenever Chileans take to the streets to protest. "Don't cry when the sun is gone," Parra wrote, "because the tears won't let you see the stars."

This 6.5-mile walk starts west of the city center at Parque Quinta Normal. In the 1930s, Parra lived at a house on nearby Calle Edison. Today, the area is home to the Museo de la Memoria y los Derechos Humanos (Museum of Memory and Human Rights), a monument to the estimated 3,000 people—including Jara—who were killed or "disappeared" by the Pinochet regime. The route then heads east toward La Moneda Palace, where Allende died in the coup, and on to the University of Chile, where Jara studied theater and sang in the choir.

It then continues east along the Alameda, Santiago's main thoroughfare, toward the Museo Violeta Parra. Finally, the walk heads north, through the Bellavista neighborhood, to the Cementerio General de Santiago, where both Jara and Parra are buried.

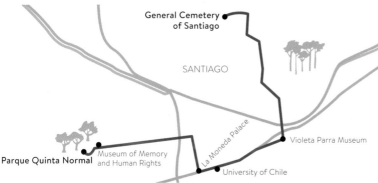

144

ISABEL ALLENDE'S
MEMORIES
Santiago, Chile

Chilean novelist Isabel Allende (1942–) was born in Lima, Peru, but spent much of her childhood in Santiago. A fictionalized version of the city features in her book *The House of the Spirits* (1982). This three-mile walk starts in Cerro Santa Lucia, a hilly park of which Allende is fond, and then cuts through downtown Santiago to the city's main street, the Alameda. The walk finishes at the Museum of Memory and Human Rights, which provides an insight into the dictatorship that forced Allende into exile.

General Cemetery of Santiago

SANTIAGO

Parque Quinta Normal
Museum of Memory and Human Rights
La Moneda Palace
University of Chile
Violeta Parra Museum

145

PABLO NERUDA'S
PART OF TOWN
Santiago, Chile

Nobel Prize-winning poet Pablo Neruda (1904–1973) lived, on and off, at the foot of San Cristóbal hill in a home he called La Chascona, a nickname he gave to his third wife, Matilde Urrutia, due to her abundant red hair. This two-mile walk starts by exploring the house, now a museum, before winding through the Bellavista neighborhood via El Venezia, one of Neruda's favorite restaurants. From here it heads west to the Central Market, where seafood joints serve *caldillo de congrio* (eel stew), a classic dish to which Neruda dedicated a poem.

UP AND DOWN PABLO NERUDA'S "DISHEVELED HILLS"

Valparaíso, Chile

Walk with: Pablo Neruda (1904–1973)

Route: The Barrio Puerto to the Plaza de los Poetas

Length: 2.8 miles

Essential reading: *Twenty Love Poems and a Song of Despair* (1924)

ABOVE: Chile's well-loved poet Pablo Neruda.

TOP LEFT: The wonderful disheveled hills of Valparaíso.

LEFT: If the uphill walk gets too much, there's always the creaky funiculars.

"Valparaíso,
how absurd
you are,
how crazy,
crazy port,
what a head
of disheveled hills,
that you never
finish combing"

So wrote Pablo Neruda of a city that seemed perfectly designed for him. Spread across dozens of steep hills, Valpo—as the city is commonly known—combines edginess and elegance, seediness and sophistication. During the 1960s and early 1970s, Neruda spent much of his time in the city, combining poetry with his political career.

This 2.8-mile walk starts in the Barrio Puerto, the crumbling port district, and passes landmarks such as the Turri Clock Tower, plus several historic restaurants and bars from Neruda's day, most notably Bar Inglés and La Cinzano. Up Ascensor Concepción, one of Valpo's creaking funicular lifts, the walk continues through two of the most atmospheric areas in the city, Cerro Concepción and Cerro Alegre.

At the top of Cerro Concepción, Avenida Alemania snakes over to the east, offering panoramic views of the city below, until it meets Calle Ricardo de Ferrari. This is the location of La Sebastiana, another of Neruda's homes that has been turned into a museum. Nicknamed *la casa en el aire* (the house in the air), thanks to its lofty position, the home's eccentric decor—including a stuffed Coro-Coro bird and a wooden horse—provides an insight into the poet's idiosyncratic character.

The walk finishes just south of La Sebastiana in a small square, the Plaza de los Poetas. Here bronze statues of Neruda and his fellow poet and former teacher, Gabriela Mistral, stand alongside each other.

ON THE TRAIL OF CHE GUEVARA

Ruta del Che, Bolivia

Walk with: Ernesto "Che" Guevara (1928–1967)

Route: Pucará to Quebrada del Churo

Length: 11 miles

Essential reading: *The Bolivian Diary* (1968)

ABOVE: Argentinian-born Ernesto "Che" Guevara.

TOP RIGHT: Che overlooks the main street of La Higuera.

RIGHT: In Vallegrande, there are several murals of the famous revolutionary.

Ernesto "Che" Guevara arrived in La Paz on November 3, 1966, disguised as a balding Uruguayan businessman and with an ambitious plan to launch a South America-wide revolution. Less than a year later, he was killed in the wilds of southeast Bolivia. "In a revolution," he had noted, "you triumph or you die."

Che's plan may have failed, but his efforts—and the enigmatic photos of his Christ-like corpse—helped transform him into an enduring global symbol of revolution. The final stage of his life—recounted, in part, in his book *The Bolivian Diary*—has been turned into the Ruta del Che, which stretches for about forty miles from the town of Vallegrande—where Che's dead body was laid out before being buried in an unmarked grave—to the isolated hamlet of La Higuera, where he lost his life.

The most dramatic section of the trail is an eleven-mile hike starting in the sleepy village of Pucará. A rough track heads south through rugged jungle terrain to La Higuera, which is filled with murals, artworks, and statues dedicated to the revolutionary. The night can be spent at the Casa del Telegrafista, which was used by Che's guerrillas and the C.I.A.-backed Bolivian soldiers who pursued them.

The trail continues below La Higuera to the Quebrada del Churo, a dramatic steep-sided ravine where Che was finally captured. It finishes in the hamlet's old school, where he was executed. His last words, reputedly, were: "Shoot, coward, you are only going to kill a man."

Pucará

BOLIVIAN
ANDES

La Higuera

Quebrada
del Churo

148

BRUCE CHATWIN'S SEARCH FOR BUTCH AND SUNDANCE

Patagonia, Argentina

One of the most memorable stories in Bruce Chatwin's (1940–1989) lyrical, if not entirely truthful, travelog *In Patagonia* (1977) is of Butch Cassidy and the Sundance Kid. This six-mile hike starts in the isolated Andean hamlet of Cholila, not far from the Chilean border. It heads north along the RP-71 road, before breaking off onto a dirt track that leads to the Cholila Ranch, where the bandits lived incognito at the start of the twentieth century. Their cabin has been restored since Chatwin's visit in the 1970s, but it remains an evocative place.

149

FOLLOWING CARLOS GARDEL'S BEAT IN BUENOS AIRES

Buenos Aires, Argentina

A singer, songwriter, and actor, Carlos Gardel (1890–1935) played a major role in popularizing tango in Argentina and around the world in the early twentieth century. This 6.5-mile walk starts in the Chacarita Cemetery, where Gardel is buried, and then heads southeast to the Abasto neighborhood, where he once lived. His old home is now a museum and the area is filled with street art, murals, and statues dedicated to the "dark-haired guy from Abasto." The route continues southeast to the famous Cafe Tortoni, much frequented by Gardel, and finishes in San Telmo at El Viejo Almacén, one of the city's most famous tango venues.

150

PAY TRIBUTE TO ALFONSINA STORNI IN MAR DEL PLATA

Mar del Plata, Argentina

Born in Switzerland, Alfonsina Storni (1892–1938) moved to Argentina as a child and went on to become a groundbreaking poet and champion of women's rights. Tragically, her life came to an early end, after she discovered that her breast cancer had returned in 1938. In despair, she took a train from Buenos Aires to the seaside resort of Mar del Plata. After mailing her last poem, "I am Going to Sleep," to a newspaper, Storni walked down to La Perla beach and drowned herself. This 3.5-mile walk goes from the railway station to the beach and finishes at a moving monument to the poet.

151

HOPSCOTCH THROUGH JULIO CORTÁZAR'S BUENOS AIRES

Buenos Aires, Argentina

In the spirit of Julio Cortázar's (1914–1984) most famous book, the experimental, stream-of-consciousness "counter-novel" *Hopscotch* (1963), this 10.5-mile route can be reordered according to personal taste, and diversions are highly encouraged. It starts at the Escuela Mariano Acosta, a school Cortázar attended in Balvanera, and then heads to Plazoleta Cortázar, a square named for him in Palermo. It meanders on to leafy Barrio Agronomía, where Cortázar lived and which inspired some of his short stories. Cortázar was a big jazz fan, so the route finishes back in Palermo at the famous jazz venue Thelonious.

LEFT: Wander in Patagonia where Butch Cassidy and the Sundance Kid hid out.

WALK SLOWLY IN THE COMPANY OF JORGE LUIS BORGES

Buenos Aires, Argentina

Walk with: Jorge Luis Borges (1899–1986)

Route: Palermo Viejo to Constitución

Length: 6.5 miles

Essential reading: *Fictions* (1962); *The Aleph* (1945)

ABOVE: Jorge Luis Borges is one of Buenos Aires' most famous sons.

TOP RIGHT: The local bar of La Biela was one of Borges' favorite haunts.

RIGHT: The market of San Telmo.

"Hard to believe Buenos Aires had any beginning," wrote Jorges Luis Borges in his poem "The Mythical Foundation of Buenos Aires" (1929). "I felt it to be as eternal as air and water." Few authors have better captured the timeless nature of Argentina's capital than Borges.

This 6.5-mile walk is best approached in a typically Borgesian fashion: "I walk slowly," he wrote, "like one who comes from so far away he doesn't expect to arrive." It starts in Palermo Viejo, the neighborhood in which Borges grew up. His early years were spent at the house at Calle Serrano 2135, and today a plaque marks the spot (a section of the street has since been renamed in his honor). Growing up, Borges was captivated by the raucous stories of the men at the local *almacén* (a shop-bar) on the adjacent street corner.

The route heads southeast into the upscale Recoleta neighborhood, site of the Fundación Internacional Jorge Luis Borges, which has a small museum. Northeast of here is Recoleta Cemetery, where many members of Borges' family—though not Borges himself—are buried. Nearby is one of his favorite haunts, La Biela, a classic Buenos Aires-style café-bar.

From here, head south toward the city center, calling at Calle Tucumán 840, where a plaque marks his birthplace. And then on to two neighborhoods that captured the imagination of Borges and inspired much of his writing: Montserrat and San Telmo.

Finally, the walk heads west to the Constitución neighborhood and Avenida Juan de Garay, the setting for one of Borges most famous works, *The Aleph*. One of the cellars on this street, in that short story, contains a "point in space that contains all other points" in the universe.

EUROPE

In the lands where the Romantics introduced walking for pleasure as a concept, trace the old paths left by Wordsworth and Brahms, and the new ones formed by Andy Goldsworthy and Christa Wolf.

JULES VERNE'S CENTER OF THE EARTH

Snæfellsjökull, Iceland

Walk with: Jules Verne
(1828–1905)

Route: Up Snæfellsjökull
volcano

Length: 5 miles

Essential reading: *Journey to
the Center of the Earth* (1864)

French author Jules Verne was a pioneer of science-fiction writing. His stories were adventurous and fantastical—and prolific. He wrote more than sixty adventures, including *Twenty Thousand Leagues Under the Sea* (1870), *Around the World in Eighty Days* (1873), and *Journey to the Center of the Earth* (1864).

This last was set in Iceland, a country Verne had never visited, but which he thoroughly researched in Paris' Bibliothèque Nationale. It follows eccentric professor Otto Lidenbrock on his quest to explore volcanic tubes leading to the center of the earth.

Visitors to Iceland today can hike to the volcano of the novel— Snæfellsjökull—even if they can't quite go inside. Its barren slopes rise up five thousand feet from the rocky moss-covered lunar landscape below. In the summer months, it is a five-hour hike to the crater. Verne's description of "the stones, adhering by no soil or fibrous roots of vegetation, rolled away from under our feet, and rushed down the precipice below with the swiftness of an avalanche," will feel very much like fact rather than fiction.

The weather on the glacier-covered summit can be misty. However, those who are rewarded with views may well feel like the professor: "I was thus steeped in the marvelous ecstasy which all high summits develop in the mind; ... I was forgetting where and who I was ... I felt intoxicated."

ABOVE: Master of science-fiction writing, Jules Verne.

RIGHT: The glacier-covered top of Snæfellsjökull volcano.

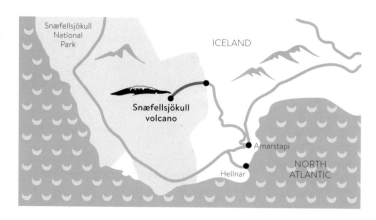

Snæfellsjökull
National
Park

ICELAND

Snæfellsjökull
volcano

Arnarstapi

NORTH
ATLANTIC

Hellnar

FIND POETIC INSPIRATION IN CONNEMARA

Ballynahinch Lake, Connemara, Ireland

Walk with: Seamus Heaney (1939–2013)

Route: Around Ballynahinch Lake

Length: 4 miles

Essential reading: "Ballynahinch Lake" (1999)

RIGHT: It's easy to see why Ballynahinch Lake inspired Seamus Heaney to write a poem

Ballynahinch Castle Hotel is surrounded by hundreds of acres of rugged Connemara landscape that has long captivated writers, painters, and photographers. Poet Seamus Heaney was a regular visitor here, right up until his death in 2013. In his poem, "Ballynahinch Lake," Heaney and his wife pause to look at the view of Ben Lettery rearing up above the stretch of water beside the hotel:

"So we stopped and parked in the spring-cleaning light
Of Connemara on a Sunday morning
As a captivating brightness held and opened
And the utter mountain mirrored in the lake
Entered us like a wedge knocked sweetly home
Into core timber"

The Ballynahinch grounds offer a range of trails to walkers keen to experience the "captivating brightness" for themselves. Stepping away from the hotel, cross the bridge on the main avenue and then veer left toward the lakeside, keeping an eye out for peregrine falcons, pine martens, Atlantic salmon, and red deer—protected species on the estate.

The path joins up with the Connemara Greenway by a smaller lough. This stretch is the first completed section of what is hoped will become a forty-seven-mile trail connecting Clifden to the west with Galway in the east. It follows the old Clifden to Galway railway line, last used in the 1930s, and here at Ballynahinch, it passes the old station building. Cross back over the river, where the road steers right, leading up to the back gate lodge and past the walled garden, before returning to the castle for a well-earned whiskey by the crackling log fire.

155

AN ISLAND
OFF IRELAND
Connemara, Ireland

Writer, artist, and
cartographer Tim Robinson
(1935–) set up his studio
on the quayside of remote
Roundstone, on the west
coast of Ireland. This marked
the start of a study of the
Connemara landscape that
would begin with a series of
maps, before continuing to
books, which would lead a
newspaper critic to write:
"Robinson is perhaps the
only writer alive who can
make a sequence about
sphagnum moss seem
page-turningly thrilling."
The small island of Inishnee
in Roundstone Bay is
connected to the mainland
by a narrow bridge and the
Inishnee Loop is an easy
3.75-mile walk, passing
by boggy hills, bracing
coastline, and, probably,
sphagnum moss.

156

GREEN ROAD ON
THE EMERALD ISLE
Connemara, Ireland

Philosopher Ludwig
Wittgenstein (1889–1951)
was a frequent visitor to
Ireland in the 1930s and
1940s, creating some of his
finest work here. It began
with his first visit to the
hamlet of Rosroe, a place to
which he would return, to
work on the posthumously
published *Philosophical
Investigations* (1953). The
nearby 5.5-mile Green Road
provides a tranquil meander
on which to ponder those
philosophical questions of
life and death.

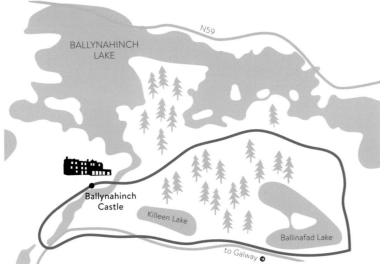

157

A MOUNTAIN HIKE

Ben Bulben, Sligo Bay, Ireland

The looming flat-topped rock of Ben Bulben was immortalized in the work of Irish poet William Butler Yeats (1865–1939), leading this part of the emerald isle to become known as Yeats Country. "Under bare Ben Bulben's head/In Drumcliff churchyard Yeats is laid," he wrote in "Under Ben Bulben" in 1938—as indeed he now is, buried in that same churchyard in the shadow of the mountain (although there is some debate as to whether the bones are really his). The summit of "Sligo's Table Mountain," as it is known, is accessible via a moderate hike up the south side (beware, the north side is hazardous).

"ARISE AND GO NOW, AND GO TO INNISFREE"

Lough Gill, Ireland

Walk with: W. B. Yeats (1865–1939)

Route: Slish Wood, Sligo

Length: 2 miles

Essential reading: "The Lake Isle of Innisfree" (1890)

The Isle of Innisfree is an uninhabited lake isle, sitting in Lough Gill in Sligo, on the northwest coast of Ireland. William Butler Yeats spent his summers here as a child, and its charm never left him. He was inspired to write "The Lake Isle of Innisfree" after he was struck by a sudden memory of his childhood, while walking down London's Fleet Street in 1888.

"I hear lake water lapping with low sounds by the shore;
While I stand on the roadway, or on the pavements grey,
I hear it in the deep heart's core."

It's a yearning many Irish emigrants around the world will be able to empathize with—and lines from this poem feature in the Irish passport.

Today it is easy to escape to the Emerald Isle, as Yeats did. Lough Gill is surrounded by nature trails—including a short one at the small hill of Dooney Rock, which inspired another of Yeats' works, "The Fiddler of Dooney" (1892). For a longer walk, try Slish Wood, which features in some of his poetry as "Sleuth Wood." From the car park, a circular forest walk leads to spectacular views of the lake and Innisfree. At the fork, after about one mile, keep right to complete the loop, or veer left to continue on to the long-distance Sligo Way toward Dromahair (6.2 miles away).

ABOVE: W. B. Yeats, who shared his memories of Innisfree with the world.

TOP LEFT: Who wouldn't yearn for the tranquility of the Lake Isle of Innisfree?

LEFT: A walk through Slish Wood leads to spectacular views of Lough Gill and its famous isle.

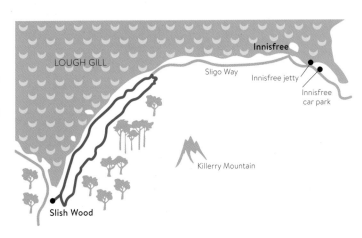

WALK ON THE WILDE SIDE

Dublin, Ireland

Walk with: Oscar Wilde (1854–1900)

Route: Dublin, Ireland

Length: 0.6 miles

Essential reading: *The Importance of Being Earnest* (1895)

ABOVE: Dublin-born Oscar Wilde.

RIGHT: The house in which Wilde grew up, in Dublin.

Flamboyant playwright, poet, novelist, and all-round conversational wit Oscar Wilde was born at 21 Westland Row, Dublin (now home of the Oscar Wilde Centre for Irish Writing, Trinity College). When he was a year old, the family moved a three-minute walk south to 1 Merrion Square Park, where his parents held soirées with Dublin's writers, artists, and raconteurs.

Wilde's life in Dublin didn't stretch far from here. He went on to read classics at Trinity College, practically on his doorstep, and he lived in the family home until he left for Oxford to complete his studies. He only ever returned to Ireland three times, and then only briefly.

The Oscar Wilde Memorial Sculpture in Merrion Square Park features a statue of Wilde wearing his Trinity tie. The odd expression on Wilde's face—one half smiling, one somber—is intended so visitors can see one side of Wilde when approaching and another when walking away—the witty public face, and the broken man he became following his incarceration in Reading jail for homosexuality.

Complete a circuit of the small park and retrace your steps to celebrate Wilde's charmed but complicated life with a pint in Kennedy's, a former grocery shop where Wilde earned his first pennies with a Saturday job, and where he would later spend them on stout, alongside other great Irish writers. With its close proximity to Trinity College, patrons here today could quite possibly be sitting beside the next great Irish writer.

160
A SHORT PUB CRAWL
Dublin, Ireland

For many Irish writers, their haunts were local pubs, but nineteenth-century poet William Butler Yeats (1865–1939) was famed for only going to one—Toners on Kildare Street—before declaring to his friend, "I have seen the pub, now please take me home." Toners is a ten-minute walk from the National Library, where Yeats was much more at home (go via Henry Moore's statue of the poet on St. Stephen's Green). Head north and over the River Liffey to the Abbey Theatre, which was cofounded by Yeats.

161
A DAY WITH JAMES JOYCE
Dublin, Ireland

Number 7 Eccles Street is where Leopold Bloom—the protagonist in James Joyce's (1882–1941) opus magnus *Ulysses* (1922)—begins his single epic day in Dublin. He walked through the city, crossing the Liffey at O'Connell Bridge (where he buys a cake to throw at the seagulls) before heading to St. Stephen's Green, where the trees "were fragrant of rain and the rainsodden earth gave forth its mortal odor." Purists can retrace their steps back to Eccles Street, to end where the novel does, with its forty-page monolog featuring just two punctuation marks.

162

DRAMATIC SCENES FROM MAGGIE O'FARRELL

Omey Island, Ireland

Maggie O'Farrell (1972–) is the queen of family dramas, with her sixth novel, *Instructions For A Heatwave* (2013), exploring the aftermath when a father walks out on his family. The novel ends on Omey, a small tidal island off Connemara's west coast. Accessible on foot at low tide, "The strand out is a gleaming white path through the waves, which foam and turn on either side," writes O'Farrell. Check tide times before crossing between the markers on the golden sand.

163

GET CAUGHT IN VAN MORRISON'S BELFAST

Belfast, Northern Ireland

Any fan on a walk through George Ivan "Van" Morrison's (1945–) native Belfast should start on Cyprus Avenue, in homage to the singer's eponymous song. The song contains a number of references to places in the area, as does "Madame George" (1968), another track from the Northern Irish singer/songwriter. Start your walk at the Eastside Visitor Centre, where you can grab a map before heading to Elmgrove Primary School, The Hollow, The Beechie, Hyndford Street, Orangefield Park, Cyprus Avenue, St. Donard's Church, and Cyprus Avenue Restaurant for more Van Morrison hotspots.

RIGHT: Cross between the markers to reach the dramatic tidal island of Omey.

VISIT NARNIA WITH C. S. LEWIS

Mourne Mountains, Northern Ireland

Walk with: C. S. Lewis
(1898–1963)

Route: Cloughmore Trail,
Rostrevor, Northern Ireland

Length: 2.5 miles

Essential reading: *The Lion, the
Witch, and the Wardrobe* (1950)

RIGHT: Cloughmore Stone was
almost certainly C. S. Lewis'
inspiration for the Stone Table
in Narnia.

C. S. Lewis was born and spent the first ten years of his life in Belfast, Northern Ireland. He lived in a large Victorian house on the outskirts of the city which very possibly inspired the house of his *Chronicles of Narnia* series with its famous wardrobe.

However, this walk takes place in the heart of Narnia itself, near the small town of Rostrevor, where the young Lewis spent many holidays.

"That part of Rostrevor which overlooks Carlingford Lough is my idea of Narnia," he wrote to his brother of this magical spot with its green valleys, looming mountains, and sparkling sea.

Begin the walk in the upper car park of Kilbroney Park and follow the waymarked trail through the forest until you emerge at the Cloughmore Stone—a fifty-five-ton granite boulder sitting at the top of the hill.

Pause here to reflect on a passage near the end of *The Lion, the Witch, and the Wardrobe*: "They were on a green open space from which you could look down on the forest spreading as far as one could see in every direction … There, far to the East, was something twinkling and moving. 'By gum!' whispered Peter to Susan, 'the sea!' In the very middle of this open hilltop was the Stone Table … a great grim slab of grey stone supported on four upright stones." How can you not believe you are in Narnia?

WANDER INTO THE CORNISH WORLD OF ALFRED WALLIS

St. Ives, Cornwall, England

Walk: Alfred Wallis
(1855–1942)

Route: St. Ives Railway station
to Porthmeor Beach

Length: 0.6 miles

Essential viewing: *The Blue Ship* c.1934

TOP RIGHT: The Digey is typical
of many of St. Ives' narrow
cobbled streets.

RIGHT: The wildness of
Porthmeor beach inspired
Alfred Wallis

Alfred Wallis was a retired fisherman from St. Ives who took up painting at seventy, to occupy his time. With very little money, he painted on scraps of wood and cardboard using mostly household paint. The naivety of his work and methods were a breath of fresh air to the sophisticated trained artists who moved there from London.

From St. Ives railway station make your way north toward The Warren, the old coastal path with its limestone seawall on your left. Continue toward the harbor and you will see some tiny fishermen's cottages on the right. About 500 feet farther on, there is an opening on the right called Pednolva Walk. From here, enjoy the view across to the harbor mouth and lighthouse, which has changed little since Wallis's time. It was from this spot that he painted *The Blue Ship, Harbor with Two Sailing Lighthouses and a Motor Vessel* (1932–1934), and many others.

Continue along this walkway until you reach St. Andrew's Street, turning right and continuing past the beautiful fifteenth-century parish church until you reach Fore Street, St. Ives' main thoroughfare, a narrow pedestrianized street with a cornucopia of shops and cafés. At the end of Fore Street, fork left into The Digey, which brings you on to Porthmeor Beach, the setting for several other Wallis paintings including *St. Ives* (1928). These two views have continued to inspire artists ever since.

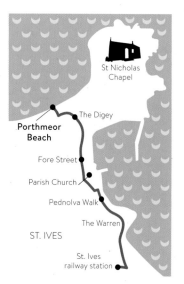

St Nicholas
Chapel

The Digey

**Porthmeor
Beach**

Fore Street

Parish Church

Pednolva Walk

The Warren

ST. IVES

St. Ives
railway station

166
BARBARA HEPWORTH
St. Ives, Cornwall, England

Artists have long been attracted to live and work in St. Ives, where the landscape is enhanced by the quality of the natural light. Studios and workshops have been here for at least one hundred years, and the St. Ives Society of Artists formed in the 1920s. English sculptor and artist Barbara Hepworth (1903–1975) established her studio in 1949. Left to the nation upon her death, visitors can walk around the inspirational Barbara Hepworth Museum and Sculpture Garden, for a new perspective on the working practises of one of Britain's most important sculptors.

167

THE RUINED CASTLE THAT INSPIRED A SYMPHONY

Tintagel, Cornwall, England

At the end of his Second Symphony, Sir Edward Elgar (1857–1934) printed the words "Venice—Tintagel." Later, he explained that the openings of the second and third movements were inspired by St. Mark's Basilica in Venice. Less clear is which part of the music can be identified with the area around Tintagel, with its ruined castle and wild clifftops. Elgar visited his friend Alice Stuart Wortley and her husband Charles here and enjoyed many walks along the coastline. To follow in his footsteps, walk the Tintagel Circular up to the castle and along the clifftops.

168

JOIN ARTHUR CONAN DOYLE ON DARTMOOR

Dartmoor, England

In 1888, Arthur Conan Doyle (1859–1930) wrote: "'Where there is no imagination, there is no horror." This sentiment found its apogée in his later story *The Hound of the Baskervilles* (1902). To relive the chilling sense of the book, visit Fox Tor, a site 1,440 feet above sea level on Dartmoor, arguably the bleakest place on earth. Even on a clear sunny day, it's not hard to imagine the bitterly cold swirling fog of a winter's evening. Just over half a mile to the north below the Tor is Fox Tor Mire, the boggy setting for the incident where the evil Stapleton, a character in the story, warns Sherlock Holmes that: "A false step yonder means death."

169

HIKE ENGLAND'S MOST POETIC RAILWAY LINE

River Camel, Cornwall, England

Sir John Betjeman (1906–1984) once described the railway line running along the Camel Estuary to Padstow as "the most beautiful train journey I know." Today, the line is a seventeen-mile-long walking and biking trail, passing through countryside that inspired many of the Poet Laureate's greatest works. For Betjeman, Cornwall was a world of "golden unpeopled bays," where "gorse turns tawny orange." Betjeman grew up holidaying at his father's property in Trebetherick, eventually moving to live in Cornwall toward the end of his life.

170

FIND J. D. SALINGER IN THE UK

Tiverton, Devon, England

A ramble around the rural town of Tiverton in Devon is a walk away from the hustle and bustle. J. D. Salinger (1919–2010) was stationed in this peaceful town for three months during the Second World War, and it was the slower pace of life here that gave him the chance to reflect on his writing and the characters he was creating for his landmark novel, *The Catcher in the Rye* (1951). The experience of the countryside and the matter-of-factness of its people led him to create a more sympathetic and less sarcastic Holden Caulfield. Retrace some of the steps Salinger would have taken via the Grand Western Canal, passing under twenty-four bridges.

LEFT: The ruins of Tintagel Castle in Cornwall, inspired Elgar's Second Symphony.

ON THE TRAIL OF AGATHA CHRISTIE IN TORQUAY

Torquay, Devon, England

Walk with: Agatha Christie (1890–1976)

Route: The Agatha Christie Mile (The Grand Hotel to The Imperial Hotel)

Length: 1.3 miles

Essential reading: *Sleeping Murder* (1976); *Agatha Christie: An Autobiography* (1977)

ABOVE: The doyenne of mystery, Agatha Christie.

TOP RIGHT: The Agatha Christie Mile takes visitors on a tour of sites linked to the author's life.

RIGHT: Christie was from Torquay, and she often chose small Devon towns as the setting for her murder-mysteries.

Agatha Christie is so intrinsically linked to her hometown of Torquay, in Devon, that the town hosts a biennial literary festival in her honor.

Christie based many of her works in Devon, preferring a backdrop of small towns and tight-knit communities for her dramatic murder mysteries. "I specialize in murders of quiet, domestic interest," she explained, staging her crimes in holiday resorts and at village fetes.

In Torquay, The Agatha Christie Mile leads visitors in a neat arc around the town's harbor, calling at twelve locations linked to the author's life. Christie's two famous detectives, Miss Marple and Hercule Poirot, may also make an appearance. The two never met in her books, but both visited Torquay. A little detective work—with those "little gray cells" engaged, as Poirot would say—should uncover their footprints.

Beginning at the Grand Hotel, the walk leads around the bay to the Princess Pier, a favorite spot of the author's during her youth. Nearby, the exotic palm trees and stunning coastal views of the Princess Gardens feature in *The ABC Murders* (1936).

The "Mile" ends at The Imperial, an elegant Victorian hotel at the top of Beacon Hill, where Christie attended many social functions. This was also a setting for several of her novels, masquerading as The Majestic in *Peril at End House* (1932). The hotel's terrace, with its sweeping views of Torquay's bay, was the setting for the last chapter of Miss Marple's final case, *Sleeping Murder* (1976).

172
A BEAUTIFUL SPOT FOR A MURDER
Burgh Island, Devon, England

A small tidal island off the coast of Devon, Burgh Island was the setting for two of Agatha Christie's best-loved books. Starting out from Bigbury-on-Sea at low tide it's possible to walk across the sands to the island. Take the footpaths past the luxurious, art-deco Burgh Island Hotel and over the hill to the dramatic coastline on the farthest side of Burgh, where "there is no such thing as a really calm sea. Always, always, there is motion." These are the cliffs from which Dr. Armstrong was pushed to his death in *And Then There Were None* (1939), and nearby lies the cove where Arlena Stuart met her end in *Evil Under the Sun* (1941).

WALKING THE COLERIDGE WAY

Somerset and Devon, England

Walk with: Samuel Taylor
Coleridge (1772–1834)

Route: Coleridge Way

Length: 51 miles

Essential reading: *The Rime of
the Ancient Mariner* (1798)

RIGHT: The Coleridge Way
runs from Nether Stowey
to Lynmouth through
the Quantock Hills.

"On springy heath, along the hill-top edge,
Wander in gladness, and wind down, perchance,
To that still roaring dell, of which I told;
The roaring dell, o'erwooded, narrow, deep,"

This is the opening to "This Lime-Tree Bower My Prison," a poem
Samuel Taylor Coleridge wrote in 1797 when his friends went off to
explore the countryside, leaving him to languish at home beneath a tree
after he'd had an accident involving a pan of scalding milk.

The countryside in question is the Quantock Hills, and the friends fellow
Romantics William Wordsworth and Charles Lamb. The locals were so
suspicious of the poet and his friends' eccentric pastime of walking that
they suspected Coleridge was spying for the French.

Coleridge could walk from his home in Nether Stowey to Porlock,
twenty-four miles away, in a day (it was a visitor from here who famously
interrupted his "Kubla Khan" composition, and "person from Porlock" has
come to mean "someone who disrupts creative endeavors").

Today, the Coleridge Way is a footpath more than twice that length,
running from Coleridge's cottage via Porlock to Lynmouth, crossing the
peaceful Exmoor National Park. The path traverses a variety of landscapes,
including open moors and ancient woodland, with a scattering of pretty
villages to stop at and explore en route.

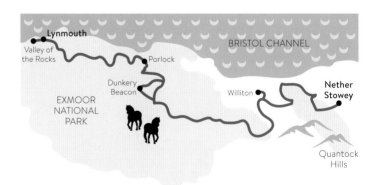

177
SEE LIFE THROUGH MARTIN PARR'S LENS

Bath and Bristol, England

British documentary photographer and photojournalist Martin Parr (1952–) is known for his documentation of the vast realms of British heritage, and it is his love for walking which has led him to some of his most iconic photos. Today Parr lives in Bristol, and it's the variety of landscapes that inspire his daily life, regularly walking with his wife on a Sunday morning. Take your own camera on an adventure via the Bath Skyline Walk, with six miles of meadows, ancient woodlands, and secluded valleys to capture.

178
EXPLORING DAPHNE DU MAURIER'S CORNWALL

Fowey, Cornwall, England

With its windswept coastline and rugged beaches, Cornwall is the setting for many of Daphne du Maurier's (1907–1989) novels, and where she lived for most of her life. Strike out west along the dramatic South West Coast Path from Fowey (home to the Daphne du Maurier Literary Centre), and follow the scenic route toward Gribben Head to pass Polridmouth Cove 2.2 miles away—the secluded beach that was one of her favorite bathing spots. It lies just below Menabilly House, where du Maurier spent many years writing and which was the inspiration for the house of Manderley in *Rebecca* (1938), with its famous opening line: "Last night I dreamt I went to Manderley again."

179
A COLORFUL JAUNT IN THE DORSET HILLS

Dorset Hills, England

New Zealand landscape and still-life artist Frances Hodgkins (1869–1947) spent most of her working life in England. In the 1920s, she moved into a studio in Burford, Oxfordshire, and, as she wrote in a letter at the time, "found the Cotswold country very paintable and the air splendidly bracing." A circular walk east from the town, following the River Windrush then on through the medieval villages of Swinbrook and Widford, explores the area where Hodgkins painted, capturing the bare essential forms of the landscape in an abstract style that would come to embrace modernist hallmarks.

180
JOIN A JOHN FOWLES DRAMA ON THE JURASSIC COAST

Lyme Regis, Dorset, England

A challenging 3.5-mile stretch of the South West Coast Path takes hikers from Seaton to Lyme Regis through the Undercliffs. It was to this dramatic, isolated part of the Jurassic Coast that John Fowles (1926–2005) moved in 1965 and began work on *The French Lieutenant's Woman* (1969). The novel features striking descriptions of the local area, a place that is, Fowles wrote, "perched like a herring gull on a ledge, suspiciously peering both ways into Devon and Dorset." End the walk at The Cobb harbor, where the French Lieutenant's woman stood alone, gazing out to sea.

RIGHT: The colorful town of Fowey in Cornwall.

181
JOHN CONSTABLE'S SALISBURY CATHEDRAL

Salisbury Wiltshire, England

Recapture the essence of John Constable's (1776–1837) romantic views of Salisbury Cathedral, painted in 1820. Enter St. Anne's Gate on Exeter Street and walk along North Walk until you reach Sarum College of Theology, which has been here since medieval times. Opposite the College is Bishop's Walk and your first view of the Cathedral. Continue to the end of North Walk, where it meets West Walk, and continue until you are facing the West Front of the Cathedral. Along West Walk, past the Salisbury Museum, is Leaden Hall, where the artist stayed in 1820.

182
WALK BETWEEN THE POEMS OF LAURIE LEE

Slad Valley, Gloucestershire, England

Slad, a steep-sided valley nestled in the charming Cotswolds area of England, has been immortalized in the writings of Laurie Lee (1914–1997), particularly in his much-loved memoir *Cider with Rosie* (1959). The Laurie Lee Wildlife Way is a six-mile circular walk through the valley, where "lemon-green the vaporous morning drips" and "hedges choke with roses fat as cream." Ten cedar posts, each printed with one of Lee's poems, mark significant spots along the trail, which also takes in Lee's local, the Woolpack pub in Slad village.

183
RICHARD LONG AND THE LEGEND OF SILBURY HILL

Avebury, Wiltshire, England

In 1970, artist Richard Long (1945–) created *A Line the Length of a Straight Walk from the Bottom to the Top of Silbury Hill* for an exhibition in New York. The work was a photograph of Silbury Hill—the largest man-made Neolithic site in Europe—with a text explaining its ancient legend on the wall of the gallery and a spiral of chalky footprints, whose overall length was 120 feet, the distance Long covered walking from the base to the top of the hill, on the floor beneath. All of Long's work contains aspects of paths that he has trodden. "My art is the essence of my experience, not a representation of it," he says. It's not possible to climb Silbury Hill now, but there is a lovely walk around its base starting in Avebury.

184
IN THE WORDS OF EDWARD THOMAS

Dymock, Gloucestershire, England

Until 1914, Edward Thomas (1878–1917) was a biographer and literary critic, through which work he became great friends with the American poet Robert Frost, who lived in Dymock in Gloucestershire. Thomas visited Frost often, and Frost encouraged Thomas to turn his hand to poetry. In 1914, Thomas did so, and all his poems were written between then and 1917, when he died. Thomas and Frost roamed the countryside together. His poem "The Sun Used to Shine" was written about the walks the two of them used to take. Retrace their footsteps on a walk up May Hill, near Boxbush, where Thomas began to write his famous poem "Words."

LEFT: The Neolithic Silbury Hill in Wiltshire was the inspiration for a Richard Long artwork.

185

PLAY AT BEING JANE AUSTEN IN THE LANES AROUND HER HOME

Chawton, Hampshire, England

Walk with: Jane Austen (1775–1817)

Route: The Writers' Way

Length: 11 miles

Essential reading: *Jane Austen's Letters* (1932)

English novelist Jane Austen grew up in Steventon in Hampshire and spent a few short years in Bath before the death of her father forced the family into genteel impoverishment. When Jane was thirty-two, her brother Edward inherited Chawton House and estate and offered Jane, her sister, and their mother a cottage to live in rent-free for life.

The pretty seventeenth-century red-brick cottage about which Austen wrote, "Our Chawton House how much we find already in it to our mind, and how convinced that when complete it will all other houses beat," is now the Jane Austen's House Museum.

The Writers' Way traces an 11-mile path from Jane Austen's home through gently rolling countryside. From Chawton, the trail passes through the market town of Alton, before going over a steep hill and into sunken Watery Lane. The trail winds through woods, lanes, and villages until it reaches Farringdon, where just after Massey Folly, the circular route heads back to Chawton via St. Swithun's Way, which uses, in part, the line of the old Meon Valley Railway.

Finish your walk at the Tearoom of Chawton House, where Jane's brother lived and which she referred to in her letters as the "Great House."

ABOVE: British national treasure, Jane Austen.

TOP RIGHT: Massey's Folly in Farringdon is an interesting eccentricity along the route.

RIGHT: The cottage in Chawton where Jane Austen lived is now a museum.

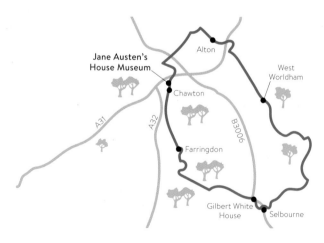

186
JANE AUSTEN'S REGENCY BATH
Bath, Avon, England

At the turn of the nineteenth century, Jane Austen lived in Bath for a few short years. Two of her novels, *Northanger Abbey* (1817) and *Persuasion* (1818), reveal Austen's initial excitement, which eventually turned to weariness of crowded rooms and forced frivolity. Exploring Bath, with its pale-gold Georgian crescents, reveals sites that Jane Austen knew well. Walk from the Pump Rooms to Sally Lunn's House, toward Pulteney Bridge, and then north from the Theatre Royal to The Royal Crescent, The Circus, and the Upper Assembly Rooms for a feel of life in an Austen novel.

187

ENJOY J. M. W. TURNER'S PAINTERLY VIEWS OF AND FROM THE THAMES PATH

Gloucestershire to London, England

Walk with: J. M. W. Turner (1775–1851)

Where: Cotswolds, Gloucestershire, to London

Length: 184 miles

Essential viewing: *Windsor Castle from the Thames* (c.1805), *Isleworth* (1819)

In southern England, an idyllic stretch of river known as the Thames Path travels 184 miles—from Cricklade, near Cirencester in the Cotswolds, through the Chiltern Hills, to Oxford, before meandering on via Windsor and Hampton Court, passing Teddington, Twickenham, Richmond, and Hammersmith, to Greenwich, London. The English artist Joseph Mallord William Turner painted stretches of the river at many locations along the path over the years. Many views today are exactly as they were in Turner's day, unspoilt by the spread of urban living.

Turner's views of Oxford included landscape sketches created close to the riverside. Others from along the path include *Windsor Castle from the Thames* (c.1805), *The Thames near Walton Bridges* (c.1807), and *Dorchester Mead, Oxfordshire* (1810). *Isleworth* (1819) was possibly painted while aboard a boat. Viewing the river from water was a tactic employed by Turner at sea, too, once tying himself to a mast in a storm to sketch torrential waves.

In 1840, Turner designed and built his own house, Sandycombe Lodge, in Twickenham. Open to the public, it is a pleasant eleven-minute walk from the Thames Path at Twickenham, crossing the tip of Orleans Gardens through to Marble Hill Park.

ABOVE: J. M. W. Turner was the master of the watery view.

TOP RIGHT: The Thames Path is 184 miles long and has many unspoiled rural sections.

RIGHT: The river at Richmond on a summer's day is a hive of leisurely activity.

188
SEA VIEWS IN MARGATE
Margate, Kent, England

"...The skies of Thanet are the loveliest in Europe," remarked English artist J. M. W. Turner about this corner of Kent. Turner first visited aged eleven, staying with an uncle in Margate. He returned regularly to paint the sea and skies, renting accommodation in a house close to where the Turner Contemporary gallery now stands. Over one hundred paintings by Turner feature the East Coast and Margate. A walk along Marine Drive, passing in front of the Turner Contemporary to stand on the tip of Harbour Arm, will give glorious sea views, unchanged since Turner stayed here.

189
PETWORTH PARK
Petworth, West Sussex, England

During J. M. W. Turner's visits to Petworth House, West Sussex, between 1809 and 1837, he was allocated a permanent art studio space by the mansion's owner, the Third Earl of Egremont. A series of landscapes created for the Earl include the glorious *Petworth House from the Lake: Dewy Morning* (1810) and *The Lake, Petworth: Sunset, Fighting Bucks* (1829–1830). On a visit to Petworth House and Park, Turner's romantic views of the estate, on display in the house, can be visualized while strolling through the 700 acres of parkland.

190

BRITISH SEA POWER

Firle, East Sussex, England

Walk with: British Sea Power

Route: Firle to Lullington Church

Length: 6.5 miles

Essential listening: "The Smallest Church in Sussex" (2015)

TOP LEFT: A view of Firle Beacon on the South Downs.

LEFT: The smallest church in Sussex inspired a British Sea Power song.

While much is made of how walking and the countryside inspired the romantic poets, composers, and artists of yesteryear, there are far fewer modern examples. One British pop group, however, that celebrates its love of walking as something that is inherent to the creative process is the band British Sea Power. "[The countryside is] seen as the antithesis of rock music, but walking in the outdoors gives you the same exhilaration as music," guitarist Martin Noble said in an interview with the *Guardian* newspaper. "It can move you in the same way that music does."

The six-piece band spent many years based in East Sussex and launched their first album in The Ram Inn at Firle, where they then camped in the pub garden.

This walk starts here and heads uphill to the Firle Beacon for magnificent views across the Sussex countryside and to the sea at Eastbourne. Follow the South Downs Way eastward for a couple of hours until it drops down into the village of Alfriston. Near the main church, cross the river and take the footpath up to Lullington Church—or "The Smallest Church in Sussex," as British Sea Power rightly called it. The tiny church seats about twenty people. It still holds services, although not on a daily basis.

The spot—and the church—captivated Neil Hamilton Wilkinson, songwriter, bass guitarist, and vocalist with the band, and the church's organ features in the song.

FOLLOW VIRGINIA WOOLF ACROSS THE SOUTH DOWNS

Rodmell, East Sussex, England

Walk with: Virginia Woolf (1882–1941)

Route: Monk's House, Rodmell, to Charleston Farmhouse

Length: 6 miles

Essential reading: *Between the Acts* (1941); *A Writer's Diary* (1953)

Virginia Woolf may be more associated with London, with *Mrs. Dalloway*'s Westminster and the bohemian Bloomsbury Set, but much of her life was spent in rural East Sussex. Those who chase the ghost of the British author are inevitably drawn to Monk's House, an "unpretending house, long and low, a house of many doors," in the village of Rodmell. Leonard and Virginia Woolf bought Monk's House in 1919 and it became a rural retreat, for the couple and their literary friends.

A six-mile walk across the River Ouse and along the South Downs leads from Rodmell to Charleston Farmhouse. Once the home of Woolf's sister, Vanessa Bell, the house was another haunt for the intellectuals and artists of the day, and is still filled with their work.

It is a walk that Woolf made countless times to visit her sister. "What I wouldn't give," she wrote in 1921, "to be coming home through Firle woods, dusty and hot, with my nose turned home." It was on this same route that, in 1941, Woolf drowned herself in the River Ouse; her ashes were scattered in the garden of Monk's House.

The walk offers spectacular views across the South Downs, of which Woolf once wrote: "Too much for one pair of eyes, enough to float a whole population in happiness, if only they would look."

ABOVE: Virgina Woolf spent many years in Sussex.

TOP RIGHT: Monk's House in Rodmell was Virginia Woolf's rural retreat.

RIGHT: Charleston Farmhouse, home of Woolf's sister, Vanessa Bell, is a six-mile walk away.

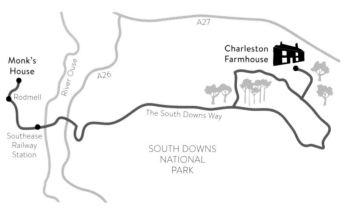

192
TO THE LIGHTHOUSE
Isle of Skye, Scotland

Fans of Virginia Woolf's introspective novel *To the Lighthouse* (1927) may not recognize the Isle of Skye from its pages. Although set on the Hebridean island, much of the landscape was inspired by St. Ives in Cornwall. The house where the Ramsay family holiday in the novel, for example, was based on Talland House where Woolf's own family holidayed in St. Ives. But echoes of the novel's landscapes can nonetheless be found across Skye. A walk to Brother's Point on the northeastern coast offers views of the wild island of Rona, where a small lighthouse lies perched on a hill "running purple down into the distant heather," across a "sea without a stain on it."

193

WALK ON WATERSHIP DOWN

Ecchinswell, Hampshire, England

Watership Down in Hampshire is the setting for Richard Adams' (1920–2016) eponymous adventure story about a group of rabbits. Set off south from the village of Ecchinswell to enter Adams' beloved countryside, passing Nuthanger Farm—as featured in the novel—on the way.

194

ENJOY HUNDRED ACRE WOOD

Ashdown Forest, East Sussex, England

Hundred Acre Wood, home of A. A. Milne's (1882–1956) Winnie the Pooh, that "bear of very little brain," is based on Ashdown Forest, East Sussex. A circular trail through the woodland crosses Poohsticks Bridge and other landmarks such as Roo's Sandy Pit.

195

ADVENTURES WITH ROALD DAHL

Great Missenden, Buckinghamshire, England

Roald Dahl (1916–1990) lived in Great Missenden in Buckinghamshire for more than thirty years. Walking through the streets, the inspirations for his books' characters and locations can be spotted in the local pub, in the Red Pump Garage, Crown House, and Atkins's Wood, where he walked.

KIPLING'S SOUTH DOWNS

Burwash, East Sussex, England

Walk with: Rudyard Kipling (1865–1936)

Route: Circular route around Burwash and Bateman's

Length: 2.25 miles

Essential Reading: "The Land" (1917)

ABOVE: Rudyard Kipling, forever associated with colonial India.

TOP LEFT: Kipling's family home of Bateman's, in Sussex.

LEFT: The study where Kipling wrote many of his later works.

Rudyard Kipling—whose views have dated less well than his work, such as the stirring poem "If" (1896) and *The Jungle Book* (1894)—loved "our blunt, bow-headed, whale-backed Downs," and settled on them from 1897—initially in Rottingdean, then near Burwash in a house called Bateman's—described by Kipling as "a good and peaceable place."

This walk starts at Burwash's Bear Inn and threads south through the Sussex fields to Bateman's. It's now a National Trust property and visitors can see the rooms as the family lived in them, including the study where Kipling wrote books like *Puck of Pook's Hill* (1906).

They can also walk the 330-acre estate, about which Kipling wrote "The Land," in which the narrator gets the story of the mill brook from a fictional local everyman called Hobden:

"So they drained it long and crossways in the lavish Roman style—
Still we find among the river-drift their flakes of ancient tile,
And in drouthy middle August, when the bones of meadow show,
We can trace the lines they followed sixteen hundred years ago."

And so can today's visitors. From the front of the house, the path heads to the mill pond and continues to the right of the mill stream, before crossing a footbridge, then northward back over the fields until it meets the A265, which runs east to Burwash.

197
HELEN ALLINGHAM'S
THATCHED COTTAGES

Witley, Surrey, England

Born in Derbyshire and raised in Birmingham, artist
Helen Allingham (1848–1926) eventually made her
home in Sandhills, near the town of Witley in Surrey.
Originally an illustrator—including supplying drawings
for Thomas Hardy's *Far from the Madding Crowd*—after
her marriage to the poet William Allingham, she
was able to return to her first love of watercolors.
In particular, she painted the local thatched cottages
that were starting to disappear with the arrival of
the railways. Begin this walk at Witley station, on the
footpath that takes you over the railway. Soon after, it
joins a lane, which will lead you past Allingham's former
home of Sandhills, recognizable from her paintings.

198
CROSS WATER MEADOWS IN
WINCHESTER WITH JOHN KEATS

Winchester, Hampshire, England

The English Romantic young poet John Keats
(1795–1821) wrote lines of one of his most famous
odes, "To Autumn" (1819), while staying in Winchester.
From his lodgings, thought to be on the north side
of Winchester Cathedral, he took walks daily, passing
through Cathedral Close and crossing the water
meadows alongside the River Itchen chalk stream,
to reach the medieval almshouse of the Hospital of
St. Cross. Travelers arriving on foot can receive the
Wayfarer's Dole—bread and ale. Those walking in
the fall will experience Keats'"season of mists and
mellow fruitfulness."

199
CHARLES DARWIN'S
"THINKING PATH"

Down House, Downe,
Kent, England

In 1846, Charles Darwin (1809–1882) rented a patch
of land near Down House, his home in rural Kent, and
constructed a stone-and-sand path around a copse of
trees. This quarter-mile circuit, the Sandwalk, became
his "thinking path." For forty years, Darwin walked
along it almost every day, meditating on his work.
When he completed a lap, he added a stone to a pile;
his children often removed stones when he wasn't
looking to trick him into walking farther. Today,
the Sandwalk is open to the public, and offers views
across grassy meadows, a soundtrack of birdsong, and,
occasionally, the chance to spot a wild deer.

200
DISCOVER KENT'S MORE
MODERNIST SIDE

Dungeness, Kent, England

Following the Dungeness Trail along the beach of
this windswept corner of Kent leads walkers past a
distinctive black fisherman's house with a sprawling
garden. English film director, artist, and author Derek
Jarman (1942–1994) bought Prospect Cottage on a
whim, and the house quickly became an escape. "My
garden's boundaries are the horizon," he wrote on the
very first page of his meditative diary *Modern Nature*
(1991); and he's right. The garden leaks into the shingle
of the beach, mingling into the local flora until it's no
longer clear where Prospect Cottage ends, encapsulating
this idea of escape.

RIGHT: Derek Jarman's
coastal cottage merges into
the beach at Dungeness.

201

BENJAMIN BRITTEN'S EAST ANGLIAN SOUNDSCAPE

Aldeburgh, Suffolk, England

The six-mile pathway along the estuary from the Suffolk village of Snape to the seashore at Aldeburgh echoes with the music of Benjamin Britten (1913–1976). Born in Lowestoft, the composer is intrinsically linked with this part of East Anglia. Nicknamed the Sailor's Path, the trail starts near the Snape Maltings concert hall—founded by Britten—and skirts the nature reserve. Here, among the cries of the abundant water birds, walkers might pick out the sound of the curlew, inspiration for *Curlew River* (1964). On the beach at Aldeburgh, one can almost hear the footsteps of the titular character of Britten's opera *Peter Grimes* (1945) among the crash of waves against the shingle.

202

WALK DOVER BEACH WITH MATTHEW ARNOLD

Dover, Kent, England

Fans searching for the spot captured so beautifully in Matthew Arnold's (1822–1888) famous poem, "Dover Beach," should head to the coast on a clear evening. Walk the shingle beach, where "sea meets the moon-blanched land" and listen to the "grating roar" and "tremulous cadence" of pebbles swept by the surf. Arnold visited Dover on his honeymoon, and later wrote what is often called his most radical poem. The setting is a worthy one for a beach walk, where the "cliffs of England stand, Glimmering and vast, out in the tranquil bay," welcoming travelers to the country.

DISCOVER CHARLES DICKENS' HIGHAM

Higham, Kent, England

Walk with: Charles Dickens
(1812–1870)

Route: Around Dickens' home

Length: 3.1 miles

Essential reading: *Great
Expectations* (1861);
The Pickwick Papers (1836)

RIGHT: Charles Dickens first
saw Gad's Hill Place as a boy and
dreamed of living there, which,
once he became a successful
novelist, he did.

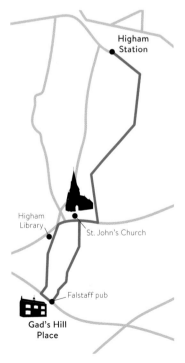

Charles Dickens was born in Portsmouth and came to represent Victorian London, but to some extent his heart was always in Kent. As a boy, when his father worked in Chatham, he had walked past Gad's Hill Place in Higham and resolved to one day live there; by 1856, he could afford to buy it, and he lived there for the rest of his life.

The trail starts at the railway station. Over the railway bridge is a footpath through open fields to The Landway; up to the right is Whitehouse Farm, after which the path heads across to St. John's Church, whose vicar sold Gad's Hill Place to Dickens (and who was allowed to stay there until a vicarage was built). As a public reader, Dickens advised the curate that "reading more from the chest and less from the throat" would aid audibility.

Round the corner from the church, on Forge Lane, is Higham Library, with an 1864 map contemporary to Dickens. Farther down Forge Lane and slightly left on Gravesend Road is Gad's Hill Place itself. Dickens wrote: "I used to look at it as a wonderful mansion (which God knows it is not) when I was a very odd little child with the first faint shadows of all my books in my head."

If Gad's Hill was full, Dickens would often station guests at the Falstaff pub opposite, which is still open. Telegraph Hill, which runs past the Falstaff, runs back up to Hermitage Road just past St. John's Church; retracing back to the station from there creates a 3.1-mile walk that Dickens would have seen as paltry—he walked 12 miles a day. His eldest daughter, Mamie, wrote that "walking was perhaps his chiefest pleasure."

Higham
Station

Higham
Library

St. John's Church

Falstaff pub

Gad's Hill
Place

ROOKERIES
OF LONDON

**The Arches, Charing
Cross, London, England**

"The neighborhood was a
dreary one at that time; as
oppressive, sad, and solitary
by night, as any about
London." Charles Dickens
was describing a tannery near
Charing Cross, but, in truth,
it's a description that fits
many of the London places
associated with the great
author. Much of "his"
London has changed little
since his time—bar the
lighting. To enhance this
walk, take it on a winter's
evening after dusk. Start
at St. Michael's Church in
Cornhill, and walk into St.
Michael's Alley, at the end of
which is the site of London's
first coffee house. Now turn
right into Castle Court
to reach the George and
Vulture restaurant, often
visited by Mr. Pickwick of
The Pickwick Papers (1836)
when it was a "chop house."

205

DISCOVER LONDON THROUGH CLAUDE MONET'S EYES

Bankside to Westminster, London, England

Walk with: Claude Monet (1840–1926)

Route: Tower Bridge to Westminster Bridge

Length: 2.5 miles

Essential viewing: *The Thames Below Westminster* (1871)

RIGHT: Stand near the spot where Monet painted his view of the Houses of Parliament.

At the turn of the nineteenth century, Claude Monet stated that: "Without fog London would not be beautiful."

The artist had originally come to London in 1870 to escape the Franco-Prussian War, staying for several months and painting views of London. At low tide it is possible to stand slightly up river from Tower Bridge, where he painted *The Pool of London* and *Boats in the Pool of London*, both dated 1871. The chimneys and warehouses have now long gone but in the middle distance on the right are the Customs House and Billingsgate Fish Market buildings, which are still there.

Walk along the north embankment for about two miles, imagining how much more hectic, noisy, and polluted it was in Monet's day, when this was the busiest docks in the world. Continue underneath London, Southwark, and Blackfriars bridges, and climb the steps of Waterloo Bridge to the street level above. A little way past here on the same embankment is the rear entrance of the Savoy Hotel where Monet painted views of the Thames from 1899 to 1901. Look up to the fifth floor where his apartment was situated. A little farther along the embankment is the Golden Jubilee footbridge, from where it is possible to see an identical view of Monet's painting *The Thames Below Westminster*, depicting the Houses of Parliament.

On the south side of Westminster Bridge is St. Thomas' Hospital, from where Monet painted so many of his ethereal paintings of the Houses of Parliament in the fog.

206
CLIMB TREES WITH PETER BLAKE

Chiswick Garden, London, England

Some of pop artist Peter Blake's (1932–) more recent works, such as *The Climbing Tree,* have been inspired by peaceful moments with his family in the tree-lined gardens of Chiswick House.

207
FRANCIS BACON'S SOHO

Soho, London, England

The paintings of Francis Bacon (1909–1992) depict the loneliness he found at the heart of man, often as he cruised the streets of Soho.

208
WHISTLER'S CHELSEA

Chelsea Embankment, London, England

James Abbott McNeill Whistler's (1834–1903) *Nocturnes* of the River Thames were painted in Chelsea. His statue is at the end of Battersea Bridge; he lived along Cheyne Walk at Lindsey House and painted Cremorne Gardens.

209
HOGARTH'S LONDON

Smithfield, London, England

For William Hogarth's (1697–1764) London, explore the alleyways off Cloth Fair, which in his time were full of low-life. Continue to St. Bart's Museum and the huge Christian narrative that he painted for free.

The Savoy

The Thames

Blackfriars Bridge

Waterloo Bridge

Golden Jubilee Bridge

Westminster Bridge

St. Thomas' Hospital

LONDON

Custom House

The Tower of London

London Bridge

Tower Bridge

210
SYLVIA PLATH'S PRIMROSE HILL

Primrose Hill, London, England

American poet Sylvia Plath (1932–1963) arrived in London in 1955, attending lectures at the Bedford College for Women. The college is gone but there is a plaque at Bedford Square. On the other side of the British Museum is the church of St. George the Martyr, where she married Ted Hughes in 1956. From here, head through Regent's Park—where Plath used to take her daughter to London Zoo—to 3 Chalcot Square in Primrose Hill, where she and Hughes rented a top-floor flat and she wrote *The Colossus* (1960) and *The Bell Jar* (1963). After splitting from Hughes, Plath moved in to 23 Fitzroy Road, where, tragically, she committed suicide, weeks after writing in her journal: "When I came to my beloved Primrose Hill, with the golden leaves, I was full of such joy."

211
DISCOVER MRS. DALLOWAY'S LONDON

Westminster to Bloomsbury, London, England

"I love walking in London," declares Mrs. Dalloway in the opening pages of Virginia Woolf's (1882–1941) novel. This is one of many similarities between the titular character and the author, who wrote in her essay "Street Haunting" that "to walk alone in London is the greatest rest." Woolf wrote *Mrs. Dalloway* (1925) on returning to London after ten years of living in Surrey, and her pleasure at being back is reflected throughout the novel. Walk from Mrs. Dalloway's home in Westminster, near Dean's Yard, and follow her footsteps through Green Park to Bond Street. End in Bloomsbury, littered with the former homes and haunts of the Bloomsbury Set, including Woolf's in Gordon Square and Tavistock Square.

212
A TOUR OF ZADIE SMITH'S "NW" CORNER OF LONDON

Willesden, London, England

Born and raised in Willesden, British author Zadie Smith (1975–) and her writings are deeply associated with north London. Toward the end of *NW* (2012)—named after the postcode for northwest London—one of the central characters, Keisha, walks from her home near Queen's Park across north London. Mapped out with loyal precision, the road names and landmarks overlap with real life. It's possible to follow Keisha's footsteps by chapter titles alone: "Willesden Lane to Kilburn High Road" and "Hampstead to Archway," ending, eventually, at "suicide bridge" on Hornsey Lane.

213
FEEL THE EYES WATCHING YOU WITH GEORGE ORWELL

Islington, London, England

A short walk from Highbury and Islington station is 27b Canonbury Square, where the writer George Orwell (1903–1950) lived from 1945 and where he wrote his dystopian novel *Nineteen Eighty-Four*, published in 1948. The story focuses on the totalitarian control of society by the government through its all-seeing mass-surveillance program. Orwell's prophecy has some resonance today, with London having four times more CCTV surveillance than any other city in the western world. Take a short walk from his house to the junction of Canonbury Square and New North Road and count how many cameras you can spot.

RIGHT: Dean's Yard where Mrs. Dalloway lived and walked.

214

THE BALLAD OF PECKHAM RYE

Peckham Rye, London, England

Muriel Spark (1918–2006) lived in Camberwell, south London, when she wrote *The Ballad of Peckham Rye* (1960)—a nearby area. The novel takes place in some imaginary, but many real, locations. Two of the pubs mentioned on the first page can be visited: The White Horse on Nigel Road and, a short walk away, the Rye (which was the Rye Hotel in the book) along the left-hand fork of Peckham Rye. Opposite The Rye, behind some trees, look for the blue cement structure, which is all that is left of the Peckham "swimming baths" mentioned in the book, before enjoying a stroll around Peckham Rye itself—a constant presence in the tale.

215

NATURE IN THE CEMETERY

Nunhead Cemetery, London, England

Aminatta Forna's (1964–) novel *Happiness* (2018) begins on Waterloo Bridge and is firmly rooted in a modern London—both its people and its wildlife. The story focuses on the lives of two visitors to London, one of whom goes jogging in Nunhead Cemetery. "The innumerable hues of green: bright moss, candescent pale lichen on the gravestones, dark ivy which smothered every tree…" This atmospheric spot in southeast London has paths that wind through the trees to a viewpoint of the distant dome of St. Paul's Cathedral.

216

AROUND HILARY MANTEL'S HAMPTON COURT PALACE

Hampton Court, East Molesey, Surrey, England

History piles up on itself around Hampton Court Palace, strong-armed off Cardinal Wolsey by Henry VIII in 1529, as dramatized in Hilary Mantel's (1952–) *Wolf Hall* (2009) novels. The palace grounds can be approached directly down Chestnut Avenue—Bushy Park's grand processional parade, designed for King William III and Queen Mary II by St. Paul's architect, Christopher Wren. However, the more dramatic approach is from the west, past Wren's blue-plaqued house at the end of Hampton Court Road: from here, the drive sweeps up to the unmistakable Tudor frontage. The palace's south and east faces are resplendent in the Versailles-style Baroque with which William and Mary intended to replace the whole palace—even monarchs run out of money sometimes.

217

TAKE A WALK ON THE WILD SIDE

Piccadilly, London, England

It was one of Lord Byron's (1788–1824) lovers, Lady Caroline Lamb, who famously noted that he was: "Mad, bad, and dangerous to know." By the time Byron married his wife Annabella in 1815 and moved into the elegant Georgian mansion at 139 Piccadilly, he was already famed for his womanizing, gambling, and debauched behavior. Unsurprisingly, his marriage lasted barely more than a year. While here, across the road from Green Park, he wrote one of his most tragic works, "*Parisina" (1816).*

It is the hour when from the boughs
The nightingale's high note is heard."

Wander through Green Park and listen out for that nightingale.

LEFT: Hampton Court Palace, with its distinctive Tudor style.

218
GET SOME SATISFACTION IN RICHMOND PARK

Richmond, London, England

The Rolling Stones lived in Chelsea in their early years, but it was their residency at the Crawdaddy Club in Richmond-upon-Thames in 1963 that catapulted them into the limelight. The club has moved on, but the link between Richmond and The Stones continues. Front man Mick Jagger (1943–) and his then wife, Jerry Hall, lived in a large Georgian property on Richmond Hill during the 1990s and into the 2000s. Cross the road to Terrace Gardens for the view of the River Thames that has been painted by Joshua Reynolds and J. M. W. Turner. Continue up the hill into Richmond Park and follow the tracks to Pen Ponds. There is a 750-year-old oak tree, known as the Royal Oak, which Jagger has called his favorite tree in the park.

219
WANDER IN AMY WINEHOUSE'S LONDON PLAYGROUND

Camden, London, England

Amy Winehouse's (1983–2011) untimely death at twenty-seven, adds another layer of sadness to her expressive jazz-soul albums. Her extraordinary singing and mature songwriting had already led to multiple Grammys and worldwide sales, but her heart was always in London's gritty Camden, which she referred to as her "playground." Winehouse spent many hours on nearby Primrose Hill. Half a mile down from there is The Roundhouse—the venue where Winehouse played her final UK gig on July 20, 2011. Farther down Chalk Farm Road, in the Stables Market, is a lifesize bronze statue of the singer, while around the corner on Castlehaven Road is her regular haunt, The Hawley Arms. Winehouse died on July 23, 2011, in her home at 30 Camden Square.

220
FOLLOW THE SOUNDS OF THE WESTMINSTER CHIMES

London, England

Ralph Vaughan Williams (1872–1958) first began his *London Symphony* (1914) at the suggestion of his friend and fellow composer George Butterworth, to whom the piece was dedicated. Although Williams attributes numerous physical locations to the various movements of the piece, one theme that returns throughout is the Westminster chimes. Of the third movement, he wrote that the listener should: "imagine himself standing on Westminster Embankment at night, surrounded by the distant sounds of The Strand." Head, then, from Westminster Bridge toward The Strand, accompanied by the sprawling and poetic *London Symphony*.

221
WALK THE TRAIL OF A ROYAL CONCERT

River Thames, London, England

George Frideric Handel's (1685–1759) *Water Music* was written to be performed on water. The piece was commissioned by King George I to accompany a grand royal cruise along the Thames. On July 17, 1717, the king boarded his Royal Barge at Whitehall Palace along with a group of aristocrats, and sailed to Chelsea. Alongside, on a separate barge, Handel himself conducted fifty musicians in his lavish, three-part suite. Begin at the Banqueting House to follow the same route along the Thames to Chelsea's Cadogan Pier.

RIGHT: Amy Winehouse loved the vibrancy of Camden.

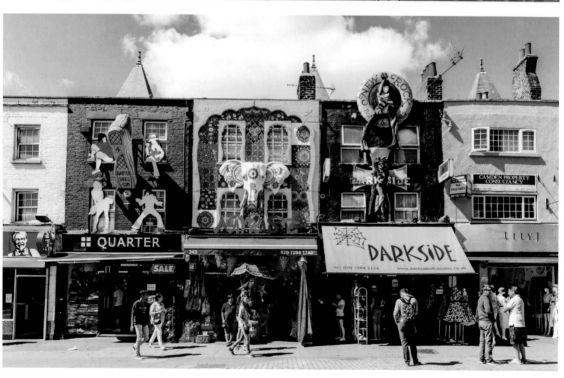

RETRACE THE ROUTE OF CHAUCER'S PILGRIM'S WAY

London to Canterbury, England

Walk with: Geoffrey Chaucer (1343–1400)

Route: Southwark, London, to Canterbury, Kent

Length: 60 miles

Essential reading: *The Canterbury Tales* (1387–1400)

TOP RIGHT: The George Inn on Borough High Street is typical of an inn from Chaucerian times.

RIGHT: The goal of the walk, Canterbury Cathedral.

In 1170, the Archbishop of Canterbury, Thomas Becket, was murdered inside Canterbury Cathedral on the supposed orders of King Henry II. Within a short time the Pope canonized Becket and, soon after, his shrine became a pilgrimage destination.

Geoffrey Chaucer began writing his *Canterbury Tales* in 1387, as a series of stories told by pilgrims to entertain one another while on this pilgrimage to Canterbury. The first tale is *The Knight's Tale*, which was of courtly love and chivalry at court, followed by twenty-three others, including the altogether more lurid and bawdy *The Miller's Tale*.

Chaucer's walk begins at The Tabard in Southwark, but as this inn is no longer standing, this walk starts at the nearby George Inn on Borough High Street instead. The cobbled courtyard is typical of taverns and inns of the medieval period.

The route from Borough High Street passes the St. George the Martyr church and turns left on to the Old Kent Road. This leads you to Blackheath and views back to Southwark, then on down Shooters Hill and into Kent.

The full pilgrimage to the Cathedral takes five to six days, but there are plenty of stories to tell on the way.

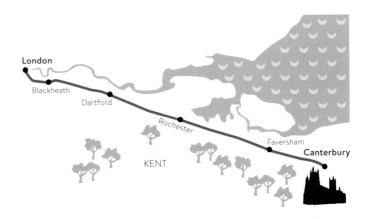

London
Blackheath
Dartford
Rochester
Faversham
Canterbury
KENT

223
VINCENT VAN GOGH'S WALK
Ramsgate to London, England

Before he was an artist, Vincent van Gogh (1853–1890) spent a few months in Ramsgate, working without payment as a boarding-school teacher at 6 Royal Road. The young Vincent loved walking. His sister Anna was staying in Welwyn Hatfield, about ninety miles away in Hertfordshire. He walked from Ramsgate to visit her, getting the occasional lift from a passing horse and cart. His journey took him through the poorest parts of London, which was reflected in his art when he became a painter in 1880. He wrote of these walks in wonderfully expressive letters home, many of which are published in *Vincent van Gogh: A Life in Letters* (2020).

WALK THE DYLAN THOMAS TRAIL

Ceredigion, Wales

Walk with: Dylan Thomas, (1914–1953)

Route: Llanon to New Quay

Length: 25 miles

Essential reading: *Under Milk Wood* (1954)

As one of his most oft-quoted lines urges, Dylan Thomas did not "go gently into that good night." Thomas was born in Swansea in 1914 and died in New York in 1953, aged just thirty-nine. But what a life. Almost as well known for his riotous boozing and frequent philandering as his rich and rhythmic poetry, Thomas raged both in life and on the page, drunk on beer and language, producing some of the most visionary verse of the twentieth century.

Though he spent time elsewhere, Thomas was very much a Welsh poet; his homeland stimulated some of his best writing. In the 1940s he lived briefly in the west Wales coastal town of New Quay. It was here that he penned the prose poem "Quite Early One Morning," which recounts a walk along the cliffs as the village starts to stir.

The Dylan Thomas Trail runs through the Ceredigion countryside that so inspired him. Starting at the village of Llanon, it sneaks inland through oak woods and quiet valleys to Talsarn, where Thomas stayed for a while in the county house of Plas y Gelli. The trail then turns back toward the sea, tracing the coast south from Aberaeron to New Quay. In the latter you'll find the little bungalow of Majoda, where Thomas lived; The Black Lion Inn, his favored drinking den; and the terraces that seem like Thomas' fictional village of Llareggub brought to life.

ABOVE: Dylan Thomas, arguably Wales' greatest poet.

TOP RIGHT: The Black Lion Inn in New Quay was Thomas' favored drinking den in the area.

RIGHT: The Dylan Thomas Trail passes along the charming harbor at Aberaeron.

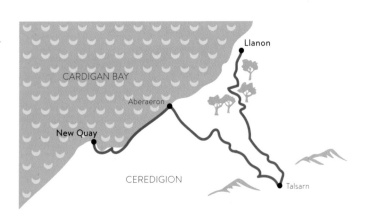

225
DYLAN THOMAS BIRTHDAY WALK
Carmarthenshire, Wales

Dylan Thomas spent his last years in the village of Laugharne, an eccentric spot that slips off the end of the Taf estuary. In 1944 Thomas wrote "Poem in October," about a stroll he took here on his thirtieth birthday, when he rose:

*"in rainy autumn
And walked abroad in a
   shower of all my days."*

You can follow him, on a two-mile route that begins at the Boathouse (his former home), passes the crumbling castle, skirts the harbor, and climbs Sir John's Hill for fabulous views over the estuary. Benches carved with the poet's words dot the route.

226
WALKING ON THE BLACK HILL WITH BRUCE CHATWIN

Brecon Beacons, Wales

On the Black Hill (1982) was a departure for the travel writer and novelist Bruce Chatwin (1940–1989), being a story of twin brothers who, far from roaming, live out their lives in a farmhouse on the Welsh/English border. "The border of Radnor and Hereford was said to run right through the middle of the staircase." Their home—called The Vision—is a real farmhouse north of Llanthony, bordering the east of the Brecon Beacons National Park, and the Black Hill behind it is accessible on a 4.5-mile steep circular walk from Llanthony, along the top of the scenic Hatterall Ridge.

227
A WALK IN THE VALLEY OF THE ELWY

Elwy Valley, Wales

"Lovely the woods, waters, meadows, combes, vales, All the air things wear that build this world of Wales," is how Gerard Manley Hopkins (1844–1889) portrayed the Elwy Valley in a poetic love letter to this tranquil region in north Wales. Plenty of walking trails traverse this landscape, from short riverside strolls in St. Asaph to a 6.2-mile route from Llansannan, following the paths northward on both sides of the Afon Aled, over woods, waters, meadows, combes, vales. The walk will introduce you to the nature and environments of the valleys surrounding the Elwy, exactly how Hopkins described it.

228
SHIRLEY BASSEY'S TIGER BAY

Cardiff, Wales

Since Shirley Bassey (1937–) was born in Tiger Bay, both person and place have undergone significant gentrification. The future Dame Shirley who sang "The Girl From Tiger Bay" (plus three Bond themes) left long before the dockside area's major modernizations. Bassey's first regular booking, as a fifteen-year-old watched by drinkers including Dylan Thomas, was at 36 James Street: The Ship & Pilot pub, now renamed Mischief's but still hosting live music. She was born around the corner at 116 Bute Street, which leads into Cardiff city center. Walk to Queen Street and the Edwardian New Theatre, where Shirley went professional, aged just seventeen, in *Hot From Harlem*. By the age of twenty, she was recording in New York.

229
CHANCE UPON LED ZEPPELIN'S MOUNTAIN RETREAT

Machynlleth, Powys, Wales

In 1970, Led Zeppelin's chief songwriters Jimmy Page and Robert Plant decided they needed to head for the hills after being on tour for eighteen months. They retreated to an eighteenth-century cottage called Bron-Yr-Aur on the outskirts of Machynlleth, Wales, where the young Plant had holidayed with his family. There, he and Page wrote songs including "Bron-Yr-Aur" and the incorrectly spelled "Bron-Y-Aur Stomp." Bron-Yr-Aur is a private home, but the hills around it are a hiking hotspot. The 135-mile Glyndwr's Way includes a beautiful but demanding 9.5-mile stretch from Aberhosan. Climbing to the green track high above the valley of Cwm Cemrhiw, the trail strides above Machynlleth.

LEFT: The dockside in Shirley Bassey's Tiger Bay.

230

THE WYE VALLEY VIEWPOINT THAT SO INSPIRED WILLIAM WORDSWORTH

Wye Valley, Wales

Walk with: William Wordsworth (1770–1850)

Route: Whitestone Walk

Length: 2 miles

Essential reading: "Lines Composed a Few Miles above Tintern Abbey, On Revisiting the Banks of the Wye during a Tour" (1798)

TOP RIGHT: A view down to the wonderful bends of the River Wye.

RIGHT: The ruins of Tintern Abbey have long been popular with poets and painters.

At the end of the eighteenth century, when Grand Tours of Europe were the height of fashion, somehow sleepy Wye Valley became something of a destination. It was *de rigueur* to take a boat tour along the Rye from Ross to Chepstow and admire the landscape and crumbling ruins of Tintern Abbey from the water. Poets and painters arrived clutching William Gilpin's bestseller, *Observations on the River Wye*.

The great English Romantic Poet William Wordsworth preferred to explore the picturesque lower Wye Valley on foot—wandering "lonely as a cloud" shaped him as a man and a poet. His 1798 visit to the Welsh/English border was Wordsworth's second:

"Five years have past; five summers, with the length
Of five long winters! and again I hear
These waters, rolling from their mountain-springs
With a soft inland murmur."

He composed *Tintern Abbey* while climbing the hills above the village of Llandogo and today the easiest access to these magnificent views down into the Wye Valley are from the Whitestone car park (ten miles north of Chepstow). As the trail ascends, with the River Wye to the east, each viewpoint has a bench engraved with lines from Wordsworth's poem: the third and highest bench is said to be where the poet was inspired. Along the right-hand fork at the T-intersection, the trail continues via an ancient track to Cleddon Falls, perhaps where Wordsworth penned:

"the sounding cataract
Haunted me like a passion: the tall rock,
The mountain, and the deep and gloomy wood."

THE QUANTOCK HILLS

Holford, Somerset, England

William Wordsworth and his sister Dorothy lived in the Quantock Hills for just a year between 1797 and 1798. They took a house near Holford to be close to their dear friend Samuel Coleridge in Nether Stowey, and the writers walked between each other's homes most days, crossing glens, glades, and woodland. An eight-mile loop trail between the villages takes in part of the Coleridge Way, Walford's Gibbet, and Holford Combe, with fine views of the Somerset Coast. Plough Inn in Holford is a great spot for lunch and there's a short mile-long extension out to Alfoxton House and estate (closed to the public), where the Wordsworth's lived.

232

ALAN BENNETT'S GROCERY BAG OF A MEMORY LANE

Headingley, Leeds, England

Playwright Alan Bennett (1934–) might have described his youth as, "a childhood dull, without color, my memories done up like the groceries of the time in plain, utility packets." Nonetheless, he has often returned, in person and prose, to the streets of Headingley in Leeds where he grew up above his father's butcher's shop (which closed in 2005) at 92A Otley Road. "My bedroom was at the back, looking up Weetwood Lane." Up Weetwood Lane, Bennett remembers, "my mother hiding buttered bread under the table at Bryan's Fish and Chips so we could have chip butties." Beyond Bryan's (still serving), Weetwood Lane climbs up to The Hollies, a park with a steep wooded ravine formed by Meanwood Beck, said to have influenced Leeds University lecturer J. R. R. Tolkien—plus, of course, the teenage Bennett.

233

FOLLOW ELGAR IN THE MAJESTIC MALVERN HILLS

The Malvern Hills, Worcestershire, England

The Malvern Hills inspired the music of English composer, Malvern-born Sir Edward Elgar (1857–1934). A good day's trek starts at St. Wulstan's Church in Little Malvern, where Elgar, his wife, Lady Elgar, and their daughter Carice are buried. From here, head up to the Worcestershire Beacon, the highest point of the hills, at 1,395 feet and with fabulous views. Then walk down to the city center of Worcester and the sublime Worcester Cathedral, where Elgar played in 1884. A memorial window, placed a year after his death, depicts one of Elgar's most famous works, *Dream of Gerontius* (1886).

234

AT COLLEGE WITH IRIS MURDOCH

Oxford, England

Born in Dublin, Iris Murdoch (1919–1999) went to Oxford's Somerville College in 1938 to study philosophy. Over time, she became one of Britain's greatest philosophers and novelists. Although Murdoch traveled extensively throughout her life, some say it was Oxford that made her, and suitably so, for the city of dreaming spires has produced many great writers and philosophers. Start from the college and walk toward the River Thames, up the Thames path and then turn right to return by the ancient Port Meadow, to be among the wild ponies, birds, and flowers—plenty of nature to stimulate the philosopher's thoughts within.

235

FRIENDLY ENCOUNTERS AMONG THE DREAMING SPIRES

Oxford, England

J. R. R. Tolkien (1892–1973) wrote *The Hobbit* (1937) and *Lord of the Rings* trilogy (1937–1949) while living in Oxford. Walking from either Pembroke or Merton College (he was a professor for both at various times) one passes Exeter College, where Tolkien was a young student in 1911. From here it's a short walk to The Eagle and Child pub at 49 St. Giles' Street, where, as one of "The Inklings" literary group, he met his friends and colleagues, including writer C. S. Lewis. The Banbury Road northward passes 20 Northmoor Road, where Tolkien lived for many years. Concluding a walk of around 4.5 miles, continue north toward Wolvercote Cemetery, where Tolkien is buried.

TOP LEFT: Iris Murdoch studied philosophy among the dreaming spires of Oxford.

LEFT: It's a pleasant stroll from the city of Oxford to the meadows by the river.

THE REAL *LARK RISE TO CANDLEFORD*

Oxfordshire, England

Walk with: Flora Thompson (1876–1947)

Route: From Juniper Hill to Bicester, Oxfordshire

Length: c.7.5 miles

Essential reading: *Lark Rise to Candleford* (1945)

TOP RIGHT: The countryside around Bicester is full of open fields and pretty woodland.

RIGHT: This walk traces the changes from rural to urban, ending in the town of Bicester.

In Flora Thompson's trilogy of novels *Lark Rise to Candleford*, she describes the family relations, society, and environment that surrounds the protagonist, Laura Timmins, as she moves from Lark Rise to Candleford. Published separately between 1939 and 1943, the stories roughly follow Thompson's own early life.

In her books, she described Lark Rise (Juniper Hill in reality) as a: "hamlet stood on a gentle rise in the flat wheat-growing north-east corner of Oxfordshire," and that to a passerby with observation, they'll find the life here, "as seething with interest and activity as a molehill."

Thompson's novels describe the effect of the changes in society on the quiet and peaceful environment of the impoverished farming community as the mechanization of agriculture and the closure of common land caused the decline in rural peasantry and the migration of the rural population into larger towns, such as Bicester.

At the age of fourteen, just like her character in the novel, Thompson left the village to work in the post office. To follow her, walk southeastward, over farmlands and country lanes, through the village of Cottisford, where Thompson received her early education into Fringford, or Candleford Green, as readers know it, then continue on Fringford Road to eventually arrive at Bicester Post Office.

237
D. H. LAWRENCE'S BLUE LINE TRAIL
Eastwood, Nottingham, England

English writer and poet D. H. Lawrence (1885–1930) has his roots firmly in the town of Eastwood in Nottinghamshire. From his birthplace at 8a Victoria Street, which now houses the D. H. Lawrence Museum, to the Three Tuns Pub where he would drink, the town is filled with the literary influences of Lawrence's first twenty-three years. Follow the Blue Line Trail, which links various Lawrence-related sites, and see the places which feature in works such as *Lady Chatterley's Lover* (1928 in Italy, 1960 in the UK) and *Women in Love* (1920).

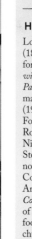

238
EXPLORE *HOWARDS END*
Forster Country, Hertfordshire, England

London-born E. M. Forster (1879–1970), is renowned for novels such as *A Room with a View* (1908) and *A Passage to India* (1924). His masterpiece, *Howards End* (1910), is set in a house that Forster lived in as a child, Rooks Nest, close to St. Nicholas Church, near Stevenage. This rural area is now known as Forster Country. A sculpture by Angela Godfrey, *Only Connect* (1994) (the subtitle of *Howards End*), next to the footpath from St. Nicholas churchyard, makes a good starting point for a pleasant walk signposted with Forster Country Walk waymarkers.

TAKE A WALK WITH THE BARD

Stratford-upon-Avon, England

Walk with: William Shakespeare (1564–1616)

Route: Shakespeare's Way

Length: 146 miles

Essential reading:
Shakespeare's Way, a Journey of Imagination by Peter Titchmarsh (2006)

Often regarded as the greatest writer, poet, and playwright in the English language, William Shakespeare's stories are still read, performed, and made into film productions all around the world.

Shakespeare's Way is a route dedicated to this master of words, roughly following Shakespeare's journey from his birthplace of Stratford-upon-Avon toward London, where he worked, performed, and found eternal fame.

Scholars derive that Shakespeare probably arrived in London in mid-1580 and spent the rest of his working life traveling between the capital and Stratford. He established himself in the theatrical communities and his plays became well received among the population at the time—even Queen Elizabeth I went to his shows.

This walking route starts from the house of his birth in Stratford-upon-Avon, through the north of the Cotswolds toward Blenheim Park, on to the dreaming spires of Oxford, through the woodlands and fields of the Chilterns, reaching the River Thames at Marlow, roughly following its flow to meet the Grand Union Canal near Hayes, and eventually ending at Shakespeare's Globe on Southbank in London. The whole route takes walkers between ten to fifteen days to complete.

ABOVE: The unmistakable face of William Shakespeare.

TOP RIGHT: Shakespeare's Way roughly follows the route The Bard would have taken from Stratford-upon-Avon to London.

RIGHT: Shakespeare's birthplace and family home is now a popular visitor attraction.

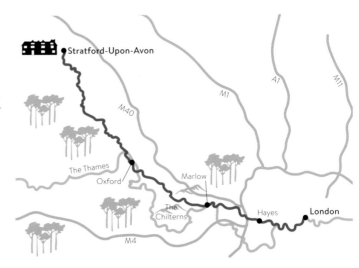

THE SHAKESPEARE FAMILY

Stratford-upon-Avon, Warwickshire, England

Visitors to the historic market town of Stratford-upon-Avon simply cannot escape references to William Shakespeare, and a short 0.6-mile walk around town traces his life from birth to death. Starting from Shakespeare's Birthplace to the New Place, to Hall's Croft, and finally to the Holy Trinity Church, the resting place for William Shakespeare and his wife, Anne Hathaway. Each location offers a different perspective on Shakespeare's personal and family life to those who stop to explore. For the energetic, walk a farther 1.5 miles to Shottery and Anne Hathaway's Cottage, to learn about the woman behind Shakespeare's success.

241
A CORNER WHICH IS FOREVER GEORGE BERNARD SHAW

Ayot St. Lawrence, Hertfordshire, England

For forty-four years, George Bernard Shaw (1856–1950) lived in the village of Ayot St. Lawrence, which is now forever stamped as Shaw's village. A circular walk from Wheathampstead, 2.5 miles away, gives a perspective on the nature and landscapes that inspired Shaw. See the old station platform he would have waited on, and stop by Lamer Park, home of explorer and Shaw's great friend Apsley Cherry-Garrard. Finish at Shaw's Corner, Shaw's house which is now a museum dedicated to the great playwright.

242
HENRY MOORE'S SCULPTURAL LANDSCAPE

Much Hadham, Hertfordshire, England

The one-time home and studio of the British sculptor Henry Moore (1898–1986) can be visited in the summer months. Aside from the house and studio, there are seventy acres of land in which The Henry Moore Foundation has placed over twenty of his monumental works. On leaving the Visitor Centre, walk north to be greeted almost immediately by one of the earliest works, *Family Group,* from 1948. Farther north on the Sculpture Lawn is the large *Two Piece Reclining Figure No. 2,* but the most imposing of all can be seen at the most northerly point of the grounds, The Meadow, where *The Arch* is situated.

243
FIND NATURE THAT JOHN CLARE WOULD DELIGHT IN

Swaddywell Pit, Lincolnshire, England

Known as the "Peasant Poet," John Clare's (1793–1864) love of his surroundings inspired his poems that celebrate English rural life while portraying his frustration and sadness at the disappearance of natural spaces such as the Swaddywell Pit, near the cottage in which Clare lived. Clare dedicated two poems personifying Swaddywell (Swordy Well), disapproving of the changes to his beloved English countryside. Thankfully, today Swaddywell Pit is a protected nature reserve with a five-mile trail that is buzzing with bees and butterflies and rich in birdlife, nurtured back to the natural glory John Clare would have loved.

244
FIND STANLEY SPENCER'S "VILLAGE IN HEAVEN"

Cookham, Berkshire, England

Stanley Spencer (1891–1959) was born and lived most of his life in the tiny Thames-side village of Cookham, a place that inspired much of his narrative paintings. Begin the walk on the High Street at Fernlea, his childhood home that bears a blue plaque to him, before making your way to the riverside and Cookham Bridge, depicted in several of his paintings. Before reaching the river, on the left is Holy Trinity churchyard, the location for his most famous painting called *The Resurrection, Cookham* (1924–1927) in which, on an enormous eighteen-feet-wide canvas, he depicted his living friends rising from the tombs.

RIGHT: Visitors can walk around Henry Moore sculptures at his former home in Hertfordshire.

245
REVEL IN JOHN CONSTABLE'S SUFFOLK

East Bergholt, Suffolk, England

Opposite St. Mary's Church in the village of East Bergholt, where John Constable (1776–1837) was baptized, is the aptly named Flatford Road. Walk the 0.7 miles along here until you arrive at the scene of Constable's *Hay Wain,* painted in 1821. Little has changed here since his day, with the river's edge and Willy Lott's Cottage on the left. The only thing missing today is the angler and the hay cart. To the right of where you are standing is Flatford Mill, which appeared in other paintings by Constable.

246
SEE SATURN FROM THE MARSHES OF EAST ANGLIA

Southwold, East Anglia, England

W. G. Sebald (1944–2001) is that rarity among local authors, in that he didn't actually write in the local language. He came to East Anglia from Germany, and his *Rings Of Saturn* was first published in 1995 in German. Its idiosyncratic blend of historic fact and fiction—text and images—centers around a descriptive ramble along the Suffolk coast, albeit one with long digressions into far away, far off times. One such meander takes him the nine miles south from Southwold to Dunwich—across the River Blythe, through the marshes of Walberswick, and, at low tide, along the shore to the tiny village of Dunwich, once one of the largest ports in England.

247
TAKE IN ANOTHER VIEW OF THE SEA

Crosby Beach, Liverpool, England

A short walk from Crosby Leisure Centre, north along the promenade, a series of motionless figures stand dotted along the beach, some close to the esplanade, others farther out to sea, often partially submerged in the soft sand. In all, there are one hundred of these figures, made of hollow iron cast from a mold of the artist's own body. The artist, Sir Antony Gormley (1950–), created the figures, collectively known as *Another Place* (2005), to explore man's relationship with nature. At high tide, the figures can disappear altogether.

248
FIND GEORGE ELIOT'S MILBY

Nuneaton, Warwickshire, England

George Eliot (1819–1880) didn't just have a *nom de plume* for herself (original name Mary Ann Evans), she also renamed her birthplace of Nuneaton in Warwickshire as Milby in her novels. The town now has a quotation trail which joins various commemorative places. There's a statue in Newdegate Square; round the corner, near where Bridge Street crosses the River Anker, is the George Eliot Inn, described (as The Red Lion) in *Janet's Repentance* (1857). A look up Church Street gives some flavor of Eliot's Orchard Street that is at the heart of this novel. Off Mill Street is the 1952 George Eliot Memorial Garden, with a riverside Eliot obelisk. Upstream, the Museum and Art Gallery houses Eliot artifacts in a recreated drawing room complete with the writing desk from which she sent her hometown around the world.

LEFT: One of Antony Gormley's *Another Place* figures looks out to sea from Crosby Beach.

JOIN THE BRONTË FAMILY FOR A BRACING YORKSHIRE WALK

Haworth, Yorkshire, England

Walking with: The Brontë sisters Charlotte (1816–1855), Emily (1818–1848), and Anne (1820–1849)

Where: Haworth

Length: 10.4 miles (one way)

Essential reading: All novels by the Brontë sisters

There is an area in the north of England across the East Lancashire Pennines and West Yorkshire that is commonly known as Brontë Country after the three Brontë sisters, all of whome were talented writers of nineteenth-century contemporary fiction.

The Brontë sisters lived in the village of Haworth, Yorkshire, at Haworth Parsonage on the edge of the moors, where their father was a curate. Their mother died here in 1821. Charlotte is best known for *Jane Eyre* (1847), Emily for *Wuthering Heights* (1847), and the youngest, Anne, authored *The Tenant of Wildfell Hall* (1848). Their books have become classics in the genre of romantic fiction, weaving the Pennine moors as a dramatic backdrop in stories of adventure, intrigue, social class, love, and revenge.

There is a long-distance walk known as the Brontë Way that stretches for forty-three miles from Oakwell Hall, near Birstall, which Charlotte visited and used in her novel, *Shirley*, to Gawthorpe Hall in Padiham, which was the home of Charlotte's friend, John Kay-Shuttleworth.

A shorter ten-mile walk begins at Thornton, where the sisters were born, crossing the moorlands—vividly portrayed in Brontë narratives—to Haworth and their former home, which is now the Brontë Parsonage Museum. From Haworth, head to the sisters' favorite picnic spot at Brontë Waterfall, and below it, the Brontë Bridge. From there, one can walk on to Top Withens, a ruined building, said, by Ellen Nussey, a lifelong friend of Charlotte, to be the inspiration for the Earnshaw family house in *Wuthering Heights*.

ABOVE: The Brontë sisters as painted by their brother.

RIGHT: All of the Brontë sisters were inspired by the countryside in which they lived.

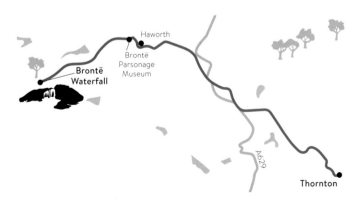

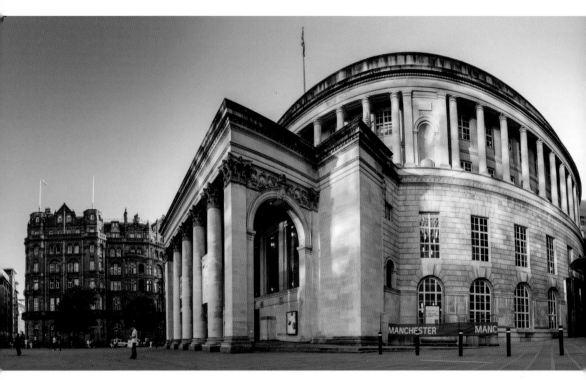

MANCHESTER AS ELIZABETH GASKELL SAW IT

Manchester, England

Walk with: Elizabeth Gaskell (1810–1865)

Route: A walking trail around Manchester city

Length: 3.4 miles

Essential reading: *Mary Barton: A Tale of Manchester Life* (1848); *North and South* (1854)

ABOVE: A woman with a social conscience, Elizabeth Gaskell.

TOP LEFT: Manchester's Central Library reflects the city's civic pride.

LEFT: The Royal Exchange was the epicenter of business during the Industrial Revolution.

In the eighteenth and nineteenth centuries, Manchester was widely believed to be the city of example for the development of industrialization—the creation of jobs and wealth allowing the city to boom. However, through the eyes of Elizabeth Gaskell, the boom ushered in wider social divisions and poor living conditions.

Born in London, Gaskell moved to Manchester after she married. The city had a great impact on her life and writing, and her works became a voice for combating poverty and ignorance.

She writes of Manchester at the time as, "ugly, smoky Manchester, dear, busy, earnest, noble-working Manchester; where their children had been born, and where, perhaps, some lay buried; where their homes were, and where God had cast their lives; and told them to work out their destiny."

Visit some of Gaskell's frequented locations on foot with this walk, starting at the Royal Exchange house that would have been the center of trading activities during the industrial revolution, to Portico Library, where she was provided books through her husband (women were excluded from membership at the time). Roughly follow the railway lines past the Manchester Town Hall and Central Library toward the Science and Industry Museum by the canals, locations which would have been busy with industry in Gaskell's day, then head over to the universities' area, and finally end at Elizabeth Gaskell's House on Plymouth Grove for an intimate look into her life in Manchester.

SIMON ARMITAGE'S PENNINE POETRY

Yorkshire, England

Walk with: Simon Armitage (1963–)

Route: Stanza Stones Trail and Pennine Way

Length: 47 miles

Essential reading: *Walking Home* (2012)

In 2012, seven years before he was named the UK's Poet Laureate, Simon Armitage walked the 268-mile Pennine Way toward his home in the Yorkshire village of Marsden, performing every night to earn his bed and board, and writing about the experience in his book *Walking Home*.

That same year, Armitage also wrote six poems which have been carved into rocks, creating the forty-seven-mile Stanza Stones Trail, which follows the Pennines between Marsden and Ilkley.

From Marsden train station, the trail takes the canal towpath to the 1811 Standedge Tunnel, climbing past a reservoir, with views back to Armitage's hometown. The trail tacks west along the Standedge escarpment toward Pule Hill Quarry's carved Snow Stone poem: "The sky has delivered its blank missive. The moor in coma…"

Soon afterward, the Stanza Stones Trail joins the northbound Pennine Way, passing a hilltop radio mast and taking a vertiginous bridge across the M62. After the highway's echoing din comes the serene solitude of Blackstone Edge's oddly shaped gritsone outcrops and the curious Aiggin Stone (of which Armitage wrote: "a crudely cut and cryptically coded waymarker"). The incorrectly named Roman Road (actually a 1700s cobbled causeway) leads to the concrete-walled Broad Head Drain, and another chiseled Armitage poem at the Rain Stone: "…let it teem, up here where the front of the mind distils the brunt of the world."

After a couple of windswept reservoirs, the trail reaches Stoodley Pike, with its monument to the Napoleonic Wars and its stunning views over the South Pennines. Thereafter, the trail starts to drop down from the heights into a wooded valley that leads to Hebden Bridge.

ABOVE: Keen walker and poet, Simon Armitage.

TOP RIGHT: Armitage's hometown of Marsden.

RIGHT: The monument of Stoodley Pike offers stunning views over the South Pennines.

252

TED HUGHES' YORKSHIRE

Calder Valley, Yorkshire, England

Ted Hughes' (1930–1998) poetry encapsulates nature's brutal majesty. In certain weather, a walk around his home valley in Yorkshire can fully explain the inspiration behind his line: "Through the brunt wind that dented the balls of my eyes." Hughes was born in Mytholmroyd, a couple of miles up the Calder Valley is the Stubbing Wharf pub, immortalized by Hughes as he describes trying to persuade his wife, Sylvia Plath, to move there:
"*Up that valley*
A future home waited for both
  of us –
Two different homes."
Farther on is the eighteenth-century millowner's house called Lumb Bank, which Hughes bought and is now a writers' retreat.

253

A GALLERY WITHOUT WALLS

West Bretton, Yorkshire, England

The Yorkshire-born Henry Moore (1898–1986) was one of the first patrons of the Yorkshire Sculpture Park at Bretton Hall. His sculptures, of monumental proportions, were clearly intended for sitting in outdoor locations such as this—a gallery without walls. The 500-acre site is an inspiring place to walk.

254
THE IMAGINATIONS OF DARESBURY WONDERLAND

Daresbury, Cheshire, England

Alice in Wonderland (1865) is a story filled with magic and imagination, and for Lewis Carroll (1832–1898) it was the charm of his childhood home in the Cheshire village of Daresbury that perhaps brought the adventures of Alice and the characters alive. Take a walk starting at the Lewis Carroll Centre at the All Saints' Church to learn about Carroll's childhood. Then a short walk from here takes visitors to Carroll's childhood home and Alice in Wonderland-themed Davenports Tea Room. Heading away from the village to find Wonderland, take a 5.6-mile return walk to the pleasant Lewis Carroll Centenary Wood.

255
WALK FROM WARTER WITH DAVID HOCKNEY

Millington, East Riding of Yorkshire, England

The artist David Hockney (1937–) was born and raised in Yorkshire but in his early career led a peripatetic lifestyle between England and California, U.S.A.. In the 1990s he spent more time in Yorkshire, visiting his mother where he began a series of landscape paintings, some on a huge scale, of his native homeland. One of the most remarkable was the forty-feet wide *Bigger Trees Near Warter* of 2007, made up of fifty canvases. A walk from Warter to another favorite location of Hockney's, Millington, about four miles northwest, opens up views of the magnificent Yorkshire Wold as the artist sees it.

256
ON THE TRAIL OF DRACULA WITH BRAM STOKER

Whitby, Yorkshire, England

The Whitby Dracula Trail is a 4.25-mile circular walk that begins and ends in the fishing town that inspired Bram Stoker's (1847–1912) great novel. Heading east along a short cliff-top section of the Cleveland Way, the route includes a detour up the iconic 199 steps to the imposing gothic ruins of Whitby Abbey ("it is a most noble ruin, of immense size, and full of beautiful and romantic bits") which Dracula ran up, in dog form, after his ship was wrecked on the shore. Wander through the graveyard at St. Mary's Church next to the Abbey to find the gravestone of Swales—Stoker took the name for Dracula's first victim in Whitby from this.

257
WHERE LENNON MET McCARTNEY

Woolton, Liverpool, England

When John Lennon (1940–1980) wrote about the places he'd remember all his life, in "In My Life" (1965), he was partly thinking of when he met his future Beatles buddy Sir Paul McCartney (1942–). In 1957, sixteen-year-old Lennon's skiffle group, the Quarrymen, played a gig at Woolton Fete. Fifteen-year-old McCartney was watching, met Lennon afterward, and was enrolled into the band. In 1959 they played a gig around the corner at Woolton Village Club, 23 Allerton Road. Lennon had been brought up by his Aunt Mimi at nearby 251 Menlove Avenue. Just up Menlove Avenue on Beaconsfield Road, the grounds of the former Salvation Army children's home, Strawberry Field, reopened in September 2019.

RIGHT: Strawberry Field in Liverpool, made famous by the Beatles.

BEATRIX POTTER'S WORLD IN THE LAKE DISTRICT

Cumbria, England

Walk with: Beatrix Potter (1866–1943)

Route: Wray Castle to Bowness Bay

Length: c.8 miles

Essential reading: *The Tale of Peter Rabbit* (1902)

This walk begins at Wray Castle, on the northwest side of Lake Windermere. This nineteenth-century edifice is where Beatrix Potter came as a sixteen-year-old on holiday with her parents, and fell in love with the area. From the ramparts of the castle, enjoy extensive views south along the lake, with mountains in the distance.

From here, walk southwest downhill toward Hawkshead, a distance of three miles, enjoying the wonderful views that inspired Beatrix Potter to write and illustrate her collection of children's stories such as *The Tale of Peter Rabbit*. At the village, follow the signs to the Beatrix Potter Gallery on Main Street.

Head south for two miles, following the east side of Estwaite Water, until reaching the tiny village of Near Sawrey. At its heart is Hill Top, Beatrix Potter's home for nearly forty years. The village itself is littered with clues that were inspirational for the creation of her stories and characters. Continue this route for another 1.5 miles, toward Far Sawry, and then on to Claife Viewing Station on the shore of Lake Windermere. From here, there are extensive views of the Claife Heights and the lake.

Close by is the foot ferry that takes you across the lake to Bowness Bay, the location of the tourist attraction, The World of Beatrix Potter, where the young at heart can interact with Peter Rabbit and the other characters created by Beatrix Potter. The author would approve; she once wrote: "If I have done anything, even a little, to help small children enjoy honest, simple pleasures, I have done a bit of good."

ABOVE: Beatrix Potter, whose children's stories have been read by millions.

TOP RIGHT: Potter fell in love with the Lake District when she visited Windermere with her parents.

RIGHT: As an adult, Potter made her home in the pretty village of Near Sawrey.

SWALLOWS AND AMAZONS

Coniston, Cumbria, England

Arthur Ransome (1884–1967) was a journalist working in London before living permanently in the Lake District, where he wrote his most famous children's novel, *Swallows and Amazons,* in 1929. Although its exact location is unspecified in the book, there are enough references to suggest it is in fact Lake Coniston. Begin at the southernmost point of the lake, which is the estuary of the River Crake, fictionalized by Ransome as Octopus Lagoon. Continue north along the east side of the lake until reaching a small peninsula. Just beyond is Peel Island, which is renamed Wild Cat Island in the novel.

260

STAND ON TOP OF ENGLAND WITH A FEMALE WALKING PIONEER

Scafell Pike, Cumbria, England

Walk with: Dorothy Wordsworth (1771–1855)

Route: Corridor Route up Scafell Pike

Length: 8.7 miles

Essential reading: *The Grasmere Journals* (1897)

LEFT: Walkers tackle Scafell Pike, one hundred years after Dorothy Wordsworth made the ascent.

In 1818, walking for pleasure was still relatively uncommon and especially so for women. However, that was the year that Dorothy Wordsworth and her friend, the poet Mary Barker, climbed to the top of England's highest peak, Scafell Pike in the Lake District.

Dorothy wrote about the excursion. Her brother, William Wordsworth, then published this account in his book, *A Description of the Scenery of the Lakes* (1810), with no mention that it had been written—and the adventure undertaken—by his sister, who never published any of her own writings during her lifetime.

Her descriptions vividly hold the joy and peace of reaching the top of a mountain: "The stillness seemed to be not of this world: we paused, and kept silence to listen; and no sound could be heard. We were far above the reach of the cataracts of Scaw Fell; and not an insect was there to hum in the air."

Dorothy began her walk in Rosthwaite, heading to Seathwaite and on to Scafell Pike; she returned via Sprinkling Tarn and Sty Head Tarn. Today's well established Corridor Route takes a similar line.

When you reach the top, as well as the view, take in the apparently barren rocks underfoot, as Dorothy noted, they are: "covered with never-dying lichens, which the clouds and dews nourish; and adorn with colors of vivid and exquisite beauty."

261

JOIN SAMUEL TAYLOR COLERIDGE IN HIS NATURAL HABITAT

Helvellyn, Lake District, England

Walk with: Samuel Taylor
Coleridge (1772–1834)

Route: Helvellyn via
Striding Edge

Length: 8 miles

Essential reading: *Coleridge's*
Notebooks: A Selection,
ed. Seamus Perry (2002)

TOP RIGHT: The view
from Helvellyn. ·

RIGHT: The dramatic views of
the Lake District appealed to
Samuel Taylor Coleridge.

Samuel Taylor Coleridge moved to Keswick from Somerset in July 1800, and was immediately delighted with his new home: his view across Derwent Water and the miles and miles of countryside to explore.

He famously undertook a nine-day tour of the High Peaks without a guide. He wore out his shoes, broke his fingers, got stranded on precarious ledges, and was repeatedly caught in terrible storms. But throwing himself into the landscape and putting himself at its mercy allowed him to experience the spiritual essence of nature in a way that nothing else did.

He had already written the poems for which he is now best known: "Kubla Khan," "Frost at Midnight," "The Rhyme of the Ancient Mariner." However, the notebooks he kept during the Keswick years are filled with spontaneous prose-poems, written on the spot as he walked, charting both physical and spiritual sensations.

He would walk from his home in Keswick to his friends Dorothy and William Wordsworth at Dove Cottage in Grasmere, climbing up Helvellyn and taking in the entire ridge of the Eastern Fells as he did so.

"No words can convey any idea of this prodigious wilderness," he wrote on reaching the top of Helvellyn. "That precipice fine on this side was but its ridge, sharp as a jagged knife, level so long, and then ascending so boldly ... and to my right how the Crag ... plunges down, like a waterfall, reaches a level steepness, and again plunges!"

One of the best ways to experience the drama of Helvellyn is to approach from Glenridding and along the ridge of Striding Edge, returning via Swirral Edge and the summit of Catstye Cam, which gives an impressive view of the eastern crags that Coleridge would have scrambled over on his route.

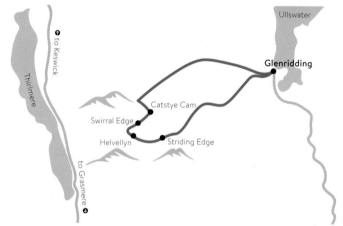

Ullswater

to Keswick

Thirlmere

Glenridding

Catstye Cam

Swirral Edge

Helvellyn   Striding Edge

to Grasmere

262
FIND WILLIAM MORRIS AND CO.
Brampton, Cumbria, England

The Brampton area, near Carlisle, is farming country, and the air is clean and fresh in a landscape of woods, fells, rivers, and streams. Designer-craftsman William Morris (1834–1896) stayed nearby in Naworth Castle with his host George Howard, Ninth Earl of Carlisle, to discuss a new church for Brampton. Naworth Castle is a private home but can be seen from the nearby Lanercost Priory, from where it is a pleasant 2.5-mile walk to Brampton and St. Martin's Church at the far end of Front Street, adorned by Morris & Co.'s stained-glass windows.

263
WANDERING WITH WORDSWORTH
Cumbria, England

The Rydal Water Walk in Grasmere is also known as the Wordsworth Walk, due to its links to the great Romantic poet William Wordsworth (1770–1850). Start in St. Oswald's churchyard, where Wordsworth is buried, before embarking on a six-mile circular walk that passes both Dove Cottage and Rydal Mount, two of Wordsworth's previous homes. It also takes in Wordsworth's Seat, where the poet would sit to take in the view over Rydal Water. Wordsworth wrote that the Vale of Grasmere was "the loveliest spot that man hath ever found."

NAN SHEPHERD'S CAIRNGORMS

Cairngorms, Scotland

Walk with: Nan Shepherd (1893–1981)

Route: To the peak of Meall a'Bhuachaille

Length: 5 miles

Essential reading: *The Living Mountain* (1977)

TOP RIGHT: Meall a'Bhuachaille turns purple with heather in the late summer months.

RIGHT: The panoramic view from the top of Meall a'Bhuachaille.

Nan Shepherd sat on her best-known work for three decades. She was already a noted novelist and poet when, during the Second World War, she wrote *The Living Mountain*, a nonfiction work about walking in the Cairngorms. It combines memoir and metaphysical meditation in the manner of Henry David Thoreau or John Muir, her fellow Scot who did so much to praise and preserve the American wilderness. After it was rejected by one publisher, she left it in a drawer until 1977; but Shepherd's lightly worn knowledge and erudite amazement—"However often I walk on them, these hills hold astonishment for me. There is no getting accustomed to them"—have influenced nature writers ever since.

The five-mile hike up Meall a' Bhuachaille ("Mound of the Herdsman"), six miles from the ski resort of Aviemore, is an excellent taster of the Cairngorms. Starting from the car park at Glenmore Forest, a well-signposted trail toward Nethy Bridge passes Glenmore Lodge's outdoor training center before diving into one of many nearby forest remnants dating back nine millennia. As Shepherd wrote, "When the aromatic savour of the pine goes searching into the deepest recesses of my lungs, I know it is life that is entering."

Passing the stunning An Lochan Uaine—"Green Lake," which Shepherd might describe as "a green like the green of winter skies"—the path breaks above the treeline. At the emergency shelter of Ryvoan Bothy, the path to the left climbs to the summit of Meall a'Bhuachaille. There, at 2,657 feet above sea level, is a glorious panorama of the kind that induced Shepherd to write, "Details are no longer part of a grouping in a picture of which I am the focal point, the focal point is everywhere. Nothing has reference to me, the looker. This is how the Earth must see itself."

265
BRITAIN'S LAST
TRUE WILDERNESS
Rannoch Moor, Scotland

In *Mountains Of The Mind* (2003), Robert Macfarlane (1976–) explores our historical and emotional fascination with mountains, and his follow-up, *The Wild Places* (2007), does the same for the wilds of Britain and Ireland. A 12.4-mile hike west from Rannoch station to the Glencoe mountain pass crosses a desolate swathe of blanket bog. Macfarlane writes: "So expansive was the space within which we were moving that when I glanced up at the mountains west of the Moor, to try to gauge the distance we had come, it seemed as though we had not advanced at all."

HUNTER DAVIES ON HADRIAN'S WALL

Bowness-on-Solway, Tyneside, England

From Wallsend, Tyneside, on the east coast, to Bowness-on-Solway on the west coast of northern England, the seventy-three-mile Hadrian's Wall has been a UNESCO World Heritage site since 1987. It was commissioned by order of Emperor Hadrian in AD122 as a military fortification to mark the edge of the Roman Empire, and is now a global destination for walkers. Writer and broadcaster Hunter Davies (1936–) has walked the Wall over the years. His book, *A Walk Along the Wall: A Journey Along Hadrian's Wall* (1974) is a good companion. Must-sees are Housesteads, Vindolanda, Corbridge, and Birdoswald.

FEEL THE MAGIC OF J. K. ROWLING'S EDINBURGH

Edinburgh, Scotland

Harry Potter might exist in a fantastical world of Muggles and Quidditch, but the boy wizard's adventures first took shape in the cafés of Edinburgh. J. K. Rowling (1965–) frequented places such as The Elephant House, which now declares itself "the birthplace of Harry Potter," when she set about writing the stories. The café is just off Candlemaker Row—this, and nearby Victoria Street, are colorful streets crammed with brightly painted shops, and it is easy to see how these may have inspired the magical cobblestoned streets of Diagon Alley. A short stroll away, Edinburgh Castle, with its similarities to the magical school of Hogwarts, dominates the city's skyline.

HEAR THE SOUND OF FINGAL'S CAVE

Isle of Staffa, Scotland

Within hours of returning home to his native Germany, Felix Mendelssohn (1809–1847) composed the first few bars of *Hebrides Overture*, based on his visit to the basalt columns of Fingal's Cave on the southern end of Staffa. The melodic segments set a mood of the surrounds in calm weather and are accompanied by the dramatic breakout of the thunderous rush of roaring waves during a storm. Take a walk from the boat jetty on the eastern side, take the steps to the top of the plateau, then follow the path northward, where you'll encounter puffin colonies. Follow the path to the natural walkway of broken columns into Fingal's Cave for a finale worthy of an overture.

LEFT & RIGHT: Felix Mendelssohn was inspired by the sounds of Fingal's Cave.

RABBIE BURNS IN DUMFRIES

Dumfries, Scotland

Born in Alloway, Robert "Rabbie" Burns (1759–1796), Scotland's national bard, had no interest in his parents' tenant-farming, so he worked instead as an "occasional" poet. His poems earned him wealth, which he quickly spent, which in turn led to him taking the job of an Excise Officer in Dumfries in 1789. Robert Burns Statue is found in Burns Statue Square. From here, a half-mile walk south along the High Street leads to Robert Burns House, on Burns Street, where he lived with his family. Burns died of rheumatic fever in Dumfries, aged thirty-seven, and is buried a little farther on at St. Michael's Church.

McCARTNEY'S MULL OF KINTYRE

Mull of Kintyre, Scotland

Sir Paul McCartney (1942–) immortalized the Mull of Kintyre in his 1977 titular song about the blunt headland that marks the end of Scotland. The song became his band Wings' biggest hit in Britain, with McCartney describing it as a love song to the place where he had bought a home. The Kintyre Way is a one-hundred-mile trail zigzagging north to south down the narrow peninsula, through forests, fishing villages, and moors, with the sea never far from view.

271

OFF THE BEATEN PATH WITH L. S. LOWRY

Berwick-upon-Tweed, England

Walk with: L. S. Lowry
(1887–1976)

Route: The Lowry Trails

Length: 5–6 miles

Essential viewing: *Dewar Lane*
(1936)

Much-loved British painter L. S. Lowry is famed for his industrial landscapes and urban scenes peopled with his distinctive "matchstick men" figures. He was a prolific painter of the country's northwest, including Pendlebury, where he lived and worked for more than forty years, and Salford—where the Lowry gallery, named in his honor, holds more than fifty of his paintings and nearly three hundred drawings.

Yet it is in Berwick-upon-Tweed, where Lowry regularly holidayed, that some of his lesser-known works took shape. Here, cobblestoned streets and seaside settings replaced his factories and back-to-back terraced houses. The Lowry Trail takes visitors on a tour of the sites, starting with one of his earlier drawings: the narrow medieval alley of Dewar's Lane. While walking here, keep an eye open for the prominent clock tower that reaches up from the heart of the town—this 150-foot steeple can be seen in several of Lowry's works.

A departure out along the pier leads to the lighthouse, a spectacular location in any weather, before walking the remaining walls and heading over the river to the harbor and the village of Tweedmouth, then onward around Spittal, taking in the coastal views from the promenade. Information boards along the trail show the paintings and sketches Lowry undertook at each location.

ABOVE: Mostly associated with England's nortwest, L. S. Lowry also spent time in Berwick-upon-Tweed.

TOP RIGHT: The walls of Berwick-upon-Tweed were built for defense, but make a lovely route around town.

RIGHT: The lighthouse at the end of the pier is a spectacular setting.

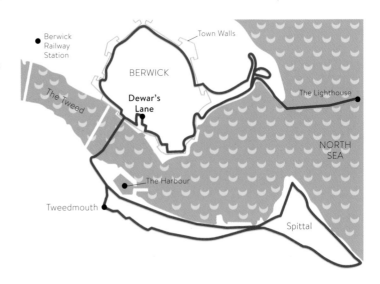

272
SURRENDER TO THE SUBLIME
Glencoe, Scotland

Although based mainly in the city of Edinburgh, the Scottish landscape artist Horatio McCulloch (1805–1867) is best known for his Romantic views of the Highlands of Scotland. Most notable is his painting of Glen Coe (1864), a breathtaking image of the mountains and glen, populated only by deer. The awe of this view can be recreated on a number of walks in the Ben Nevis and Glen Coe National Scenic Area. Arguably the most impressive of the glens, is the Buachaille, the pyramidical mountain that is the guardian to the valley.

273

AT HOME IN SKIEN WITH HENRIK IBSEN

Skien, Norway

Henrik Ibsen (1828–1906) is one of the most influential playwrights of the nineteenth century, with works such as *The Doll's House* (1879) and *An Enemy of the People* (1882). Many of his plays are set in places reminiscent of his hometown of Skien, one of the oldest cities in Norway. Begin the walking tour of the town from beside the Telemark Canal. A short stroll leads to the pedestrian street of Henrik Ibsen's Gate via the cultural space of Ibsenhuset. Complete the walk at the Telemark Museum, which has a small section on Ibsen.

274

SCREAM WITH EDVARD MUNCH AT OSLO FJORD

Oslo, Norway

Follow in the footsteps of Edvard Munch (1863–1944) from the Engebret Café in Bankplassen, Oslo, to the Ekeberg Restaurant, higher up and overlooking the Oslo Fjord. This thirty-minute walk will take you to the view that was probably the inspiration for his most famous painting, *The Scream* (1893). Looking across the fjord, he stated: "Suddenly the sky turned blood red—I paused, feeling exhausted, and leaned on the fence—there was blood and tongues of fire above the blue-black fjord and the city—I stood there trembling with anxiety and sensed an infinite scream passing through nature."

275

STRIDE WITH AUGUST STRINDBERG

Stockholm, Sweden

While Swedish playwright August Strindberg (1849–1912) once famously wrote, "I need to travel to purge myself of Sweden and Swedish stupidity," in a letter to his publisher, the Swedish capital's culture in fact inspired much of his writing. Begin your own Strindberg stride in Södermalm in southern Stockholm, where Strindberg set the opening scene of his breakthrough novel *The Red Room* (1879), before making your way to Österlånggatan, known as "that street of vice, of filth, and brawls," in the Gamla Stan area. Finally, visit The Blue Tower, the last residence of Strindberg.

276

UNEARTH THE MYSTERY OF STIEG LARSSON'S STOCKHOLM

Stockholm, Sweden

Stieg Larsson (1954–2004) is the Swedish author behind *The Millennium Trilogy*—the series of internationally famed books *The Girl with the Dragon Tattoo* (2005), *The Girl Who Played with Fire* (2006), and *The Girl Who Kicked the Hornets' Nest* (2007). Set on the Stockholm island of Södermalm, the novels reference many real-life places that can be visited in the city today. Start your tour at Bellmansgatan 1, the home of the main character Mikael Blomkvist, and walk through key locations in the books from the bar and restaurant, Kvarnen, to Lisbeth Salander's apartment in Lundagatan.

TOP RIGHT & RIGHT: Colors in the sky above Oslo Fjord inspired Edvard Munch's *The Scream*.

ENTER THE IDIOSYNCRATIC WORLD OF PIPPI LONGSTOCKING

Vimmerby, Sweden

Walk with: Astrid Lindgren
(1907–2002)

Route: Stora Torget to Näs

Length: 1.4 miles

Essential reading: *Pippi
Longstocking* (1945)

ABOVE: Astrid Lindgren, whose
books about the exploits of
Pippi Longstocking received
worldwide fame.

TOP RIGHT: The street where
many of Lindgren's characters
got in to mischief.

RIGHT: Outside Vimmerby,
there is pretty woodland.

Swedish fiction writer Astrid Lindgren's stories are filled with details
and tales from places and people that were part of her life in the southern
Swedish city of Vimmerby where she grew up. Her stories of the
free-spirited exploits of Pippi Longstocking brought her worldwide fame,
but this was just one of around ten series that she wrote for children.

Start your walk at the Astrid Lindgren statue in the main square (Stora
Torget). The statue is by Marie-Louise Ekman and features Lindgren
sitting in her workroom by her typewriter.

For the inspiration that led to the books themselves, head to
Båtsmansbacken, where cobblestoned streets were the inspiration for the
alleys in her Bill Bergson (Kalle Blomkvist) mysteries (1946–1953) and
where a fight between the two rival gangs, the White Roses and the Red
Roses, plays out.

Farther along the street is the yellow house which served as Pippi
Longstocking's sweet shop, as well as Klemens Gränd, where filming
of the *Emil* series (1963–1997) took place.

Extend your walk to the graveyard where the memorial to the Phalén
brothers is said to have partially inspired *Brothers Lionheart* (1973).
Lindgren is also buried here.

Farther on, through the fields, is Lindgren's birthplace and childhood
home, the farmyard Näs, where you can see the elm tree that found fame
as the Lemonade Tree in the stories about Pippi Longstocking.

278
A MOOMIN-INSPIRED STROLL
Helsinki, Finland

Step into the life of the lady behind one of Finland's most loved cartoons, *Moomins*, first created in 1945. Swedish-speaking Finnish writer, artist, and cartoonist Tove Jansson (1914–2001) lived in Helsinki for most of her life. Wander through the town and discover the places that were important to her, from her salmon-pink childhood home at Luotsikatu 4, to the Uspenski Cathedral and neighboring Tove Jansson Park, where she played as a little girl, finishing at The Observatory to see comets that inspired *Comet in Moominland* (1946).

279
TOVE JANSSON'S ADVENTURE WALK
Pellinki, Finland

Tove Jansson's family spent their summers walking in the forests in the Pellinki archipelago in southeastern Finland. It was on these trips that Jansson got the inspiration for *The Book about Moomin, Mymble, and Little My* (1952), which describes how a little Moomintroll walks home through the forest from the milk store, just as Jansson did as a child. There is now an adventure walk that visitors can follow which retraces the steps she would have taken from her holiday home to the village store, Söderby-Boden, an orange and white cabin where islanders have bought their supplies for nearly a hundred years.

280

FIND A SOUND WITH
JEAN SIBELIUS

Forests of Hämeenlinna, Finland

Named after Finnish composer and violinist, Jean
Sibelius (1865–1957), Sibelius Forest is around
250 acres of nature reserve in Hämeenlinna,
Finland. Sibelius, who was born here, spent his youth
wandering these forests along with his violin in search
of inspiration for his famous melodies. There are several
marked walks in the forest; choose between either
the blue route signs of the nature trail or the Sibelius
Forest hiking path, which circumnavigates Lake
Aulangonjärvi before returning to the main road
on Aulangon-Heikkilän.

281

ON THE TRAIL OF
HANS CHRISTIAN ANDERSEN

Copenhagen, Denmark

Catch a glimpse of Danish history and culture through
the eyes of the country's most famous writer, Hans
Christian Andersen (1805–1875), who penned fairy-tale
classics such as *The Little Mermaid* (1837) and *The Ugly
Duckling* (1843). Andersen moved to the Danish capital
at the age of fourteen and lived in various of the colorful
townhouses along the canal at Nyhavn during his life.
From here, head to The Little Mermaid statue at
Langelinie Pier, before visiting Andersen's final resting
place at Assistens Cemetery.

282

TREAD THE PATH OF
SØREN KIERKEGAARD

Copenhagen, Denmark

"Above all, do not lose your desire to walk." This quote
from Søren Kierkegaard (1813–1855) pays tribute to
the Danish philosopher's love of walking around his
native town of Copenhagen. Heed Kierkegaard's words
as you walk from the plaque dedication at the house
in which he was born in Nytorv, to Helligåndskirken,
the church that he visited frequently in his childhood.
Finally head to Christianshavn, a place where
Kierkegaard would observe Copenhagen and wrote
in his journal that from Christianshavn, "one seems
to be far, very far away from Copenhagen."

283

FROM SKAGEN TO GRENEN
WITH P. S. KRØYER

Skagen, Denmark

The Skagen Painters were a colony of Scandinavian
artists which included the painter P. S. Krøyer
(1851–1909). They visited Skagen in the summer
months, fueling its popularity among creative types.
Pack your paintbrush for this walk which starts in
Skagen, the northernmost part of Denmark, and leads
to Grenen, where the Skagerrak and the Kattegat seas
meet and the collision of the waves is visible to the
naked eye. It was on this journey that Krøyer and other
notable artists would paint *en plein air*, inspiring works
such as *Summer Evening on Skagen Beach* (1893).

TOP RIGHT: The wild open
sands of Skagen beach.

RIGHT: The painting of the
beach by P. S. Krøyer.

WALK IN THE SHADOW OF REMBRANDT

Amsterdam, Holland

Walk with: Rembrandt Harmenszoon van Rijn (1606–1669)

Route: Rijksmuseum to Rembrandt's last home

Length: 3.1 miles

Essential viewing: *The Night Watch* (1642)

ABOVE: Rembrandt's captivating self-portrait.

RIGHT: Amsterdam's Blue Bridge, where Rembrandt used to sketch scenes of city life.

No artist epitomizes the Dutch Golden Age more than Rembrandt Harmenszoon van Rijn. Born in Leiden in 1606, he moved to Amsterdam at the age of twenty-five, where he painted prolifically. Between the 1600s and 1700s, the city saw an economic boom. Prosperous merchants built canalside houses, and adorned their homes with priceless works of art.

Located to the southwest of the city is the Rijksmuseum, which houses the most comprehensive collection of Rembrandt's works. A short walk northeast, at 218 Amstel, is the home of the Six Family, who have owned Rembrandt's portrait of Jan Six, a friend and patron of the artist, since it was painted in 1654. At the nearby Blauwbrug, or Blue Bridge, Rembrandt would spend hours observing city life and painting day-to-day scenes of beggars and wealthy merchants alike.

In 1639, Rembrandt bought a smart neighborhood home, now The Rembrandt House, the artist's house-museum. From here, a pleasant canalside walk leads to the former clubhouse of the City Guard, whose members commissioned the life-sized Rembrandt work, *The Night Watch* (which is said to have led to his ruin). Northeast, at 4 Nieuwmarkt, is the fifteenth-century Waag, where the corpse of a criminal was publicly dissected every year, inspiring Rembrandt to paint *The Anatomy Lesson of Dr. Nicolaes Tulp* (1632).

A short stroll away is the Oude Kerk, where Rembrandt's wife, Saskia, was buried. Rembrandt himself died impoverished on October 4, 1669, in his residence at 184 Rozengracht. He was given an anonymous burial and, twenty years later, his remains exhumed and discarded.

285
MULTATULI'S AMSTERDAM
Amsterdam, Netherlands

Satirical anitcolonialist Dutch author Eduard Douwes Dekker (1820–1887), better known as Multatuli (meaning, "I have suffered much"), wrote the novel *Max Havelaar* (1860) to expose what he had witnessed during his time in the Dutch East Indies. The Multatuli Museum, at Korsjespoortsteeg 20, is where he was born and died (sixty-seven years later, on the red sofa that is still there today). The museum also offers a walk through the city where he grew up, taking in the places that inspired him.

286
PIET MONDRIAN, A DUTCH MASTER
Abcoude, Netherlands

It is perhaps hard to imagine that Piet Mondrian (1872–1944) was inspired by nature when viewing his abstract paintings from the 1920s, which use pure linear geometric forms and primary colors. As he stated: "Art is higher than reality and has no direct relation to reality." Nevertheless, his earlier paintings were inspired by nature. One of his favorite walks was along the River Gein in the small village of Abcoude, south of Amsterdam. Around 1905, Mondrian painted several versions of the windmill along this stretch of river. The huge skies, often multicolored at sunset, inspired him to use unusual coloring in his imagery, an example being *Evening, Red Tree* of 1908.

287

WALK THE ST. JAMES WAY

Camino de Compostela, Spain

Walk with: Paulo Coelho (1947–)

Route: Camino de Santiago de Compostela

Length: 500 miles

Essential reading: *The Pilgrimage* (1987)

TOP LEFT: It's a long walk following Spain's Camino de Compostela.

LEFT: On arriving in Compostela, pilgrims head to the cathedral.

In 1986, Paulo Coelho was a relatively unknown Brazilian writer, about to undertake Spain's monumental pilgrimage of Camino de Santiago de Compostela. It was a decision which would lead to his literary spiritual awakening, and begin his transformation into the internationally acclaimed author he would become, just two years later, with the publication of his best-selling novel *The Alchemist* (1988).

Coelho describes his experiences in *The Pilgrimage* (1987), his autobiographical novel that is part adventure story, part guide to self-discovery. The Camino de Compostela is a religious pilgrimage to the cathedral of Santiago de Compostela in northwest Spain, where the remains of apostle Saint James are said to be buried.

Traditionally, all pilgrimages should start at home—but, thankfully, the accepted routes today don't require quite that commitment. They are all still very, very lengthy. The most common route is the Camino Frances, or French Way, starting at Saint-Jean-Pied-de-Port, on the French side of the Pyrenees, five hundred miles away from the destination. Pilgrims take, on average, thirty-five days or so to complete the path, carrying a "pilgrim's passport" that enables them to stay at hostels en route.

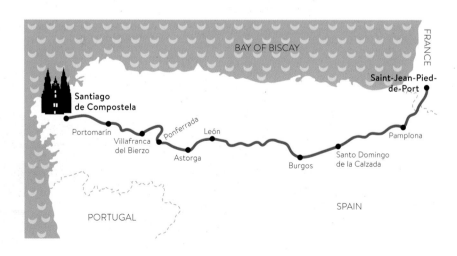

288

DALÍ'S DAYS AWAY

Cadaqués, Catalonia, Spain

Walk with: Salvador Dalí
(1904-1989)

Route: Cadaqués to Cap de
Creus via Port Lligat

Length: 4.5 miles (one way)

Essential viewing: *Port of
Cadaqués (Night)* (1918);
The Great Masturbator (1929)

Spanish surrealist artist Salvador Dalí was mesmerized by the modest beauty of Catalonia and spent much of his life there, wandering between Cadaqués and Cap de Creus. When he was young, Dalí's family had a summer home in Cadaqués and it was there that he first started painting. See the beautiful coastline that inspired many of his works on a loop walk that takes visitors along the old pilgrimage paths to the wild, rocky landscape of Cap de Creus, via Dalí's home in Port Lligat. The town and surrounding coastline feature in some of Dalí's most famous works, including *The Spectre of Sex Appeal* (1932), *The Persistence of Memory* (1931), and *Port of Cadaqués (Night)*.

In 1930, Dalí bought an old fisherman's hut near Port Lligat that he transformed into a house for himself and his wife, Gala. Today it is the Salvador Dalí House Museum Port Lligat, and visitors can see the house as it was when the artist lived there. The house is just a few minutes' walk from Cap de Creus, which is now a protected National Park. It was a favorite spot of Gala and Dalí, a romantic hideaway where they spent many hours swimming, boating, collecting washed-up debris, and creating installations. Dalí's 1929 painting *The Great Masturbator* depicts a human face in the shape of the rock formations of Cap de Creus bay. While here you can walk to the Cap de Creus lighthouse, said to be the most easterly point of the Iberian Peninsula.

ABOVE: Salvador Dalí, with his unmistakable moustache.

TOP RIGHT: Cadaqués, where Dalí first started painting while on family holidays.

RIGHT: The Cap de Creus lighthouse is a pleasant walk from Cadaqués.

CATALONIA

Cap de Creus

MEDITERRANEAN
SEA

Salavador Dali
House Museum

Port Lligat

Cadaqués

289
PABLO PICASSO
IN CATALONIA
Cadaqués, Spain

A walk around the
waterfront of the white
walled town of Cadaqués
reveals why it became so
inspirational for artists such
as Pablo Picasso (1881–
1973). This Mediterranean
town, surrounded by the
rocky outcrop of hills, is
picturesque, but also, when
viewed from a distance, a
jumbled myriad of odd
geometric shapes, heightened
by the Mediterranean sun. It
is this aspect that helped
Picasso formulate Cubism.
While taking a holiday
here in 1910, he painted
The Guitar Player.

290
YOUNG PICASSO
IN MÁLAGA
Málaga, Spain

Málaga, Andalusia, on the
southeast coast of Spain, was
Pablo Picasso's birthplace.
He was baptized in the
Apostle Santiago parish
church. The record of his
birth is on display inside
the church. Picasso went
to school at San Rafael, on
Calle Comedias, 20. From
here it is a short walk south
to reach Museo Picasso, at
Calle San Agustín, 8, which
opened in 2003. The parish
church is close by on Calle
Granada, 78. Picasso
attended his first bullfight
at La Malagueta's bullring.

291
ANTONI GAUDÍ'S BARCELONA

Barcelona, Spain

It is almost impossible to walk around the city of Barcelona without seeing the impact of Antoni Gaudí (1852–1926) and his architecture. His *magnum opus* is the organic *Church of the Sagrada Família*, but to experience the sheer genius of Gaudí, walk around the *Park Güell*, opened as a pleasure garden in 1926. Two unusually shaped organic buildings flank the entrance, but the main focus is the walk to the terrace, with its mosaic figures of fantastic creatures, quirky grottos, and finally the large beautifully decorated bench where you can sit and enjoy the spectacle of his masterpiece in full, with the city and the Mediterranean Sea beyond.

292
LOOK TO THE HORIZON WITH EDUARDO CHILLIDA

Donostía-San Sebastián, Spain

As a child, Basque artist Eduardo Chillida (1924–2002) used to love wandering to the rocks at the westernmost end of San Sebastián's bay to sit and contemplate the waves and the horizon. When he became an artist, he designed a sculpture for the same spot. Start your walk at the city's port and stroll around the beautiful bay, past another Chillida sculpture *Homage to Fleming* (1955) until you reach the majestic *Comb of the Wind* (1976). Three twisted iron anchors emerge from the rocks, lending drama to this powerful view.

293
STAY OUT LATE WITH ERNEST HEMINGWAY IN MADRID

Madrid, Spain

"Nobody goes to bed in Madrid until they have killed the night," wrote Ernest Hemingway (1899–1961), who loved the city where he was known as Don Ernesto. He stayed at Tryp Gran Via, which he mentioned in short stories *Night Before Battle* (1939) and *The Fifth Column* (1938), and where the breakfast room is a shrine to him. Across Gran Via is the early skyscraper from which Hemingway wired home Civil War reports. Along Gran Via is the Museo Chicote bar mentioned in another short story, *The Denunciation* (1938). Dogleg back through the Plaza Mayor to reach Botín, the world's oldest restaurant, where Don Ernesto set the final scene of *The Sun Also Rises* (1926) and failed to make paella. Just east, on leafy Plaza de Santa Ana, is Cervecería Alemana, where a photo of Hemingway hangs above his favorite table. Round the corner on Calle de Echegaray is sherry bar La Venencia, a Civil War time capsule.

294
THE BARCELONA OF ANA MARÍA MATUTE

Barcelona, Spain

The works of notable Spanish novelist Ana María Matute (1925–2014), who was born and died in Barcelona, were largely influenced by her experience of childhood illness and the Spanish Civil War, using elements of fairy-tale and fantasy to symbolize the betrayal and isolation felt by children in her writing. While exploring Barcelona, keep in mind that many of the sights were affected by the Spanish Civil War. At the top of the lively La Rambla was where the first shots were fired, and the former Communist Party H.Q. is a gigantic retail store. The Barcelona of Matute's novels is no longer, but visit her at Montjuïc Cemetery and walk in her memory around the hills beyond.

TOP RIGHT: Eduardo Chillida's *Comb of the Wind* in San Sebastián.

RIGHT: Antoni Gaudí's Parc Güell offers sweeping views of Barcelona.

295
FIND GOYA IN ZARAGOZA
Zaragoza, Spain

The Spaniard Francisco Goya (1746–1828), whose dramatic paintings and methods profoundly affected mid-nineteenth and early twentieth century art, moved to Zaragoza as a young child. His school was Colegio Escuelas Pías, in Calle del Conde de Aranda; from here, head to Avenue de César Augusto, to find a huge sculpture of the artist in Plaza del Pilar. Then turn south, on Calle Espoz y Mina, for the fabulous Museo Goya.

296
ON THE TRAIL OF EL GRECO
Toledo, Spain

"I was created by the all-powerful God to fill the universe with my masterpieces," said Doménikos Theotokópoulos (1541–1614). He didn't quite manage that but he made a good start in Toledo, where he lived from 1577 to 1614, and where they named him El Greco. Iglesia de Santo Tome, on Paseo Transito, includes the masterpiece *The Burial of the Count of Orgaz* (1586). Ten minutes north on the Plaza Santa Domingo, El Greco provided an altarpiece for the El Antigua monastery and similarly embellished the Capilla de San José (on Calle Nunez de Arce). The walk climaxes at the French-Gothic Cathedral (on Plaza del Ayuntamiento) with his masterpiece *Christ Being Stripped of His Garments* (1579).

DISCOVER FEDERICO GARCÍA LORCA'S GRANADA

Granada, Spain

Walk with: Federico García Lorca (1898–1936)

Route: Lorca's wanderings

Length: 2.1 miles

Essential reading: *Impressions and Landscapes* (1918); *Blood Wedding* (1932)

TOP RIGHT: Granada's Plaza de Bib-Rambla was the setting for Federico García Lorca's play, *Mariana Pineda.*

RIGHT: Lorca sat on a bench on the Avenida de la Constitución.

Although he traveled to New York, Cuba, and Buenos Aires, Spanish poet and playwright Federico García Lorca's heart was always in Granada: "If by the grace of God I become famous," he once announced, "half of that fame will belong to Granada, which formed me and made me what I am." He called the city "the perfect dream and fantasy, forever ineffable ... Granada will always be more malleable than philosophical, more lyric than dramatic." He loved to wander the city's hilltop Alhambra fortress, from where he could see the historic Albaicín hill he evoked in his first book *Impressions and Landscapes* and the church of St. Michael, which inspired his ballad of that name.

At the foot of the Alhambra hill is the Hotel Alhambra Palace, a favored Lorca haunt; in 1922, he gave a recital in its pseudo-Moorish theater. Half a mile west, downtown by the cathedral, is the Royal Chapel, resting place of Joanna the Mad, the Castilian queen for whom the young Lorca delivered an elegy; around the corner, the Centro Federico García Lorca combines museum and performance space. South across the Plaza de Bib-Rambla, where Lorca set his play *Mariana Pineda*, is Calle Acera del Darro; the young Lorca's family lived at number 46 before switching across the street to the Acera del Casino. Across the shady plaza is a restaurant called Chikito, where a plaque points out how Lorca and his friends frequently met there.

Farther west on the edge of town is Huerta de San Vicente, formerly the Lorca family farmhouse; the surrounding farmland is now a manicured park named for Lorca. The house has been time-capsuled, with the poet's bedroom, in which he worked upon his tragic play *Blood Wedding*, preserved as he suddenly left it in August 1936. Threatened by the Fascists, he fled and sought refuge nearby with a friend, but he was discovered and executed. He was thirty-eight.

DISCOVER JOSÉ SARAMAGO'S LISBON

Lisbon, Portugal

Walk with: José Saramago (1922–2010)

Route: Through Lisbon

Length: 1.2 miles

Essential reading: *Baltasar and Blimunda* (1982); *Small Memories* (1998)

LEFT: The José Saramago Foundation is in one of Lisbon's most remarkable buildings.

Portugal's most prolific twentieth-century writer, José Saramago moved to Lisbon at the age of two, where he grew up in poverty in a working-class neighborhood. His memoir, *Small Memories,* paints a vivid picture of this time of his life.

An avowed atheist and communist, Saramago was a prolific writer from a young age, although he only achieved wide recognition with the publication of *Memorial do Convento*—known as *Baltasar and Blimunda* in translation—in 1982, when he was sixty. By the age of eighty, he had published a further eight novels, received the Nobel Prize for Literature, and gone into exile on the Spanish island of Lanzarote after Portugal's government intervened in preventing his novel, *The Gospel According to Jesus Christ* (1991), from entering a European literature prize.

Despite these later years, Saramago loved Lisbon with a passion. Start this walk in Largo do Intendente, near where Saramago grew up, and stroll toward the seafront to the Casa dos Bicos on Rua dos Bacalhoeiros. This fabulously eccentric sixteenth-century building is a cultural center and home to the José Saramago Foundation. It houses a small museum dedicated to Saramago. Outside, his ashes are buried at the foot of an old olive tree. Finish your walk in the Café Martinho da Arcada in the Praça do Comercio, which was a popular haunt of Saramago's and has his photo on the wall and a table named after him.

299
LOOK FOR THE SURREAL WITH RENÉ MAGRITTE

Brussels, Belgium

Few Belgians have left a greater mark on the art world than René Magritte (1898–1967), with his surrealist take on life. Although Brussels is not full of men with apples for faces, it does hold some of the keys to his inspiration. Start at the Magritte Museum in Rue de la Regence, which has many of his works plus ephemera from his life, and walk to Rue des Alexiens for a coffee in La Fleur en Papier Doré, a truly Bohemian café which Magritte spent many hours in and where he possibly sold his first painting. Break your walk next at the art nouveau Le Greenwich, which used to be a chess bar Magritte frequented, before heading up to his former house in Jette.

300
A REALIST'S EYE ON BRUGES

Bruges, Belgium

Jan van Eyck (c.1390–1441) seemingly came from nowhere—the precise place and year of his birth are unknown—to change art forever with naturalism and almost hyperrealism. He spent the last twelve years of his life in Bruges producing masterpieces. Only twenty of van Eyck's works survive. Of these, the 1436 *Virgin and Child with Canon van der Paele* hangs in the Groeninge Museum, as does the 1439 *Portrait of Margaret van Eyck*, his wife. Two years later, he was buried at the Cathedral of Saint Donatian (on the central Burg Square), which was destroyed in 1799. He is now commemorated a little farther north with a statue on Jan van Eyckplein Square.

RIGHT: The main square of Brussels, where René Magritte developed his sense of the surreal.

301

CLAUDE MONET'S
CLIFF WALK

Pourville, Normandy, France

The painting by Claude Monet (1840–1926) known as *Cliff Walk at Pourville* was executed in 1882, following a visit there with his friend Alice Hoschedé, and is probably of her two daughters. A walk from Dieppe to Pourville along the coastal path reveals the location of this and other paintings, for example, *Low Tide at Pourville, near Dieppe* and *Chemin dans les blès á Pourville*, both dated 1882.

302

RAMBLE WITH RENOIR

Wargemont, Normandy, France

French artist Pierre-Auguste Renoir (1841–1919) was captivated by the seaside views at Wargemont, near Dieppe. This area of the Normandy coast, notable for cliffs and weather-swept panoramas, is where he painted *View of the Seacoast near Wargemont in Normandy* (1880). Amble along the steep cliffs as he did, and watch as the lighting conditions change.

303

DOCUMENTARIES OF THE DAY

Pontoise, Île de France, France

Camille Pissarro (1830–1903) lived a peripatetic life and spent some time in the small town of Pontoise, recording busy, modern, suburban life here. Two examples are *Factory at Pontoise* (1873) and *Vue du Quai du Pothuis* (1868). Begin your walk at the Musée Camille Pissarro and walk toward the road bridge, continuing south along the river, where there are panels of Pissarro's paintings at the locations of their origin.

RIGHT: Claude Monet's painting of the cliffs at Pourville.

304
ALFRED SISLEY'S TOWNSCAPES

Marly-le-Roi, Île de France, France

In late 1874, Alfred Sisley (1839–1899) moved to a house at 2 Avenue de l'Abreuvoir in Marly-le-Roi. He perfectly captures the winter scene here in his painting *L'Abreuvoir de Marly, Gelée Blanche* of 1876. A twenty-minute walk northwest along the Avenue de l'Abreuvoir will take you toward the River Seine at Port Marly. In March 1876, the heavy rain caused the river to burst its banks, and Sisley painted a number of works recording this, his most famous being *Flood at Port Marly* (1876). The views of both places have changed little since Sisley's time.

305
VINCENT VAN GOGH'S FINAL HOME

Auvers-sur-Oise, Île de France, France

Close by the railway station at Auvers is a statue to Vincent van Gogh (1853–1890), the artist who lived and tragically died in the town. Continue along the street to the town hall, where you will see a panel showing Van Gogh's painting of the building, which he made in 1890. Opposite is the Auberge Ravoux, where he lived at this time. Turn right onto Rue Daubigny until you reach the large gothic church, which was also captured splendidly by Van Gogh in a vivid blue interpretation of the building. Behind the church, walk along Rue Emile Bernard until reaching the cemetery where Van Gogh is buried, alongside his brother, Theo.

306
ÉDOUARDE MANET AT RUEIL

Rueil-Malmaison, Paris, France

The pretty suburb of Rueil on the outskirts of Paris, where Napoleon and his first wife Josephine lived at the Château de Malmaison, is also the location for one of Édouarde Manet's (1832–1883) lesser-known paintings, *House at Rueil* (1882). It was executed in the final year of his life, spending the summer here as the guest of the writer Eugène Labiche, to recuperate from the symptoms of his long-term progressive illness. The solitude of this quiet suburb inspired Manet to paint the house and garden—as an exercise in calm serenity—the empty bench, and parts of the brightly colored house cooled by the dappled shade of the trees.

307
IN THE FOOTSTEPS OF JEAN-JACQUES ROUSSEAU

Ermenonville, Oise, France

About thirty-five miles northeast of Paris is the town of Ermenonville, where the French writer and philosopher Jean-Jacques Rousseau (1712–1778) spent the last months of his life. Here, his patron, René de Girardin, created a park bearing Rousseau's name in his honor. The park was based on the English "picturesque" style of landscape garden, complete with classical follies. A walk around the park today reveals many of these features, and the site of Rousseau's tomb, on a small island in the park's lake, is where his remains lay before being reinterred at the Panthéon in Paris.

TOP RIGHT: The church at Auvers, which was painted by Vincent van Gogh.

RIGHT: Van Gogh created many paintings of the area, including *Wheat Fields at Auvers with White House* (1890).

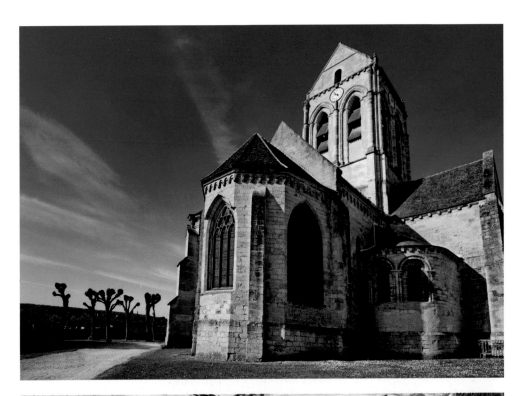

JEAN-PAUL SARTRE AND PARISIAN EXISTENTIALISM

Paris, France

Walk with: Jean-Paul Sartre (1905–1980)

Route: St. Germain des Près Metro to Montparnasse Cemetery

Length: c.2.5 miles

Essential reading: *Being and Nothingness* (1943)

TOP RIGHT: Café de Flore on Paris' Left Bank has long been a meeting point for intellectuals.

RIGHT: Both Jean-Paul Sartre and Simone de Beauvoir are buried in the Cemetery of Montparnasse.

The Left Bank of the River Seine in Paris has lost none of its edgy charm and busy bohemian atmosphere enjoyed by Jean Paul Sartre and his peers. From the St.-Germain-des-Prés Métro station, walk along the Boulevard St. Germain to number 172 and the Café de Flore, with its wonderful Art Deco interior, where intellectuals such as Sartre and his partner, Simone de Beauvoir, would meet their "family," developing existential ideas that dominated French philosophy in the postwar years.

Retrace your steps to the Église Saint-Germain-des-Prés, cross the Boulevard, and continue south along Rue Bonaparte, turning left into Rue Saint-Sulpice, to find the Café de la Mairie. It was here that Sartre and Albert Camus met for the last time. Despite both working on the radical left-wing newspaper *Combat* during the war, their political and philosophical differences later alienated them from each other.

Continue along past the church on the right until reaching the Rue de l'École de Médecines, then turn right until you reach the Sorbonne, where both Sartre and de Beauvoir were students. Now head south along the Rue de Sorbonne and meander through to the beautiful Boulevard Saint-Michel, with its brightly colored shops opposite the Tuilleries Gardens, and into the Cimetière du Montparnasse to visit the tombs of Sartre and de Beauvoir.

309

TAKE A TOUR WITH EMILE ZOLA

Paris, France

Experience the Paris of Émile Zola (1840–1902) by following in the footsteps of the newlyweds Coupeau and Gervais in his novel *L'Assomoir* (1877). The couple and their guests walk in the rain after the wedding at the Rue St. Denis, heading south to the Louvre, to kill time before the wedding feast. Once inside the museum, one of the guests then assumes the role of guide, much to the embarrassment of the others.

310

BECOME A *FLÂNEUR*

Paris, France

An essay written in 1863, by Charles Baudelaire (1821–1867) entitled *The Painter of Modern Life*, established the *flâneur* as a figure of modernity: a disengaged stroller of the Parisian streets. One has only to walk the boulevards of Paris today to see that little has changed other than the fashions.

311

LOVE WITH VICTOR HUGO

Paris, France

Victor Hugo (1802–1885) spent seventeen years writing his great novel of social injustice, *Les Misérables* (1862). Feel the romance on a walk in the Jardin du Luxembourg, where Marius catches Cosette's attention as "the sparrows were giving vent to little twitters in the depths of the chestnut trees."

312

SEEKING MODIGLIANI
AND FRIENDS

Paris, France

In 1906 Paris, the Italian-born painter and sculptor
Amedeo Modigliani (1884–1920) mixed with other
young avant-garde artists like Pablo Picasso, Constantin
Brâncuși, and Maurice Utrillo. Cheap studio space was
essential. Le Bateau-Lavoir ("laundry barge"), a former
warehouse in rue Ravignan, Montmartre, was a popular
spot where Modigliani first lived in 1906. In 1909, he
moved to another artistic hub, La Ruche (the beehive),
2 Passage de Danzig in Montparnasse. He and his artist
friends frequented cafés in the area, including Café
de la Rotonde at 105 Boulevard du Montparnasse,
where Modigliani first met his English lover, the poet
Beatrice Hastings.

313

A PARISIAN AFFAIR WITH
ANAIS AND HENRY

Paris, France

Anaïs Nin (1903–1977) and Henry Miller (1891–1980)
had an intellectual and sensual affair in Paris which had
a profound impact, especially on Nin as her inspiration
to write erotica. Nin called the bohemian neighborhood
of Montparnasse home for three years. Walk along Rue
Schoelcher where she lived, stroll over for a coffee in
Le Dôme Café, where she spent hours writing, then to
29 Rue Vavin, the location of a café where Nin and
Miller's love affair began. End your tour at Central
Hotel on Rue du Maine, where Nin experienced her
sexual awakening with Miller.

314

SOLVE THE MYSTERY OF
THE DA VINCI CODE

Paris, France

The fictional best-selling thriller *The Da Vinci Code*
(2003) by American author Dan Brown (1964–)
whizzes around Paris as American lecturer, and sleuth,
Robert Langdon tries to solve a murder. From the
luxurious Ritz Hotel in Place Vendôme, where Langdon
is staying, he crosses to the Louvre museum, in Rue de
Rivoli, half a mile away, where the murder has been
committed. It is a visual delight, which can be leisurely
retraced by walkers, to arrive at the I. M. Pei's glass
pyramid entrance to the museum. Once inside, head to
see da Vinci's *Mona Lisa* and *Virgin of the Rocks*. Both
paintings are central to the book's plot.

315

TAKE THE TRAIN WITH
EZRA POUND

Paris, France

Although born and educated in the United States,
the most creative periods for the writer and poet Ezra
Pound (1885–1972) were in London (1908–1920) and
Paris (1921–1924). He lived at 70 Rue Notre Dame des
Champs with his wife, having felt that "London had
lost its literary edge." He had already persuaded another
modernist writer, James Joyce, to move to Paris, where
they engaged with others such as Hemingway. From
Pound's house, walk the short distance to Vavin Métro
station, to relive his Imagist poem "In a Station of
the Metro":

"The apparition of these faces in the crowd;
Petals on a wet, black bough."

RIGHT: Look out at the scenes
that inspired Anaïs Nin from her
favorite café, Le Dôme.

BE INSPIRED BY THE GHOSTS OF THE PAST IN THE PÈRE LACHAISE CEMETERY

Paris, France

Where: Père Lachaise Cemetery, Boulevard de Ménilmontant

Route: Wind through 110 acres of tree-lined paths

Essential viewing: Oscar Wilde, Jim Morrison, Abelard and Heloise, *et al*

Essential reading: *Meet Me at Père Lachaise* (2010) by Anna Eriksson

LEFT: There is much inspiration to be had on a walk through the Père Lachaise Cemetery.

A wander around the Père Lachaise Cemetery is billed as the "most hauntingly romantic walk in Paris." Around 70,000 people lie buried beneath mausoleums, neo-gothic graves, simple tombs, and grave slabs of stone, set in the tranquil grounds of tree-lined paths and walkways (five thousand trees were planted when it was created).

At the time of its creation, its location outside central Paris deterred people from using the new cemetery. They were reluctant to travel to bury their dead, but the small churchyards of Parisian churches were overcrowded and unhygienic. To encourage its use, the authorities disinterred the bodies of famous French people such as the writer Molière (died 1673) and the lovers Abelard (died 1142) and Heloise (died 1164) from other cemeteries to reinter them in Père Lachaise. The plan worked, encouraging ordinary people and the famous to be buried here.

The cemetery's free map highlights the graves of the famous and popular. The grand tomb of Abelard and Heloise attracts people in love; so, too, the tomb of Italian artist Amedeo Modigliani (died 1920), reunited with his partner Jeanne Hèbuterne (died 1920), who committed suicide the day after he died. Fans of The Doors seek out the grave of Jim Morrison (died 1971). The cemetery has a very natural feel and there is an abundance of wildlife, from city foxes to flocks of birds.

317
ON THE STREETS OF PARIS WITH JEAN RHYS

Paris, France

Twentieth-century novelist Jean Rhys (1890–1979) set many of her early works in bohemian Paris of the 1920s, and it is Montparnasse where she found herself living for much of this time. Start this walk through the creative quarter at the Vavin Métro stop, past the cafés along Boulevard Montparnasse from La Closerie des Lilas, La Rotonde, Le Dôme La Coupole, to the classic 1920s Art Deco café Le Sélect. Standing at the corner of the Boulevard du Montparnasse and the rue Vavin, Le Sélect features in Rhys' first novel *Quartet* (1929), where heroine Marya has to endure a nasty scene with her lover, Heidler, and his testy wife, Lois.

318
DISCOVER SIMONE DE BEAUVOIR'S RIVE GAUCHE

Paris, France

The Paris of Simone de Beauvoir (1908–1986) is that enticing, illusory Paris of avant-garde intellectuals arguing out ideas in the smoke-filled cafés of the Rive Gauche. Begin at Les Deux Magots, the café famed as a hotspot for literary icons, de Beauvoir among them. En route to the Seine, pass by the Hotel La Louisiane, where the writer lived for a spell, and the Hotel d'Aubusson, where she enjoyed gin and jazz at the now-vanished basement bar. Doubling back, end at de Beauvoir's favorite spot in the Jardin du Luxembourg, the Medici Fountain.

319
A VIEW WITH VAN GOGH

Montmartre, Paris, France

Iconic painter Vincent Van Gogh (1853–1890) lived in two apartments when residing in the quaint area of Montmartre in Paris, but it was in the apartment he shared with his brother at 54 Rue Lepic in Montmartre that some of his most popular works were created. Trace his steps from the apartment to Moulin de la Galette, a windmill and now restaurant in the Pigalle area, that once inspired Van Gogh's *Le Moulin de la Galette* series. Artists Toulouse-Lautrec and Pierre-Auguste Renoir were similarly inspired by the landscape, so grab your paintbrush and capture the scenery as you go.

320
ENTER MARCEL PROUST'S FICTIONAL WORLD

Illiers-Combray, France

In 1971, the centenary of the birth of the writer Marcel Proust (1871–1922), the town of Illiers was renamed Illiers-Combray, as homage to Proust, who used it as the setting for the fictional town of Combray in his magnum opus *À la Recherche du Temps Perdu* (1913). The old railway station has changed little since Proust's time, (except for the name change) and, in fact, even the town's population has only grown marginally. It is easy to recognize the fictional place just walking around; the church of St. Jacques is similar to his description of the fictional St. Hilaire in the novel. A short walk away is the Marcel Proust Museum.

TOP RIGHT: Les Deux Magots café has been a mainstay of Paris' literary scene for decades.

RIGHT: The Medici Fountain in the Jardin du Luxembourg was one of Simone de Beauvoir's favorite spots.

321

JACQUES BREL'S PARIS

Paris, France

Capturing the exquisite despair of the outsider and doomed love, Jacques Brel's (1929–1978) songs define a certain view of Paris, but one that is overflowing with a love of the city. Brussels-born Brel landed there in 1953, renting a room at 3 Rue des Trois Frères—and doubtless eating frites at Chez Eugène on Place du Tertre, like the protagonists of his song "Madeleine"—while making first-rung appearances at Les Trois Baudets on Boulevard de Clichy. He worked his way up to L'Olympia theater on Boulevard des Capucines. In 2019, Paris honored Brel with a pedestrianized route in the 19th arrondissement: the Allées Jacques-Brel.

322

BARS OF SERGE GAINSBOURG

Paris, France

Any walk inspired by French singer, songwriter, and creative Serge Gainsbourg (1928–1991) has alcohol at its core. Start at the grand bar of L'Hôtel in Montparnasse, where Gainsbourg and actress Jane Birkin spent the first stages of their relationship, before heading to the Moulin Rouge bar Les Trois Baudets, where he gave his first recorded performance in 1959. The final stop is 5 Rue de Verneuil, where Gainsbourg lived for twenty-three years before dying of a heart attack.

INHALE THE AIR WHICH GAVE COLETTE HER FREE-THINKING WAYS

Saint-Sauveur, Nouvelle-Aquitaine, France

Walk with: Sidonie-Gabrielle Colette (1873–1954)

Route: Sentier Colette

Length: 3.6 miles

Essential reading: *Claudine* novels (1900-1903)

TOP RIGHT: The Musée Colette is in the town of the writer's birth.

RIGHT: The walk into the countryside begins down an avenue of lime trees.

Although Sidonie-Gabrielle Colette is firmly linked to the fast-paced Parisian lifestyle that she so enjoyed, her roots are in Saint-Sauveur-en-Puisaye in Burgundy. Her mother always encouraged her to live life on her own terms and shared her view that domestic drudgery was the death knell for creativity. When Colette had her own daughter at the age of forty, she spent little time with her.

Colette remained close to her mother, writing her thousands of letters, but she never returned to live in the town of her birth.

Instead, she recreated that town many times in fictionalized versions in her novels—most especially in the four *Claudine* novels, about a fifteen-year-old girl with a zest for life—much of which was undoubtedly based on Colette's own early life in Saint-Sauveur. The first, *Claudine at School* (1900) begins: "My name is Claudine, I live in Montigny; I was born there in 1884; I shall probably not die there."

This walk begins at the Musée Colette, based in the town's chateau, and starts with a stroll down an alley of lime trees and into the Rue Colette, where the novelist's childhood home is situated and open to the public. From here, it heads out into the charming local countryside and past the family run Batisse Pottery, which Colette used to visit as a young child, before taking a circular route via Moûtiers and back to Saint-Sauveur.

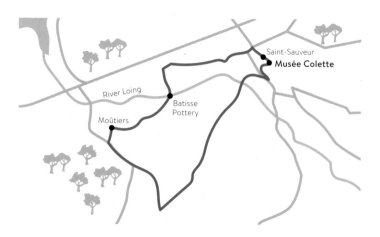

324
FORGET CONVENTION
Paris, France

Although born in the countryside, novelist Sidonie-Gabrielle Colette always seemed destined for a more libertine life in Paris. She moved there at twenty when she married Henry Gauthier-Villars—Willy— who famously locked her in their apartment while she wrote stories for which he took all the credit. This walk starts there, at 28 Rue Jacob, and crosses over the river to go past the Palais Royal, where Colette lived twice and where she died. She moved houses often and wrote about it in her novella *Trois… Six… Neuf* (1945). Continue on to Montmartre's Moulin Rouge, where Colette nearly started a riot with an on-stage kiss with her female partner, Mathilde de Morny—Missy.

325

PAUL GAUGUIN'S BRITTANY

Le Pouldu, Brittany, France

Following his stay in Arles, Paul Gauguin (1848–1903) moved to the quiet and peaceful resort of Le Pouldu in Brittany. He stayed firstly at the Hotel Destais (now renamed as the Hotel des Grands Sables), on the beachfront. Follow the short walkway, Place Gauguin, onto the main road, Rue des Grands Sables, and on the right is a reconstruction of the inn where he moved shortly after. It is now known as La Buvette de la Plage, a café that is also a shrine to the artist. A ten-minute walk away is the Chemin du Mât Pilote. Walk toward Fort Cohars and on the left is the field depicted in Gauguin's *The Harvest* (1890).

326

FEAST YOUR EYES ON DA VINCI'S HOME

Amboise, France

On the banks of the Loire river, the pretty town of Amboise is dominated by the stunning Château d'Amboise, home of French kings, situated above the town. A few hundred yards from the palace, on the edge of the town, is the smaller Château du Clos Lucé, the childhood home of François I. In 1516 the young king invited the Italian artist-engineer Leonardo da Vinci (1452–1519) to live there, as a friend and mentor to the king. It was possibly the happiest period in da Vinci's life. Today, the house, open to visitors, is furnished to recreate the period of his three-year stay.

327

LOOKING FOR THE LITTLE PRINCE

Lyon, France

The Little Prince, originally published in 1943, is one of the most translated and bestselling books ever published. Traces of author Antoine de Saint-Exupéry (1900–1944) and the adventurous Little Prince can be found in the city of Lyon—but only by those who open their eyes. Start at the amazing Fresque des Lyonnais mural on 49 quai St. Vincent—once an empty wall, it now looks like a six-story townhouse with Lyon's famous on the balconies. From here, head to the Place Bellecour, where there is a charming sculpture of the pair. Remember… "What matters most are the simple pleasures so abundant that we can all enjoy them… all we need to do is open our eyes."

328

SING *THE SONGS OF AUVERGNE*

Auvergne, France

The French composer Marie-Joseph Canteloube de Malaret (1879–1957) was born in the Auvergne-Rhône-Alpes region of southern France, in Annonay. He is best known for his orchestral interpretations of the rustic folksongs of the region, *Chants d'Auvergne* (Songs of Auvergne). He made musical arrangements for them between 1923 and 1930 which evoke the beauty of the landscape. Popular walks in the Auvergne region center on Cantal, Mont Dores, Haute-Loire, Montagne Bourbonnaise, and Chaine des Pays.

LEFT: Antoine de Saint-Exupéry appears on the spectacular Fresque des Lyonnais.

JOIN GEORGE SAND IN LOVE

Château de Boussac, France

Walk with: George Sand
(1804–1876)

Where: Château de Boussac
to Les Pierre Jaumâtres

Length: 3.5 miles (one way)

Essential reading: *Jeanne*
(1844)

Two hundred miles south of Paris, overlooking the Creuse valley, is the Château de Boussac, where the nineteenth-century traveler might have come across author George Sand—nom-de-plume of the Parisian-born Romance novelist Amantine Lucile Aurore Dupin.

Sand loved this region of France and set her novel *Jeanne* in Château de Boussac and the nearby Pierre Jaumâtres, where forty vast granite blocks balance on one another as if held magically together.

Sand first stayed at the Château de Boussac in 1841 and returned frequently. That first time she was in the company of Prosper Mérimée, another romantic novelist. She had left her husband in 1835 to begin a new life, taking with her their two children. Sand later returned to the château with her lover, Polish composer Frédéric Chopin. There was a portrait of the two of them painted in 1838 by artist Eugène Delacroix that was later cut up into two halves.

The walk from Château de Boussac to Les Pierre Jaumâtres is a pleasant day out, crossing a verdantly green landscape of fields.

ABOVE: George Sand refused to be limited by her gender.

TOP RIGHT: A recreation of Sand's bedroom in the Château de Boussac.

RIGHT: The mystical granite blocks of Les Pierres Jaumâtres.

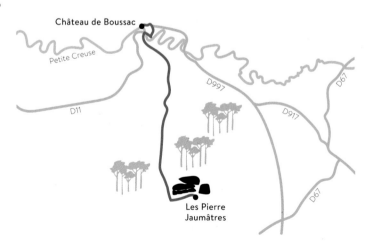

Château de Boussac

Petite Creuse

D11

D997

D67

D917

D67

Les Pierre Jaumâtres

THE CHÂTEAU OF MADAME DE STAËL

Loire Valley, France

Forced into exile by Emperor Napoleon, French woman of letters and historian Madame de Staël (1766–1817) stayed in Chaumont-sur-Loire from April to August 1810, making the most of her time to edit her book *De l'Allemagne* (1830). During her stay at the château, she invited guests to discuss literature and politics, sing, and play music. Occupying thirty-two hectares, the castle's grounds are full of scenic pathways zigzagging through lush landscapes. Madame de Staël often walked the park, enjoying unobstructed views of the River Loire.

MARGUERITE FROM DURAS

Duras, France

French author Marguerite Duras (1914–1996) was born Marguerite Donnadieu, but she chose Duras as her pen-name after the town of her father's birth. She herself only lived in the medieval town of Duras, in the Lot-et-Garonne region of southwest France, for two years between the ages of eight and ten. It would be the setting for her early novels *Les Impudents* (1943) and *La Vie Tranquille* (1944). A pleasant walk of about 4.5 miles links Duras to Pardaillan, passing farmhouses, fields and vineyards. In mid-May each year, the town of Duras holds a three-day festival in her honor.

332
BLEND NATURE AND ART WITH ANDY GOLDSWORTHY

Haute Provence, France

The Refuge d'Art is a ninety-three-mile hiking trail in the Haute Provence area of France that leads you through stunning countryside and past ten Andy Goldsworthy (1956–) artworks over the course of a ten-day hike. The concept is Goldsworthy's creation. He wanted to bring together nature, the agricultural heritage of the area, and hiking in such a way that the art only reveals itself gradually. The route, which starts in Digne-les-Bains, follows old agricultural pathways. Some of the artworks are designed as refuges built around old derelict buildings, renovated by Goldsworthy in his unique style of using the materials he finds in nature, while three are huge stone cairns—or sentinels—standing guard in the center of the valleys.

333
FOLLOW TOULOUSE-LAUTREC THROUGH HIS HOME TOWN

Albi, France

Although Henri-Marie-Raymond de Toulouse-Lautrec-Monfa (1864–1901) made his (much shorter) name in Paris as a sensational artist, it is in Albi, the town of his birth, that he can truly be found. He was born at the Hôtel de Barc into a wealthy aristocratic family, the homes and estates of which can be visited. The town of Albi is dominated by the Palais de la Berbie (bishop's residence), which towers over the River Tarn, which flows through the city. A walk through the city reveals the UNESCO sites of the Cathedral of Saint Cecilia, and the medieval citadel, familiar places to Toulouse-Lautrec, while the Musée Toulouse-Lautrec holds the largest public collection of artworks by its native son.

334
EXPLORE THE DELIGHTS OF PROVENCE WITH HENRY JAMES

Avignon, France

American writer Henry James (1843–1916) traveled through France in fall 1882, recounting his experiences in his book *A Little Tour in France* (1884). He began his travels in Touraine, traveling through Provence before heading north to Burgundy. He spent time exploring the streets of Avignon, before making his way to Villeneuve-les-Avignon. From Avignon, a series of scenic walks snake their way across the hills of Provence to Gard, where James was particularly struck by the Pont du Gard, an ancient Roman aqueduct bridge (he wrote that its impressive grandeur left him with "nothing to say"). The bridge is part of a thirty-one-mile aqueduct that carried water to the Roman town of Nîmes, which James also visited on his journey.

335
ALBERT CAMUS' PROVENCE HEAVEN

Lourmarin, France

In the last two years of his life, acclaimed French author and journalist Albert Camus (1913–1960) lived in the village of Lourmarin in Provence, where he is now buried. He originally learned of Lourmarin from his high school teacher during an excursion to the château here. After winning the Nobel Prize for Literature, he bought a house in the village. Walk along the village streets and stop by the soccer field where the former goalkeeper came to cheer on his local team. He once said, "What I know most surely in the long run about morality and obligations, I owe to football." On Rue Albert Camus you can pass his house, where his daughter still lives, and finish at the cemetery to pause by the humble stone that bears his name.

LEFT: Andy Goldsworthy's sentinel, on a walking loop in Haute Provence.

336

ONE TOWN THAT INSPIRED THREE GIANTS OF THE ART WORLD

Arles, France

Walk with: The painters van Gogh (1853–1890), Gauguin (1848–1903), and Picasso (1881–1973)

Route: Alyscamps, Necropolis to Rue Marius Jouveau

Length: 0.9 miles

Essential viewing: Vincent van Gogh's *Café Terrace at Night* (1888)

TOP RIGHT: Vincent van Gogh's richly colored *Starry Night over the Rhône*, painted in Arles.

RIGHT: The vibrant Place Voltaire buzzes with cafés.

"I cannot help it that my pictures do not sell. Nevertheless the time will come when people will see that they are worth more than the price of the paint," said Vincent van Gogh prophetically.

Attracted by the warm Mediterranean sun and bright light, van Gogh left Paris for the town of Arles in February 1888. Arles was a Roman town, and this walk begins at the Roman ruins of the Alyscamps Necropolis, where van Gogh and Paul Gauguin painted together in the fall of 1888. Walk west along the tree-lined avenue and then north for a few hundred yards to the Jardin d'été, another inspirational site used by van Gogh. Writing to his sister about a painting he made of the garden, he stated: "The picture may not present a literal image of the garden, but may present it to our minds as if in a dream."

Behind the garden is the original Roman amphitheater used in the summer for bullfights, which were regularly attended by the artist Pablo Picasso from 1912. Van Gogh painted *Arena in Arles* at this location in 1888.

Continue walking on the other side of the amphitheater, through Rue Voltaire and into the Place Voltaire, an area of shops and cafés. Gauguin and van Gogh both painted their night café scenes here. A few hundred yards farther is the Place Lamartine, where a panel displays van Gogh's *Yellow House* (1888), at its original location. The house, destroyed during the Second World War, was one he shared with Gauguin for a few weeks prior to his nervous breakdown and exile from the town.

Finally walk the short distance to the river, to the location of the painting *Starry Night Over the Rhône*, 1888. Stay after sunset, as van Gogh put it: "Often it seems to me the night is even more richly colored than the day."

337
PAINTING WITH PICASSO
Juan-les-Pins, Côte D'Azur, France

The Côte d'Azur inspired a great many artists who all succumbed to the beauty of its landscapes, most notably Pablo Picasso (1881–1973), who loved the French Riviera and stayed there for almost thirty years. There are many places to visit here, but it is the walk along the gloriously colored coast of Juan-les-Pins from Antibes that was a great inspiration for the Spanish painter, and it is here that he painted *Juan-les-Pins* in 1920. A visit to the Musée Picasso is a must for any Picasso fan. The château was Picasso's studio in 1946 and now houses a collection of his works.

338
PAUL CÉZANNE, A SOLITARY PAINTER
Aix-en-Provence, France

Paul Cézanne (1839–1906) was born in Aix-en-Provence and spent the last twenty years of his life there, virtually as a recluse. The house that his father bought in 1859, Jas de Bouffan, to the west of Aix, is the location for many of Cézanne's early watercolors of the area. A thirty-minute walk northeast through the town of Aix takes you to his purpose-built studio, complete with furnishings and equipment, that he used in the last four years of his life. A further ten minutes north takes you to the "Field of Painters," with its fabulous views toward the Mont St. Victoire, Cézanne's favorite motif.

COLLIOURE AND THE BIRTH OF FAUVISM

Collioure, France

Walk with: Henri Matisse (1869–1954) and André Derain (1880–1954)

Route: Place Fauve to Rue de la Caranque

Length: 0.6 miles

Essential viewing: Henri Matisse's *Vue de Collioure, l'église été* (1905)

LEFT: The church on the seafront in Collioure that Henri Matisse painted.

In 1905, Matisse moved to the Mediterranean resort of Collioure, where he was joined by Derain, both keen to exploit the strong light and colors the location afforded. The results were exhibited later that year at the Salon d'Automne in Paris, where the artists were ridiculed as "fauves" or wild beasts, because of the unnatural coloring used in their work. Undeterred by the criticism, they both continued to paint in this manner.

"I would like to recapture that freshness of vision, which is characteristic of extreme youth when all the world is new to it," wrote Matisse.

The walk begins at the Place Fauve on Boulevard du Boramar, where there is a board depicting Matisse's painting *Vue de Collioure, l'église été*. Look across the habor to see the view today. The tower of the church was at one time a lighthouse. Continue along this shoreline past locations of other works such as Derain's *Le Faubourge de Collioure, été* and Matisse's *Barques à Collioure, été*, both dated 1905, and on to the chapel of St. Vincent. Look back toward the town to recapture Matisse's *La porte, plage St-Vincent, été* (1905).

Back at the main church, turn right into Rue du Mirador, and at the top of the hill is the view toward the town which Matisse painted as *Les toits de Collioure* (1906). Look the other way for Derain's view of *Collioure, le village et la mer, été* (1905).

"We became intoxicated with color, with words that speak of color, and with the sun that makes colors brighter," wrote Derain.

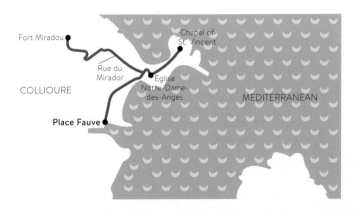

WALK WITH BETTINA VON ARNIM

Frankfurt, Germany

Walk with: Bettina von Arnim (1785–1859)

Route: Goethe Museum to Neuer Börneplatz

Length: 0.86 miles

Essential reading: *Goethe's Correspondence with a Child* (1835)

ABOVE: Bettina von Arnim was a prolific fiction writer.

RIGHT: Von Arnim had a close friendship with Goethe, which is explored at the Goethe Museum.

Born into the wealthy Brentano family in Frankfurt in 1785, German author, composer, and illustrator Bettina von Arnim was a prolific writer of fiction. She took a great interest in political and cultural affairs, and counted renowned literary and musical figures among her friends, including the brothers Grimm, Ludwig van Beethoven, and, most notably, Johann Wolfgang von Goethe.

Over the course of the years, Bettina built a close bond with Goethe. They exchanged dozens of letters and, three years after his death, she published her correspondence with him in *Goethe's Correspondence with a Child*. The Goethe Museum on Großer Hirschgraben 23–25 sheds light on this close relationship.

From the museum, it's a short walk to the Carmelite Monastery, where Bettina's parents are buried. In a letter to Goethe, Bettina wrote: "I come here every day at noon; the autumn sun shines through the church window and paints the shadow of the vine leaves here on the pavement and the white wall; then I see how the wind stirs them and how one after the other falls." Despite being brought up in the devout Brentano family, she was not particularly religious, rejecting the church as an institution: "I love better to see the lambs feeding in the church-yard, than the people in the church; better the lilies in the field, which though they spin not are nourished by the dew, than long processions tramping over them and treading them in their loveliest bloom."

Heading east is the Neuer Börneplatz, a holocaust memorial site located in what was once the Jewish quarter. Bettina would often head here to visit her Jewish friend, Violet. Many, including her sister, thought that her friendship with the girl was inappropriate, but Bettina stood her ground, and throughout her life strongly advocated the emancipation of Jews.

341

SEEK BERTOLT BRECHT'S LEGACY

Berlin, Germany

A strong supporter of Marxism and socialism, Bertolt Brecht's (1898–1956) theatrical works are deliberately devoid of emotion to allow better alignment with political thought. He wrote his *Threepenny Opera* (1928), a "play with music," in Berlin, after moving there from Bavaria. Later, after the Second World War, he and his wife established the Berlin Ensemble by the riverside to continue his theater productions. From here, walk north along Chausseestrasse for 0.6 miles and visit his last home, now the Academy of Arts and Brecht-Weigel Museum. Behind the house is the Dorotheenstädtischer Friedhof, Brecht's final resting place, alongside many other elites of German intellectuals.

342

CROSS THE DIVIDE WITH CHRISTA WOLF

Berlin, Germany

As a writer whose works spanned both sides of the wall, Christa Wolf (1929–2011) is one of the most important writers to emerge from former East Germany. Her novels often focus on the division and the reunification, which a stroll from the Brandenburg Gate—tracing the line of the former Berlin Wall—can derive. From here, follow Unter den Linden eastward for 1.6 miles over the river Spree and stop at Alexanderplatz. On November 4, 1989, Wolf delivered a speech here against the East German regime, saying that: "The people are standing on the platform now, and it is the leadership that is walking past them."

343

HUNT FOR WITCHES IN THE HARZ MOUNTAINS

Harz Mountains, Germany

Grab your broomstick and discover a region of fairy-tales and legends. The Harz Witches Trail is a sixty-mile route through the mountains of the Harz National Park, a realm famed for its legends of witches and other fascinating folklore. Most itineraries take walkers from Osterode and across the iconic Brocken Mountain to Thale, passing through vast moorlands, dense forests, dramatic canyons, and villages of medieval half-timbered houses. According to local legend, witches gather on the peak of Brocken every Walpurgis Night (April 30), a tradition which features in Johann Wolfgang von Goethe's *Faust* (1829).

344

A WALK UP DRAGON'S HILL WITH BYRON

Königswinter, Germany

After his self-imposed exile from England, George Gordon Byron (1788–1824), known simply as Lord Byron, spent much of his time in Germany's Rhineland which, in the eighteenth century, was seen as a place of romance and broken hearts. In his epic poem *Childe Harold's Pilgrimage* (1812–1818) he makes mention of "The castled crag of Drachenfels Frowns o'er the wide and winding Rhine," which references Schloss Drachenburg in Königswinter, a town near the German city of Bonn. Follow the 5.6-mile walk from Bonn along the bank of the Rhine to the town, then hike the additional 3.2-mile partly forested walking path up the hill for a sweeping view of Byron's majestic Rhine.

LEFT: The Harz Witches Trail leads walkers through forests and canyons.

ESCAPE INTO THE PFALZ REGION

Pfalz, Germany

Walk with: Anna Seghers
(1900–1983)

Route: Westhofen to
Oppenheim

Length: 13.6 miles

Essential reading: *The Seventh
Cross* (1942)

ABOVE: Anna Seghers fled Nazi
Germany for Mexico.

TOP RIGHT: The town of
Oppenheim is more welcoming
than it was in Seghers' day.

RIGHT: The character in
Seghers' novel fled through
the region's vineyards and
on to Holland.

By the time *The Seventh Cross* was published, German author Anna Seghers was living in exile in Mexico. Born Anna "Netty" Rieling, to a Jewish family, Seghers fled Germany in 1934, and wrote her suspenseful account of concentration-camp escapees while living in Paris.

Seghers set out to write, "a tale that makes it possible to get to know the many layers of fascist Germany through the fortunes of a single man." That man is George Heisler, who—along with six other prisoners—escapes the fictional Westhofen Concentration Camp, set in Seghers' native Pfalz region, not far from the city of Mainz.

Several hiking trails around Westhofen will take walkers through the countryside into which George Heisler escapes—a rich wine-producing region of rolling farmland and endless vineyards, where "the apples and the grapes ripened in the gentle, misted-over sun." The longer route all the way to Oppenheim is closest to following in the footsteps of the lead character, who makes his way into the wetlands of the Rhine before pressing on to Mainz, where he finds that, "the community that supports and surrounds every person... had been turned into a network of living traps."

As the other six escapees are captured, bound to seven crosses that the camp overseer erects for their torture, the novel centers on Heisler's journey through the countryside, ultimately escaping to Holland and leaving the seventh cross empty. The gripping story of Heisler's escape is only a small part of a cleverly woven mesh of stories and characters which ultimately reflect what life was like under a fascist regime.

STROLL DOWN THE RHINE
Mainz, Germany

One of the best-known works by Anna Seghers, *Der Ausflug der toten Mädchen* (*Outing of the Dead Girls*), is also one of her most autobiographical works. An account of the author's school friends on an outing to the banks of the Rhine, the story's narrator juxtaposes the descriptions of that pleasant day with the tragic stories that follow each character as a result of the wars. "When her hospital has been unexpectedly bombed, she will think of... the white, sun-drenched café, and the garden on the bank of the Rhine." Set out from Mainz, Seghers' birthplace, along the banks of the Rhine, following the route the girls took by steamer, in search of the countryside the author describes so lovingly.

347

TAKE A WALK IN THE PARK WITH CLARA SCHUMANN

Leipzig, Germany

A stroll around the many parks circling Leipzig's old town would have been one of the pleasures of living in this city that Clara Schumann (1819–1896) enjoyed. The daughter of an ambitious piano teacher and instrument merchant, Clara Schumann performed her first concert at the age of nine at the Gewandhaus nestled between two such parks. Fifteen minutes' walk away from the town center, on Inselstrasse, Clara and husband Robert Schumann lived for the first four years of their marriage, where there's now a museum dedicated to the couple's private and public lives.

348

TAKE AN EPIC TREK INSPIRED BY BACH

Arnstadt to Lübeck, Germany

In 1705, Johann Sebastian Bach (1685–1750) set out on foot from the central German city of Arnstadt to walk the 250 miles to the Marienkirche in Lübeck, purely to see the then-famed organist Dietrich Buxtehude play. Following this well-marked north–south path, trek through the Harz mountains, steep in war history and literary ghosts, and encounter charming villages and fairy-tale forests along the way.

349

MEET BEETHOVEN IN BONN

Bonn, Germany

Visitors to Bonn seeking composer Ludwig van Beethoven (1770–1827) often begin in the beautiful historic center, to see the house where he was born on December 16, 1770, at Bonngasse 24–26. From there, it's a short walk to the Church of St. Remigius, where Beethoven was baptized the following day. In 1792, aged twenty-two, he moved to study music under Haydn in Vienna, never returning to Bonn. Nevertheless, the city honored him in 1845 with a bronze statue to commemorate his seventy-fifth anniversary, in Münsterplatz, a short walk from the church, turning south along Kasemenstrasse.

350

FOLLOW THE BRAHMS' WAY

Rhine Valley, Germany

The Rhine Valley between Mainz and Bonn is known for beautiful hilltop fortresses, layers of vineyards, and charming villages, and is popular with walkers. There is a section of walking trail called Brahm's Way, dedicated to the Romantic-era composer Johannes Brahms (1833–1897). It is said that it was a walking tour from Mainz to Bonn along the Rhine River that inspired his *Symphony no. 3*. At this time, Brahms declared his motto to be "Frei aber froh" (free but happy), in musical terms, the notes F-A-F, and the keys of these appear throughout this symphony.

LEFT: Clara Schumann enjoyed walking in the many green parks of Leipzig.

351

FINDING INSPIRATION WITH RICHARD WAGNER IN DRESDEN

Dresden, Germany

Walk with: Richard Wagner (1813–1883)

Route: Short walk around Dresden

Length: 1.37 miles or 5.6 miles, depending on the route chosen

Essential reading: *The Wagner Compendium: A Guide to Wagner's Life and Music* by Barry Millington (1992)

TOP RIGHT: Richard Wagner took part in uprisings in Dresden's Neumarkt.

RIGHT: The extravagant Semperoper is Dresden's opera house.

Much like the complex history of the Saxon city of Dresden, Richard Wagner's musical compositions are complex in texture and rich in emotions; his operas exude the concept of Gesamtkunstwerk—a "total work of art"—as they comprise poetic, visual, musical, and dramatic elements of performing arts, filled with accentuated drama.

Wagner spent around twenty years of his life living on and off in Dresden. Dresden is considered to be the center of the German Revolutions, with Wagner himself taking part in the May Uprising of 1849 in the square of Dresden Neumarkt, where Saxon and Prussian troops confronted the revolutionaries in the week of the fighting. It is widely believed that Wagner's life in Dresden heavily influenced his artistic style; he was passionate about political and social reform.

Walk from Neumarkt along Taschenberg toward the extravagant Zwinger Palace, whose porcelain glockenspiel occasionally rings out compositions by Wagner. Admire the palace exterior by walking around its garden, looping back to the Semperoper. This was previously the Hofoper, where Wagner's fourth opera *Rienzi* was accepted to play, the event which prompted his move to Dresden after living abroad. He premiered two more operas while in Dresden: *The Flying Dutchman* and *Tannhauser*.

From the opera house, walk toward the Elbe and cross the Augustusbrücke (Augustus Bridge) to walk along the riverbank for the best view of the Dresden skyline.

Keen walkers can continue the 3.7-mile stroll along the picturesque Elberadweg toward the suburb of Neugruna to visit Wagner's school, also the oldest surviving school in Dresden, the Evangelisches Kreuzgymnasium.

352
THE COMPOSER IN BAYREUTH
Bayreuth, Germany

Richard Wagner is a divisive topic, and not just for his connections with Nazism and anti-Semitism. Some, such as Nietzsche, Baudelaire, and Wilde derided him, yet for others, including C. S. Lewis, James Joyce, and Marcel Proust, he was influential. He arrived in Bayreuth in 1870 seeking a home for his expansive operas. The Margravial Opera House on Opernstrasse, then Europe's largest opera house, wasn't big enough, but he stayed in town, initially at No. 7 Dammallee during the building of Wahnfried, the family home and now a museum. At Eule (Owl) restaurant on Kirchgasse, he over-imbibed on wheat beer, his wife, Cosima, calling it a "dietary error." Up Green Hill is Wagner's legacy, the magnificent Bayreuth Festival Theater, designed to his specifications to host his work—whether you like it or not.

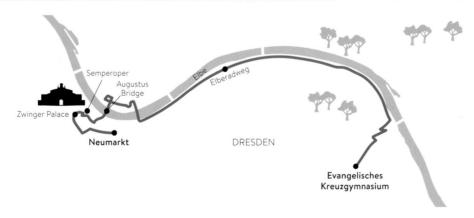

Zwinger Palace

Semperoper

Augustus Bridge

Neumarkt

Elbe

Elberadweg

DRESDEN

Evangelisches Kreuzgymnasium

LOOKING OUT FOR THE BROTHERS GRIMM'S FAIRY-TALES

Black Forest, Germany

Walk with: Brothers Jacob (1785–1863) and Wilhelm (1786–1859) Grimm

Route: The Mittelweg hiking trail

Length: Western trail: 145 miles; eastern trail: 140 miles

Essential reading: *The Complete Grimm's Fairy Tales* (1812)

ABOVE: The Grimm Brothers, whose fairy-tales are known throughout the world.

LEFT: The Black Forest inspired several of the famous fairy-tales.

Famous for its cuckoo clocks and Black Forest Gateau, the deep woods of Germany's Black Forest are both enchanting and haunting. It is believed that the Brothers Grimm were inspired by the atmosphere of the forest, the castles, and the villages among it for their stories of *Hansel and Gretel, Sleeping Beauty,* and *Rapunzel.*

Hiking is a long-established leisure tradition in the Black Forest, and the region was one of the first in the world to establish marked hiking paths. Originally laid out in 1903, the Mittelweg (Middle Way) trail leaves from Pforzheim in the north of the region to Waldshut on the Swiss border, offering diverse landscapes and storybook villages in between.

There are several viewing towers along the way, reminiscent of Rapunzel's. Traditional log cabins also appear regularly en route; although not made out of gingerbread as in the story of *Hansel and Gretel.*

354
VISIT ALBRECHT DÜRER'S FAVORITE HAUNTS

Nuremberg, Germany

Renowned for his paintings, copperplate engravings, and intricate woodcut prints, German painter Albrecht Dürer (1471–1528) lived from 1509 until his death in what is today the Albrecht Dürer House, a half-timbered building that is one of the few surviving burgher houses from Nuremberg's golden age. A five-minute walk south is St. Sebald's, Dürer's parish church, where a chapel once stood called Moritzkapelle, which was destroyed during the Second World War. Adjacent was a small restaurant where Dürer would often eat sausages. A leisurely walk south of the Pegnitz River is the Germanisches Nationalmuseum, the largest museum in the German-speaking world and home to some works by Dürer, while west is the beautifully kept St. John's Cemetery, Dürer's final resting place.

355
WHERE PAUL KLEE DISCOVERED EXPRESSIONISM

Schwabing, Munich, Germany

Paul Klee (1879–1940) lived in the bohemian neighborhood of Shwabing, Munich, at a pivotal time of his career. It was here that, in 1911, the Swiss-born artist first met his friend Wassily Kandinsky, later joining the German expressionist group Blaue Reiter (Blue Rider), of which Kandinsky was a founder. These artists had a profound influence on Klee, whose highly individual style contains elements of expressionism, cubism, and surrealism. Walk through the neighborhood along the Leopoldstraße, the main boulevard of Shwabing, to the Academy of Fine Arts in nearby Maxvorstadt, where Klee studied. Beyond it, the Lenbachhaus houses the world's largest collection of art of the Blaue Reiter.

356
HIKE TO SHERLOCK HOLMES' FINAL PROBLEM

Reichenbach Falls, Switzerland

One of the most iconic and pivotal moments in Arthur Conan Doyle's (1859–1930) much-loved Sherlock Holmes series is the showdown between Holmes and Moriarty at Reichenbach Falls, the dramatic final scene of *The Final Problem* (1893). Follow in the footsteps of Holmes and Watson on a thirty-minute walk from the funicular station outside of Meiringen to the falls, whose thundering waters "turn a man giddy with their constant whirl and clamour." At once beautiful and terrifying, the falls plunging into "a tremendous abyss" make a spectacular setting for one of Conan Doyle's most tense moments. "It is indeed, a fearful place."

RIGHT: Many of Paul Klee's works can be seen at the Lenbachhaus.

DISCOVER SWITZERLAND'S MAGIC MOUNTAIN

Davos, Switzerland

Walk with: Thomas Mann (1875–1955)

Route: The Thomas Mann Trail

Length: 1.7 miles

Essential reading: *The Magic Mountain* (1924)

RIGHT: The views from the Thomas Mann Trail between Davos and Schatzalp are sublime in any season.

High in the mountains around Davos lies The Thomas Mann Trail. It links the former Waldsanatorium in Davos, "a long building, with a cupola and so many balconies that from a distance it looked porous, like a sponge," to Schatzalp, where a second sanitorium sits at almost six-thousand feet above sea level. Thomas Mann's wife, Katia, was one of the first patients to be admitted to Davos's Waldsanatorium, and it was the Nobel Prize winning author's numerous visits to her that inspired his modernist classic *The Magic Mountain*.

The sanatorium is now a luxury hotel, the Waldhotel Davos, and is where this walk starts. Set out from the hotel, on its "low, projecting, meadow-like plateau," which offers views of the "bewitched valley" that so enthralled the novel's lead character, Hans Castorp.

The trail ends at the second former sanitorium—and the only one mentioned by its real name in the novel—which is now also a luxury hotel, the Schatzalp. This sanatorium was built so far up the mountain that "they have to bring their bodies down on bobsleds, in the winter." The hotel's Art Nouveau architecture remains almost as it was a hundred years ago, creating the same atmosphere of bourgeois grandeur so exquisitely captured on the pages of Mann's novel.

Although Mann describes a world of "eternal snow," summer does indeed reach this corner of Switzerland. When it does, the Thomas Mann Trail crosses Alpine meadows thick with colorful wildflowers.

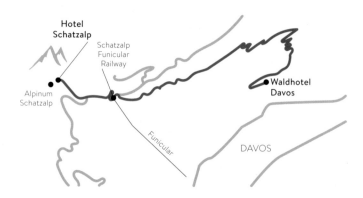

358
SEARCH FOR TOLKIEN'S MIDDLE-EARTH

Interlaken, Switzerland

In the summer of 1911, writer J. R. R. Tolkien (1892–1973), aged nineteen, took a walking holiday in the Lauterbrunnen Valley, Switzerland, with a large group of friends and a local guide. The Swiss valley has 72 stunning waterfalls. The author's later description of the fictional Rivendell valley in Middle-earth, in *The Hobbit* (1937) and three-volume series *Lord of the Rings* (1954–1955), bares close similarity to what Tolkien saw and experienced while walking in Switzerland. Recreate his route on a stunning five-mile trail between Lauterbrunnen and Stechelberg.

359
WALK THE SWISS COUNTRYSIDE WITH HERMANN HESSE

Montagnola, Switzerland

In 1919, Hermann Hesse (1877–1962) left his wife and moved alone to the village of Montagnola in the Swiss canton of Ticino. There he stayed for the rest of his life, later describing his first year in the region as "the fullest, most prolific, most industrious and most passionate time of my life." A circular hike dedicated to the writer leads from the village and along the cypress-lined Friedhofsweg (Cemetery Road) to the Church of St. Abbondio, where Hesse is buried. Arcing back through the forest, the trail passes by his home of Casa Rossa, through the landscapes which Hesse so loved.

360
GOTHIC HORROR IN GENEVA WITH MARY SHELLEY

Lake Geneva, Switzerland

In June 1816, during an unseasonably cold and wet summer, five young creatives from England gathered in Villa Diodati, near the village of Cologny, Switzerland, on the shore of Lake Geneva. To pass the time while stuck indoors, they tried to scare one another with ghost stories, little knowing that one—Mary Shelley's (1797–1851) *Frankenstein* (1818)—would become not only a beloved classic gothic horror novel, but also arguably the first ever example of science fiction. Much of the action takes place around the area here—it's an easy shoreline stroll three miles south into the city of Geneva, where a statue in Plainpalais marks the location of the monster's first murder.

361
HIKING IN HEIDILAND WITH JOHANNA SPYRI

Swiss Alps, Switzerland

Of the many literary works set in the Swiss Alps, the most famous has to be Johanna Spyri's (1827–1901) classic children's book, *Heidi* (1881)—so much so, in fact, that the pretty east Switzerland setting of her books has become known as "Heidiland." "I want to go about like the light-footed goats," says Heidi in the story. And at Flumserberg, a ski resort and hiking area in the heart of Heidiland, you can. The Seven Peaks Tour is a day-long moderate hike taking in fourteen lakes along with the seven mountains, starting at the mountain station of Maschgenkamm and ending with a fantastic view over Lake Walen.

LEFT: Could Switzerland's Lauterbrunnen valley have been the inspiration for J. R. R. Tolkien's Middle-earth?

362

IN THE STEPS OF
LESLIE STEPHEN

Trentino, Italy

Father of English novelist Virginia Woolf and painter Vanessa Bell, Leslie Stephen (1832–1904) was an author and pioneering mountaineer, dedicating many of his summers to climbing the Alps. He would walk thirty to forty miles a day, establishing new walking routes and climbing up peaks. Leslie was the first to climb the Cima di Ball, or Ball Peak, in Trentino, in 1869. Ideal for beginners, the first section of the Nico Gusella walk includes a *via ferrata*, a mountain route with ladders, ropes, steel cables, and walkways in place to aid climbers. The pathway leads on to the Stephen Pass, named after the mountaineer, from where it's possible to climb up to the panoramic summit of Val di Roda, which offers impressive views of the jagged peaks of the Dolomites.

363

TAKE IN LANDSCAPES THAT
INSPIRED ALBRECHT DÜRER

Trentino, Italy

In 1494, German painter Albrecht Dürer (1471–1528) made his first trip to Italy, traveling through the Val di Cembra to reach Venice. The Adige River, Italy's second-longest river, had overflown its banks, forcing Dürer to make his way to Venice along a path from Egna to Segonzano, today known as the Dürer Way. The walk meanders through shaded forest and areas of inspiring natural beauty, many of which became the subject of Dürer's works. Having overnighted at the Klösterle, a travelers' inn in San Floriano, Dürer hiked to the village of Pochi, past the Lauco River, up to the Passo Sauch and on to Lago Santo. From here, the path descends to Cembra and on to the earth pyramids of Segonzano, passing the striking Castello di Segonzano, depicted in a number of his watercolors.

364

THE LOCATIONS
THAT INSPIRED ANDREA VITALI

Bellano, Lake Como

Born in Bellano on the eastern shore of Lake Como, Andrea Vitali (1956–) is a prolific medic-turned-writer who has written over forty novels. He often sits on a bench in the Piazza Tommaso Grossi, inspired by the lake scenery, jotting down notes and penning stories. From the piazza, it's a pleasant stroll to the town's former cotton factory, which has served as the setting for many of his novels. Tucked away behind the building is the Bellano canyon, a natural gorge characterized by caves and gushing waterfalls, while perched on the adjacent hillside is the cemetery, both of which feature in a number of Vitali's works.

365

DISCOVER ANTONIA POZZI'S
BELOVED VALSASSINA

Pasturo, Italy

Born in Milan in the early twentieth century, poet Antonia Pozzi (1912–1938) escaped from the hustle and bustle of city life, seeking refuge in the mountainous region of Valsassina. Sprinkled around the town of Pasturo are a series of panels with photographs, poetry passages, and extracts from the poet's personal diary. At Via Manzoni 1 is the poet's family home, and a short stroll along the Cariola River leads to a large garden from where Pozzi would head out to explore the mountains—recurring subjects of her poetry. Head north on Via Manzoni, past the village primary school named after Pozzi, before reaching her grave in the Pasturo Cemetery, a quiet spot where she rests.

TOP RIGHT: The Dürer Way takes the walker through many areas of inspiring natural beauty.

RIGHT: Albrecht Dürer featured the Castello di Segonzano in many of his watercolors.

FEEL INSPIRED BY THE LAKE VIEWS AS YOU WALK THE LAKE COMO POETRY WAY

Lake Como, Italy

Walk with: The writers
Pliny the Elder (AD 23–79);
Pliny the Younger (AD 61–c.112);
Ugo Foscolo (1778–1827);
Hermann Hesse (1877-1962);
Mary Shelley (1797–1851)

Route: Lake Como Poetry Way

Length: 10 miles

Essential reading: *Wandering Italy* (1920) by Hermann Hesse, *Pliny's Letters*

RIGHT: Lake Como's Poetry Way starts from the town of Cernobbio, taking in many poetic landmarks as it goes.

Lake Como has long been a fashionable holiday destination, with grand residences and holiday homes built along the shore since as far back as the Roman times. It's the birthplace of Pliny the Elder, author of the first encyclopedia, and Pliny the Younger, writer of letters, both of whom owned several villas in the area.

The Lake Como Poetry Way stretches from Cernobbio to Brunate, passing grand opulent villas. Immersed in a lush park, Villa del Grumello is home to a marble bust of Venetian writer and poet Ugo Foscolo, whose poem "Le Grazie" was partly dedicated to his lover Franceschina, who once resided in the villa.

German writer Hermann Hesse enjoyed a walk along the Como lakefront in 1913, writing about it in his book *Wandering Italy* (1920).

English novelist Mary Shelley visited the lake shortly after publishing her gothic novel *Frankenstein* (1818), whose characters are influenced by both Plinys and Como-born physicist Alessandro Volta, who invented the electrochemical battery. In 1840 Shelley enjoyed a two-month stay on the lake.

Northeast of town, a mule track snakes its way up the forested mountainside to Brunate, a pretty hilltop town offering panoramic lake views. Wooden plaques with poetry are dotted here and there along the route, while the entirety of the Lake Como Poetry Way is sprinkled with twelve free micro-libraries where you can pick up a book and enjoy a good read in inspiring surroundings.

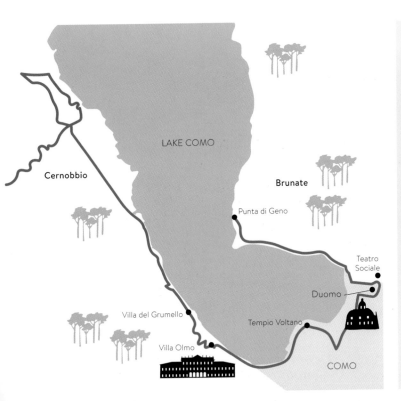

367
LAKE GARDA WITH GOETHE
Lake Garda, Italy

In 1786, at the beginning of a long trip to Italy, German poet Johann Wolfgang von Goethe (1749–1832) visited Lake Garda. His first glimpse of the lake was at Nago, where the old Roman road of Santa Lucia winds down from Castel Penede. Goethe was immediately struck by the lake's distinctly Mediterranean feel, with olive groves, figs, and lemon trees peppered here and there. "What I enjoy most of all is the fruit," he wrote in his journal. A walk along the road leads to the castle of Torbole, where Goethe gazed at the panorama of glistening blue waters, agave, and palm trees that opened up before him.

LAKE COMO

Cernobbio

Brunate

Punta di Geno

Teatro Sociale

Duomo

Villa del Grumello

Tempio Voltano

Villa Olmo

COMO

368

ALESSANDRO MANZONI'S
THE BETROTHED

Lecco, Italy

Italian poet and novelist Alessandro Manzoni (1785–1873) was brought up in Lecco, on Lake Como's eastern shore, spending his childhood and adolescence in awe of the surrounding lake scenery. "That branch of the lake of Como, which extends toward the south, is enclosed by two unbroken chains of mountains, which, as they advance and recede, diversify its shores with numerous bays and inlets," begins his historical novel *The Betrothed* (1827). A short walk southwest of his childhood home in Lecco is Piazza Manzoni, dominated by a bronze statue of the novelist, while heading east along the lakefront is Pescarenico, a small fisherman's village where Lucia and Renzo, the protagonists of the novel, are said to have fled in one of the most famous scenes of Italian literature.

369

VISIT THE ABBEY THAT
INSPIRED UMBERTO ECO

Piedmont, Italy

When writing *The Name of the Rose* (1983), Umberto Eco (1932–2016) was inspired by the striking landscapes of Piedmont's Susa Valley, most notably the ancient abbey of San Michele, which, in Eco's classic, is ravaged by fire. The Via Francigena, a historic walking route and a major pilgrimage road from northern Italy to Rome, snakes its way through the valley, which is peppered with castles, forts, and palaces. From Colle del Moncenisio the route leads down to the Novalesa Abbey and on to the Abbey of San Michele, which attracts scores of pilgrims year round. From here, the route passes through the pretty towns of Avigliana and Rivoli to Turin.

RIGHT: The Abbey of San Michele inspired Umberto Eco's *The Name of the Rose.*

370
LEONARDO DA VINCI'S MILAN
Milan, Italy

Italian Renaissance artist and inventor Leonardo da Vinci (1452–1519) called Milan his home for a number of years, moving here to work for the ruling Sforza family. Between 1495 and 1497, he worked on *The Last Supper* mural in the refectory of the Monastery of Santa Maria delle Grazie. Opposite the church is the Casa degli Atellani, a beautiful Renaissance house whose garden and vineyard were given to da Vinci as payment for his work on the mural. From here, it's a lovely walk to the Ambrosiana, which houses the Codex Atlanticus, the largest set of drawings and writings of da Vinci.

371
DA VINCI'S FEAT OF ENGINEERING
Cassano d'Adda, Italy

As an engineer, Leonardo da Vinci studied canals and navigable waterways. During his stays at the Medici Court in Milan, he visited the surrounding area, studying the course of the River Adda, designing systems for locks and river navigation. A lakefront path and cycle route winds its way along the banks of the River Adda from Lecco to Cassano d'Adda, passing the Leonardo Ecomuseum, an open-air exhibition that sheds light on da Vinci's work in the area. Walking farther downstream, a bridge leads to a path to the Villa Melzi d'Eril, where Leonardo is known to have sojourned.

372

FEEL THOUGHTFUL IN PRIMO LEVI'S TURIN

Turin, Italy

Italian-Jewish writer and chemist Primo Levi (1919–1987) wrote prolifically about his wartime experiences. "I never stopped recording the world and people around me, so much that I still have an unbelievably detailed image of them," he recounted. Levi lived at Corso Re Umberto 75, frequenting the nearby Liceo Massimo d'Azeglio as a teenager, and later receiving a degree from the University of Turin (he was one of the last Jews to do so, before laws prohibited further study on the grounds of race). From the university, it's a pleasant walk down pedestrianized Via Carlo Alberto to the synagogue, where a plaque commemorates Levi. He tragically died after falling down the stairwell of his childhood home and is buried in Turin's Cimitero Monumentale.

373

ELGAR AND HIS ITALIAN RIVIERA INSPIRATION

Alassio, Liguria, Italy

Over the winter of 1903 into 1904, the English composer Sir Edward Elgar (1857–1934) took a holiday with his wife to Alassio, on the western coast of Liguria, northern Italy, the Italian Riviera. Relaxing, walking in sunshine, and enjoying the clean air of the Ligurian landscape of hills and ice-cold mountain streams, Elgar was inspired to compose an overture. Under a Mediterranean sky, he wrote *In the South (Alassio)*, Op.50. It was premiered in 1904, the same year that Elgar received a knighthood. Take the path almost opposite the cemetery to the top of Mount Tirasso for fabulous views over the sea and green valleys.

RIGHT: The hills and sea of the Italian Riviera around Alassio.

374

DISCOVER VENICE WITH COMPOSER AND OPERA PIONEER CLAUDIO MONTEVERDI

Venice, Italy

Walk with: Claudio Monteverdi (1567–1643)

Route: St. Mark's Basilica to La Fenice

Length: 1.3 miles

Essential listening: *O beatae viae* (1621), *Il Combattimento di Tancredi e Clorinda* (1624)

TOP RIGHT: Composer Claudio Monteverdi had the role of recruiting and training musicians for Venice's St. Mark's Basilica.

RIGHT: Venice's most famous opera house, La Fenice.

The first great composer of opera, Claudio Monteverdi (1567–1643) moved from the court of his former patrons, the Gonzaga family in Mantua, to Venice to take on the role of *maestro di cappella* of St. Mark's. As part of his new position, which he held until his death in 1643, he recruited and trained the basilica's musicians and composed music for major religious celebrations.

A wonder of Venetian Renaissance art and Orientalism, St. Mark's Basilica reflects Venice's great wealth and power as a leading maritime city-state.

From St. Mark's, it's a short stroll over to the sumptuous Danieli Hotel. Once known as Palazzo Dandolo, it was the home of Monteverdi's patron Girolamo Mocenigo; it was here that the composer premiered his short opera *Il Combattimento di Tancredi e Clorinda*. From the hotel, it's a gorgeous stroll along Venice's cobbled streets to reach the Scuola Grande di San Rocco, a lay confraternity dating back to 1478, adorned with masterpieces by Tintoretto that illustrate episodes from the New and Old Testaments. It was here that Monteverdi's *O beatae viae* was performed, and he is known to have played the organ in the Scuola church. Nearby is the Basilica di Santa Maria Gloriosa dei Frari, where Monteverdi is buried in a small chapel at the end of the church. On December 9, 1643, a solemn memorial service was held to commemorate Monteverdi's life.

375
VIVALDI AND HIS VENICE
Venice, Italy

Italian composer Antonio Vivaldi (1678–1741) was born and lived most his life in Venice. Imagine him walking among the canals and narrow passageways. Begin at the gothic church of San Giovanni in Bragora, where Vivaldi was baptized. Then to Basilica di San Marco, where his violinist father took him for recitals. Trace the curve of the Grand Canal toward Ponte di Rialto, near which Vivaldi worked as a theater manager in the Sant'Angelo Theater, which was destroyed in 1804.

376
PUT YOURSELF IN A TINTORETTO
Venice, Italy

Jacopo Tintoretto (1518–1594) barely ever left Venice, but his reputation did. The son of a dyer (Tintoretto means "little dyer") was born and died here, and, in between, he painted energetically. Half a millennium later, there are seven hundred Tintoretto paintings in the city. The huge *Il Paradiso* frames a throne in the Doge's Palace. Over the Grand Canal at the Gallerie dell'Accademia is *The Miracle of the Slave*, his breakthrough work. Half a mile north is the Scuola Grande di San Rocco, where fifty paintings represent two decades' work which started when he sneaked in one night to paint for free. A mile or so north is the Madonna dell'Orto church, where he prayed, painted (ten pieces including a pair of forty-six-feet altarpieces), and was buried.

ON THE RAINER MARIA RILKE TRAIL IN TRIESTE

Trieste, Italy

Walk with: Rainer Maria Rilke
(1875–1926)

Route: Rilke Trail

Length: 2.4 miles

Essential reading: *Duino Elegies* (1923)

RIGHT: Views of the "splendid" Duino Castle from the Rilke Trail.

"Being here is splendid," wrote poet Rainer Maria Rilke when he stayed as a guest of the German noble family Thurn und Taxis in Duino Castle, a fourteenth-century fortification commanding a wonderful position on a cliff overlooking the Gulf of Trieste.

It was from the castle's first floor terrace that Rilke took inspiration when writing his *Duino Elegies*. Rilke penned his elegies on one of the castle's bastions (today named the Rilke Bastion), which commands sweeping views of the Gulf of Trieste. He would often sit back in the castle's Music Salon, where he would record his thoughts or write letters.

Connecting the villages of Duino and Sistiana, the Rilke Trail snakes its way along white limestone cliffs through beautiful karst flora and fauna, with black pines, hornbeams, and cherry trees home to reptiles, solitary sparrows, and raven. Rilke is known to have frequently walked the path, which provided him with much inspiration. It offers panoramic views of the Gulf of Trieste and the Duino Reserve, where carbonated rocks were created from shells deposited on the bed of the sea.

His friendship with Princess Marie von Thurn und Taxis was to last seventeen years, with the two exchanging about four hundred letters over the course of the years. Rilke chose to dedicate his elegies to her.

JAMES JOYCE'S OTHER HOME
Trieste, Italy

James Joyce (1882–1941) first arrived in Trieste with his wife, Nora, on October 20, 1904. He called the city his home for a number of years, and it was here that he penned *The Dubliners* (1914) and *A Portrait of the Artist as a Young Man* (1916). The couple first settled in to an apartment that looked on to bustling Piazza Ponte Rosso, where goods from Istria and Veneto daily arrived by boat. Joyce made a living teaching English at the Berlitz School, often frequenting the Caffè Stella Polare in Via Dante Alighieri as well as the city's famous Pasticceria Pirona. From here, it's a pleasant walk to Via Roma, where a bronze statue of Joyce depicts him strolling across a pretty canal bridge.

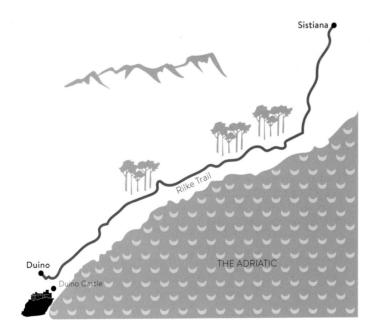

Sistiana

Rilke Trail

Duino

Duino Castle

THE ADRIATIC

379
SPOTTING MICHELANGELO IN FLORENCE

Florence, Italy

Michelangelo Buonarroti (1475–1564), sculptor, painter, and architect, was born near Florence. Wherever one walks in the city Michelangelo is there, in the palaces of the Medici, in the Bargello, Academia, and Uffizi museums. A copy of his monumental masterpiece *David* (1504) stands outside Palazzo Vecchio in the Piazza della Signoria (original in Accademia Gallery). From here it's a short walk northward on Via dei Calzaiuoli to the remarkable Medici Chapel mausoleum in the Basilica of San Lorenzo, the Medici parish church. Walk north again to the Academia, before heading in a southwest direction to visit Casa Buonarroti on via Ghibellina, housing some of Michelangelo's works. The Bargello is nearby. Turn south to find the Uffizi by the river Arno.

380
ON THE TRAIL OF AN UNKNOWN AUTHOR IN NAPLES

Naples, Italy

It is impossible to go on a real-life trail of Elena Ferrante, as her name is a pseudonym for the unknown author of the Neapolitan novels, a series of four novels following the lives of two Italian friends in postwar Naples. But the city her story brings to life is very real. The working-class area of Rione Luzzatti, behind the Centro Direzionale, is considered to be the area where Lila and Elena, the central characters, come of age. A short stroll here ends on Via Gianturco, and the dark tunnel under the railway tracks that evokes the journey the girls take in the hope of finding the sea.

381
DRAMATIC SETTINGS WITH CARLO LEVI

Aliano, Basilicata, Italy

Italian writer, painter, and activist Carlo Levi (1902–1975) is best known for his book *Christ Stopped at Eboli* (1945), in which he recounts his time spent in exile in Basilicata, at the time a poor, desolate, malaria-infested region in southern Italy. Famed for its houses made of clay, the town of Aliano has a dramatic location on a hillside, surrounded by otherworldly lunar landscapes of *calanchi*, deep gullies and chasms carved into the rock and sculpted by the rain and the wind. A gentle trek along the area's clay ridges and cliffs leads into the town, where Levi lived in forced exile at the entrance to the village.

382
ON THE TRAIL OF INSPECTOR MONTALBANO

Porto Empedocle, Sicily, Italy

Andrea Camilleri (1925–2019) is the best-selling author of the globally popular *Inspector Montalbano* fictional crime series. The first book was published in 1994, when Camilleri was seventy years old; there are now twenty-seven in the series. The fictional town of Vigata, where the inspector (Il Commissario) works, is based on Camilleri's hometown of Porto Empedocle in southern Sicily. Although many will have discovered Inspector Montalbano through the TV series, which has been filmed in other Sicilian towns, this is the original in the novels. Walk down the street of via Roma, past a statue of Inspector Montalbano, and soak up the atmosphere and the characters from the novels.

RIGHT: Inspector Montalbano keeps an eye on the streets of Porto Empedocle.

383
BERNINI'S BAROQUE ROME
Rome, Italy

No one man left more of a mark on Rome than the Baroque architect and sculptor Gian Lorenzo Bernini (1598–1680). In the seventeenth century, his output was prolific. View his legacy on a two-mile stroll, starting at the church of Santa Maria della Vittoria, home to Bernini's exquisite *Ecstasy of St. Teresa*. From here wind westward, via a checklist of his masterpieces, including the *Fontana del Tritone* in Piazza Barberini and Sant'Andrea al Quirinale, one of the architect's finest churches. Finish in the Piazza Navona: built as a racetrack in the days of the Roman Empire, Bernini reworked it into Rome's most fantastically ornate square.

384
RAPHAEL'S FRESCOES
Rome, Italy

The Renaissance transformed Rome between the mid-fifteenth and sixteenth centuries. Start at Villa Farnesina, where the walls are a flamboyance of frescoes, including Raphael's (1483–1520) *Sala di Galatea*, where the eponymous nymph cavorts. Across the Tiber lies Via Giulia. Admire the palazzo at number 85, allegedly once owned by Raphael. Cross the Tiber again to see the wedding-cake fancy of St. Peter's Basilica. Around the corner is the Vatican Museum: here lie the Raphael Rooms, a spectacular sixteen-year redecoration.

385

VISIT THE SETTINGS OF GIACOMO PUCCINI'S *TOSCA*

Rome, Italy

Walk with: Giacomo Puccini (1858–1924)

Route: Around Rome

Length: 0.9 mile

Essential listening: *Tosca* (1899)

ABOVE: Giacomo Puccini was a fan of exotic settings for his operas.

RIGHT: The third act of *Tosca* takes place in the cyclindrical fortress of Castel Sant'Angelo.

Born into a family of church musicians, Giacomo Puccini reached his zenith at the turn of the twentieth century, composing some of his most notable works, including *La Bohème*, *Tosca*, and *Madame Butterfly*. Puccini chose exotic settings for many of his operas, including Nagasaki for *Madame Butterfly* and Paris for *La Bohème*, and the Eternal City of Rome for *Tosca*.

Set in the nineteenth century, the opera is a melodramatic piece featuring some of Puccini's best-known arias; it premiered at the Teatro Costanzi in Rome in January 1900. Act I opens at the Basilica di Sant'Andrea della Valle in Piazza Vidoni, where Tosca meets painter Cavaradossi, falling madly in love with him. From the basilica, it's a leisurely five-minute stroll to Palazzo Farnese, a High Renaissance palazzo that is the setting of Act II, today the seat of the French Embassy in Italy. Started by Antonio da Sangallo the Younger, the palazzo was continued by Michelangelo and eventually finished by Giacomo della Porta. In Puccini's opera, Scarpia resides in Palazzo Farnese, and it is here that Cavaradossi is tortured and sentenced to death.

A fifteen-minute walk northwest, across the River Tiber, is Castel Sant'Angelo, a cylindrical fortress that was commissioned by Emperor Hadrian as a mausoleum. Today it is a museum housing paintings, sculptures, and military objects. The castello is the setting of the opera's third act, which tragically ends with Cavaradossi's execution and Tosca leaping to her death.

386
TRACE PUCCINI'S CAREER
Lucca, Italy

Lucca, a city with intact Renaissance-era city walls surrounded by the hills of Tuscany, can feel as beautiful as an Italian opera, especially that of Giacomo Puccini. It is a city where the Puccini family has long established musical connections and where Puccini flourished in a career in opera. Take a stroll along the path of the wall and admire the city from its perimeter, noticing the bell towers that punctuate the skyline. Back in the web of narrow streets right in the center of the city, trace Puccini's life from Chiesa e Battistero dei SS Giovanni e Reparata, where he was baptized, to Casa di Puccini Museum, and around to Cattedrale di San Martino and Teatro del Giglio, where he worked and performed.

SOAK UP PANORAMIC VIEWS WHILE HIKING THE GOETHE WAY

Innsbruck to Hafelekar, Austria

Walk with: Johann Wolfgang von Goethe (1749–1832)

Route: Goethe Way

Length: 6.2 miles

Essential reading: *Italian Journey* (1817)

LEFT: The Goethe Way takes in dramatic mountain scenery around the town of Innsbruck.

One of Germany's most celebrated writers, Johann Wolfgang von Goethe wrote prolifically for decades; his collected works comprise 143 volumes. As well as penning plays, poems, novels, and memoirs, Goethe also wrote essays on a wide range of scientific subjects, from anatomy to botany and the morphology of plants—and all of this while working as a civil servant in Weimar.

"In nature we never see anything isolated, but everything in connection with something else which is before it, beside it, under it, and over it," Goethe wrote. Walking along the Goethe Way it's easy to imagine him mulling and musing, strolling the countryside, observing nature.

Named after the writer, the Goethe Way comprises a series of trails that run through Austria, Germany, and the Alps.

From the Austrian town of Innsbruck, it's possible to join the Goethe Way as it snakes its way for six miles through the rugged Karwendel Range, undulating up and down close to the ridgetop, offering gorgeous panoramic views. The path climbs up to Mandlscharte Notch (7,592 feet), before descending through lush verdant meadows and pine fields toward Pfeishütte, where it's possible to stay overnight. From the hut, returning to the top terminal of Hafelekar, it's possible to hop on the Nordkettenbahn Gondola and Nordkette Funicular back down to Innsbruck.

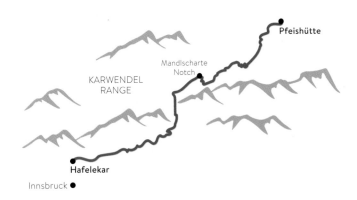

Pfeishütte

Mandlscharte Notch

KARWENDEL RANGE

Hafelekar

Innsbruck

SEE A LAKE THROUGH GUSTAV KLIMT'S EYES

Lake Attersee, Salzkammergut, Austria

Walk with: Gustav Klimt
(1862–1918)

Route: The Artist Trail—Lake Attersee to Villa Paulick

Length: 1 mile

Essential viewing: *On Lake Attersee* (1900)

Artist Gustav Klimt is most known for his portrait paintings of wealthy patrons, but it is the stunning landscapes of Lake Attersee, his summer retreat for more than fifteen years, that saw the artist move from people to places. Follow in the footsteps of Klimt on this walk which features twenty-four different viewpoints that helped inform around forty-five of his fifty known landscape paintings.

Known as The Artist Trail, this easy walk spreads along the lake shore from the center to Villa Paulick, where Klimt spent some time. The trail also references Gustav Mahler, Friedrich Gulda, Franz von Schönthan, Charlotte Wolter, and Hedwig Bleibtreu, who were also inspired by Attersee's fascinating surroundings.

The lake itself was the inspiration for *On Lake Attersee*, which is an unusual take for Klimt's normal style. While many of the landscapes in Attersee have now changed, the essence of them remains. The previously mentioned Villa Paulick is a piece of Klimt's history still intact, due to a relationship between his brother and one of the residing owners.

ABOVE: Artist Gustav Klimt.

RIGHT: Lake Attersee, which inspired forty-five of Klimt's fifty known landscape paintings.

389
IN THE SHADOW OF SCHIELE
Vienna, Austria

Egon Schiele (1890–1918) didn't always love Vienna— "There are shadows. The city is black and everything is done by rote. I want to be alone. I want to go to the Bohemian forest"—but it's where he studied and died, and where most of his expressionist works are displayed. Several are at the Upper Belvedere off Prinz Eugen-Strasse, and the city-center Albertina Museum, but the best— including *Seated Male Nude* and a *Portrait of Wally Neuzil*—are at the Leopold on Museumsplatz. His alma mater, the Vienna Academy of Fine Arts, is nearby on Schillerplatz. Conscripted in the First World War, Schiele survived the conflict but succumbed to Spanish flu on October 31, 1918.

390

TREK WITH JOHANNES BRAHMS IN SALZKAMMERGUT

Bad Ischl, Austria

Born in Hamburg, German composer Johannes Brahms (1833–1897) spent most of his summers in Bad Ischl, a popular summer holiday destination for city folk in Salzkammergut, a picturesque region of lakes and Alpine ranges. Brahms rented rooms in a cottage by the River Traun, from where he would often embark on walks in the surrounding mountains, meandering through valley forests, crossing meadows, and snaking up mountainsides. Hundreds of miles of hiking trails crisscross the region, taking in Alpine lakes, great peaks, and mountain villages, where age-old traditions remain very much alive to this day.

391

BY THE BEAUTIFUL DANUBE WITH JOHANN STRAUSS

Danube River, Austria

Originally written as a choral piece, composer Johann Strauss's (1825–1899) *The Blue Danube* was inspired by the eponymous river, the second longest in Europe. This most loved joyful waltz song intended to capture the essence of imperial Vienna while lifting the spirits of the country following a defeat by Prussia in the Seven Weeks' War. Hiking trails in Austria's Wachau Valley meander over gentle hills through vineyards and fruit orchards, offering stunning views of the river that was to so inspire Strauss. Curiously, when Austria declared independence from Nazi Germany in 1945, *The Blue Danube* was performed, as the country didn't yet have an anthem of its own.

RIGHT: Johann Strauss's *The Blue Danube* was inspired by the river.

392
MOZART IN SALZBURG
Salzburg, Austria

Wolfgang Amadeus Mozart
(1756–1791) was born in
the beautiful city of Salzburg,
Austria. A musical prodigy
encouraged by his father,
by the age of six he was
performing for European
royalty. A walk through the
historic center of Salzburg
will find his birthplace, the
Hagenauer Haus, at No.9
Getreidegasse. Here his
parents Leopold and Anna
Maria lived for twenty-six
years from 1747, in an
apartment on the third floor.
In 1773, they moved to a
house at Makartplatz 8, now
called Mozart's Residence,
a museum dedicated to
the composer. It is a short
walk away, crossing the
Staatsbrücke bridge.

393
THE GENIUS
IN VIENNA
Vienna, Austria

Vienna is a city in love
with the maestro composer
Wolfgang Amadeus Mozart.
Born in Salzburg, he moved
to Vienna at the age of
twenty-five. Over the next
ten years, he lived in many
different apartments in the
city with Constanze, his wife,
and their children. A walk
through the streets finds him
in many locations, including
Mozarthaus at Domgasse 5,
now a museum, where he
lived for three years. He
married at St. Stephen's
Cathedral in 1782, and at
Schönbrunn Palace he played
his first concert, aged six.
The St. Marx Cemetery on
Leberstrasse 6–8, is where he
was buried.

394

THE STRINDBERG WALK
FROM SAXEN TO KLAM

Saxen to Klam, Austria

In 1893, Swedish playwright August Strindberg
(1849–1912) married the Austrian author Frida Uhl
and the two creatives set up base in a castle in Saxen,
Austria. After issues arose with Uhl's family, Strindberg
relocated to the neighbouring town of Klam, where
he walked between the two places, as you can today.
Strindberg found a lot of themes for his paintings in
the canyons between Klam and Saxen, as well as for
his novels, in which he depicted the stone formations,
the hammer mill, and a pigsty in the canyon. In his
novel *Inferno* (1898), he describes the visions he
experienced during a walk through the canyon. The
Strindberg Walk is now signposted between Saxen
and Klam, so visitors can walk it with ease.

395

UNWIND WITH BEETHOVEN

Vienna Woods, Austria

In 1787, composer Ludwig van Beethoven (1770–1827)
moved to Vienna to study with Amadeus Mozart,
eventually settling here permanently in 1792. In
summer, he would escape the heat of the city, seeking
refuge in the surrounding hills and woods. It was in
the spa town of Heiligenstadt, in what is today the
Beethoven House Museum, that he wrote the
"Heiligenstadt Testament," an unsent letter to his
brothers that touches on the depths of his despair
over his worsening deafness. From Heiligenstadt, the
Beethoven Promenade winds its way up to Beethoven
Rest, where the composer often came to unwind and
seek to alleviate the mental and physical troubles that
so plagued him.

LEFT: Ludwig van Beethoven
walked in the woods around
Vienna to alleviate his troubles.

THE WALK OF PEACE—ISONZO FRONT

Soca Valley, Slovenia

Walk with: Ernest Hemingway (1899–1961)

Route: Walk of Peace Trail through the Julian Alps and Soca Valley

Length: 143 miles

Essential reading: *A Farewell to Arms* by Ernest Hemingway (1929); *Isonzo: The Forgotten Sacrifice of the Great War* by John R. Schindler (2001)

In his novel *A Farewell to Arms* (1929), Ernest Hemingway weaved a tale of life and love from the experience of an American ambulance lieutenant serving in the Italian Army during the First World War—a story based on his own experiences and love affair when he served as a volunteer ambulance driver with the American Red Cross in the same region.

The part of the war history he references is called the Isonzo Front, a series of bloody battles fought from June 1915 to November 1917 between the Italy campaign and the Austro-Hungarian Empire. Remnants of the battle are still scattered throughout the mountain region, and The Walk of Peace trail was officially opened in 2017, to commemorate the centenary of the end of the Battle of Isonzo.

Beginning from Log pod Mangartom on the northern border, this long-distance walking trail passes through the rise and lows of the Julian Alps, into valleys with crisp green meadows and farmlands. The trail roughly follows the Slovena–Italian border as well as traces the curves of the turquoise Soča (Isonzo) River. This journey is a walk into history, passing gun caverns, bunkers, and trenches preserved as open-air museums near Bovec and Volče. Turning away from the scars of war is the stunning nature that surrounded the battlegrounds, especially the sections that cut through Soča Valley, where Hemingway served during the war.

To Hemingway, this idyllic landscape and its people were broken by the war, but today, despite its scars, a walk along The Walk of Peace allows Soča Valley to shine again.

ABOVE: Ernest Hemingway, whose novel *A Farewell to Arms* was inspired by his time in Italy.

TOP RIGHT: Hemingway's protagonist lived in a house that "looked across the river and the plain to the mountains."

RIGHT: The trail follows the turquoise Soča River.

Log pod Mangartom
Ravelnik
Bovec
Julian Alps
Volče
Tolmin
ITALY
Soča River
SLOVENIA
Gorizia
Monfalcone

IMMERSE YOURSELF IN BUDAPEST'S LITERARY CAFÉ CULTURE

Budapest, Hungary

Walk with: Sándor Márai (1900–1989) and Zsigmond Móricz (1879–1942), *et al*

Route: New York Café to Hadik Kávéház

Length: 3.8 miles

Essential viewing: *The Paul Street Boys* (1906) by Ferenc Molnár

TOP RIGHT: Budapest is a city of cafés, and, as Sándor Márai said, "There is no literature without a café."

RIGHT: The Centrál Kávéház was a popular spot for Hungary's belle-epoque writers.

In the early twentieth century, coffee culture thrived in Budapest. Over five hundred cafés were sprinkled around town, with many serving as a meeting place for artists, writers, poets, and journalists. Ink, pen, and paper were readily available for free, while a "writer's menu" offered bread, cheese, and charcuterie at an affordable price.

Hungarian writer and journalist Sándor Márai would frequently visit New York Café, one of the city's most opulent cafés, with frescoed ceilings, marble columns, and bronze statues. Hungarian novelist Ferenc Molnár is known to have penned his novel *The Paul Street Boys* (1906) at one of the tables, and other writers are known to have come here for inspiration, including poet Mihály Babits, writer and journalist Géza Gárdonyi, author Frigyes Karinthy, and poet Dezső Kosztolányi.

From here, take your "café crawl" toward the river to another favorite, Gerbeaud on Vörösmarty tér, which was opened in 1870. Its esteemed guests included composer Franz Liszt, and Austrian Emperor Franz Joseph I and his wife, Empress Elizabeth (famously nicknamed "Sisi"). Its sumptuous interiors feature glittering chandeliers and draped salons.

A twenty-minute stroll to the southeast, is Centrál Kávéház, which dates back to 1887. Warm and cozy, it became another magnet for Hungary's belle-epoque writers, who settled in to the first-floor gallery.

Finish across the Danube, on trendy Bartók Béla út at Hadik Kávéház, another of the city's famed twentieth-century institutions. Frigyes Karinthy, Dezső Kosztolányi, and Ferenc Molnár are all known to have frequented the establishment (their portraits feature on the staircase mural today).

398
STEFAN JÄGER'S PLACE
Banat, Romania

Romanian painter Stefan Jäger (1877–1962) painted the Swabian community to which he belonged. Banat—an area that straddles parts of Romania, Serbia, and Hungary—served as the setting for many of his paintings. His workshop in Jimbolia, a small Romanian town close to the border with Serbia, today houses the Stefan Jäger Museum, with paintings and personal objects on display. From his studio, Jäger would set out into the countryside and walk through Swabian villages, sketching local life and the surrounding nature of Banat to recreate in oil and watercolor paintings.

399
HEAR THE HARMONIES
Budapest, Hungary

Although Franz Liszt (1811–1886) is closely associated with Budapest and performed here many times, he never truly settled in Hungary's capital, but traveled between here, Rome, and Weimar. He had an apartment in the music academy that bore his name, which is now the Franz Liszt Memorial Museum on the corner of Vörösmarty and Andrássy streets; the academy has moved to Franz Liszt Square, where there is a statue of the maestro playing an imaginary piano. In his older years, Liszt became very devout and would pray regularly at the Saint Francis' Church and the Budapest Inner-City Mother Church of the Blessed Virgin.

400

WHERE IT ALL STARTED FOR GUSTAV MAHLER

Jihlava, Czech Republic

When Gustav Mahler (1860–1911) was a few months old, he moved with his parents to the pretty Bohemian town of Jihlava, where he lived for the next fifteen years. The large open space of the town center, known as Masarykovo Square, is where Mahler would have listened to brass-band concerts. There are two magnificent eighteenth-century fountains within the square. At the northern end, turn into Benesova Street and walk for two hundred yards until reaching Gustav Mahler Park, complete with a statue to the composer. Return to the square and head south along Znojemska street, to see the house where Mahler lived, which was also a tavern and distillery run by his father.

401

FIND FRANZ KAFKA IN PRAGUE

Prague, Czech Republic

"Prague never lets you go… this dear little mother has sharp claws."

In order to understand Franz Kafka (1883–1924), one needs to visit his museum in Prague, in the Little Quarter, close to Charles Bridge. After visiting the museum, cross over the bridge and head north into the Jewish Quarter, where Kafka lived for most of his short life. Inspired by his short story *Description of a Struggle* (1912) is a large bronze sculpture that depicts an empty man's suit carrying the writer on its shoulders. Now head south to the street called Narodni and the Café Louvre, a favorite meeting place for Kafka.

402

ALPHONSE MUCHA AND ART NOUVEAU

Prague, Czech Republic

Most people will know of Alphonse Mucha (1860–1939) through his Art Nouveau posters, and there is a splendid display of these for viewing at the Mucha Museum in the New Town district of Prague. As the museum will reveal, there is a lot more to him than graphic design. A ten-minute walk north into the Old Town district will take you to Municipal House, an Art Nouveau extravaganza that is lavishly decorated inside with works by Mucha and others of his time. Mucha's masterpiece is the Mayor's Hall, with its fabulous ceiling and wall paintings, and stained glass by the Master of Art Nouveau.

403

MOZART AND HIS PRAGUERS

Prague, Czech Republic

Wolfgang Amadeus Mozart (1756–1791) was born in Salzburg, and spent his last decade in Vienna, but he had a mutual love affair with the capital of Bohemia; while it is now unsure whether he actually said "My Praguers understand me," the affection was unquestionable. There's a mini-museum at Villa Bertramka, the former home of his friends the Duscheks. Up the hill is the Strahov Monastery, where Mozart delighted locals by improvising on the church organ on the day of the *Don Giovanni* premiere; farther along the crest is Hradcanske Square, where more formal concerts were held. Across the picture-postcard Charles Bridge in downtown Prague is the Estates Theater, where *Don Giovanni* and *La Clemenza di Tito* premiered, and in the beautiful central square is St. Nicholas's Church, where a requiem was held after Mozart's death at the age of 35; Praguers turned out in their thousands to mourn the composer they adored.

LEFT: Alphonse Mucha's masterpiece, the Mayor's Hall in Prague.

THE NOBEL FOOTSTEPS OF GÜNTER GRASS

Gdansk, Poland

Walk with: Günter Grass
(1927–2015)

Route: Leisure route around
the suburb of Wrzeszcz

Length: 1.9 miles

Essential reading: The Danzig
Trilogy

ABOVE: Günter Grass, winner of
the Nobel Prize for Literature.

RIGHT: The city of Gdansk is
full of interest and intrigue for
the walker.

Although Günter Grass only spent his childhood here and never returned to live in the city in his adult life, his memories of the Free City of Danzig, as the city was known during Grass' time, inspired him to set his major works in Gdansk.

Interested and highly active in politics, Grass used many world events, as well as his experience in the military during the Second World War, as themes in his stories. His most notable works, The Danzig Trilogy, is about the rise of Nazism and how it affected Danzig at the time.

Start the walk from the Wrzeszcz suburb of Gdansk, near the railway station, where his parents had a house. Then it's on to the Sacred Heart of Jesus Church, where the family attended mass. Through the railway duct passing Kuźniczki Park beyond the brewery buildings is the Comprehensive School No.2, which was formerly the common school that Grass attended. On a bench by the fountain in the Wybicki Square to the right of the school complex is Oskar, a character from *The Tin Drum*. A short walk from here is the house where Grass lived during his childhood at 13 Lelewel Street; nearby is the Strzyża Stream, which features in his books. Onward for 150 yards, then left along Leczkowa Street in the direction of Clinical Hospital, where Grass was born.

While on the walk, be sure to look closely at other interesting sights in Gdansk. Located at an ambiguous crossroad of historical status between Prussia, Germany, and Poland, it is a fascinating city in its own right.

405
IN SEARCH OF BOHEMIA
Riesen Mountains, Poland

Spanning what is today the Czech–Polish border, the Riesengebirge (Giant Mountains) once divided the historic regions of Bohemia and Silesia. Bohemia was a source of constant inspiration to the German Romantic painter Caspar David Friedrich (1774–1840), and the Giant Mountains themselves appear in many of his landscapes. On the Polish side, a hiking trail through the Karkonosze National Park leads along a ridge between the range's highest summits, Mt. Śnieżka and Mt. Szrenica, offering views that could easily have been lifted from one of Friedrich's oil paintings.

406
A MUSICAL WALK WITH CHOPIN
Warsaw, Poland

Frédéric Chopin (1810–1849) is a bit of a national symbol for Poland, who expressed his patriotism through his music. This walk around Warsaw passes fifteen of the city's "Chopin's Benches." Located at various sites relating to the great composer, the benches contain information about Chopin as well as a piece of his music played on demand. From the Holy Cross Church, to Krasińskich Square, to Saxon Garden, to as far as Łazienki Park and his various homes around the city, treat this walk like a Chopin treasure hunt.

VENTURE BACK IN TIME WITH WILLIAM BLACKER

Romania

Walk with: William Blacker (1960–)

Route: Breb to Creasta Cocosului

Length: 6.2 miles

Essential reading: *Along the Enchanted Way* (2010)

TOP RIGHT: A distinctive church in Breb, in the Maramures region of Romania.

RIGHT: The craggy rock formation of Creasta Cocoşului, above the town of Breb.

Following the collapse of the Berlin Wall in 1989, British author William Blacker ventured east to explore the "new" countries of Eastern Europe, intrigued to visit these far lands so shrouded in mist, whose names conjured images of howling wolves, peasant cottages, and snowy forests filled with bears.

Upon arriving in northern Romania after the collapse of the Ceauşescu regime, he stepped into a lost medieval world far away from the hustle and bustle of modern British life. "The trees beside the road were white with frost, and I had entered a country frozen in time," he wrote. Horse-drawn sleds trundled along snowy dirt tracks, while traveling Romany gypsies roamed the area. Villagers grew their own vegetables and made their own clothes.

In the town of Breb, in the region of Maramures, Blacker befriended Mihai and Maria, an elderly couple with whom he stayed with on and off for a number of years. Here, Blacker fully immersed himself in Romanian traditions, joining the villagers in their ways of life, scything the meadows, and drinking palinka, traditional fruit brandy. From Breb, hiking trails lead up to Creasta Cocoşului, a craggy rock formation that offers wonderful views of the area, while a series of picturesque trails snake through the nearby Iza Valley and Rodna Mountains National Park.

408
TAKE THE LONG ROAD
Romania to Paris

In 1903 and 1904, Romanian sculptor, painter, and photographer Constantin Brâncuși (1876–1957) embarked on an epic trek to complete his art studies, walking from his Romanian village of Hobita to Paris, hiking through Austria and Germany. He would call Paris his home for fifty-three years, working with stone, marble, metal, wood, and bronze, creating works that would make him one of the most influential sculptors of the twentieth century. Born near the Carpathian Mountains, most of his art is now in France, having bequeathed it to the French state when he died (the communist government refused his offer to leave his work to his native Romania).

FINDING HOMER AND HIS ODYSSEY IN GREECE

Ithaca, Greece

Walk with: Homer (850–800 BC)

Route: Ithaca island

Length: 1.2 miles (one way)

Essential reading: *Odyssey* (800 BC)

TOP RIGHT: The island of Ithaca is peppered with ruins which date back to Homer's time.

RIGHT: Near Exogi are the archaeological remains of ancient windmills.

The epic poem the *Odyssey*, presumed written by the Greek poet Homer, author of the *Iliad*, recounts the tale of the warrior-king Odysseus' journey, after the ten-year Trojan War, returning to his wife, Penelope, and son, Telemachus, waiting for him on the Ionian island of Ithaca, his homeland. Incurring the wrath of Poseidon, great god of the seas, meant a disrupted voyage for Odysseus, taking him ten years, instead of weeks, to get home.

Steered by Poseidon toward strange lands and peoples, Odysseus encounters creatures such as Cyclops, the one-eyed giant, eater of men, whom he outwits. At home, on Ithaca, Penelope, with the aid of her son, fends off over one hundred suitors camped out in her palace, lolling about, eating her food, waiting to claim Odysseus' wealth for themselves. When Odysseus finally returns to the palace, he is so unrecognizable that only his elderly dog, Argos, recognizes him.

To search for Odysseus, a good starting point is the modern town of Stavros in northern Ithaca, where an ancient acropolis has been discovered nearby. From here, archeological finds are spread mainly between Exogi and Platrithias, situated in a northerly direction from Stavros, toward the coast. A slightly longer walk of around five miles (one way) can include Exogi and Platrithias. The location of the palace is said to be between these two landmarks with breathtaking views of the sea.

A CHILDHOOD ON CORFU
Corfu, Greece

Gerald Durrell (1925–1995) was ten when his family lived on the Greek island of Corfu for four years. This period of his life had a profound impact on him, for he describes his childhood on Corfu as a time of pure happiness and wrote extensively about it in his book *My Family and Other Animals* (1956). He writes of villas of "strawberry pink," "snow white," and "daffodil yellow," and used the nature of the island's interior as a playground. As much as Durrell has fond memories of Corfu, his family is also well remembered by the older generation there, who have dedicated a hiking trail to the family, the Durrell Trail.

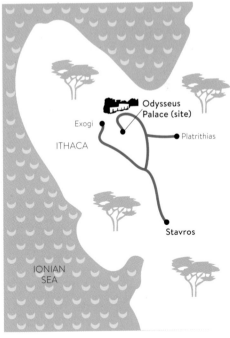

Odysseus Palace (site)
Exogi
Platrithias
ITHACA
Stavros
IONIAN SEA

IN PURSUIT OF HAPPINESS

Stoupa, Outer Mani, Greece

Walk with: Nikos Kazantzakis (1883–1957)

Route: Stoupa to Kardamyli (plus Viros Gorge)

Length: 4.5 miles (plus 7.5 miles)

Essential reading: *Zorba the Greek* (1946)

RIGHT: The story of *Zorba the Greek* is based on a friendship formed in Stoupa.

Greek writer Nikos Kazantzakis' fame spread to the English-speaking world with the cinematic adaptation of his most famous novel, *Zorba the Greek*, in 1964. The movie was made in Crete. The story itself, however, was inspired by a real-life Zorba, and is based on the time Kazantzakis spent with him at Stoupa, a village on the coast of the southern Peloponnese peninsula in Greece. Kazantzakis wrote the novel after hearing of the death of his friend—he wanted to keep his memory and the life lessons he had learned from him alive.

Today Stoupa is a popular holiday destination, thanks to its gorgeous beaches and surrounds. Just like the narrator in his novel, Kazantzakis had come here, in 1917, to set up a mine (the entrance to it can still be seen in a hillside nearby) and met Zorba, who became his foreman. A ten-minute walk north from here, the quintessential Kalogria beach sits in a sheltered cove among palm trees and tavernas. There is a bust of Kazantzakis on the cliff overlooking the beach. Stroll a farther ten minutes north to Delfinia beach, a crescent of small pebbles backed by a lush olive grove—the perfect spot for snorkelling. Hiking paths lead inland from here, or continue north to Kardamyli, which is the start of a six-to-seven-hour hike to Viros Gorge and back (a twelve-mile round route), through woodland and rocky paths, then down into the deep-sided dry gorge, filled with huge white boulders.

412

NO NONSENSE IN THE GREEK HILLS

Chalkida, Greece

"To travel in Greece during spring time is like walking over a fragrant carpet of wild flowers." Edward Lear (1812–1888) is best remembered for his nonsense verse, but he loved to travel and adored Greece, drawing and painting "these lovelinesses, these pure grey-blue seas, these clear skies, cut chiselled hills." In 1848, he roamed all over the Isle of Evia. Much of what Lear drew has been replaced, but he would surely have loved the Red House, built in 1884. Just south of it is the statue-topped Lyceum and the waterfront path which leads to the beach where Lear watched "boys jumping off the bridge top into the Euripus water."

413

"LET ME BEND MINE EYES"

Mount Cika, Albania

Lord Byron (1788–1824) visited Albania in 1809 as part of his grand tour of the Mediterranean. He wrote of "magnificent dresses," of the Albanian traditions, and included inspirations from his journey in *Childe Harold's Pilgrimage* (1812). On part of his travels, he visited Llogara National Park surrounding Mount Cika. Trails scale high mountain passes with hidden caves and pass traditional villages with citric and olive plantations, historic castles, and orthodox churches. The view from the Llogara Pass is especially pleasant, looking to the peak of Cika and the coast of the Albanian Riviera.

AFRICA AND THE MIDDLE EAST

From the poets of ancient Persia,
to the global musical stars of West Africa
and the freedom fighters of apartheid-era
South Africa, the variety of this
continent is endless.

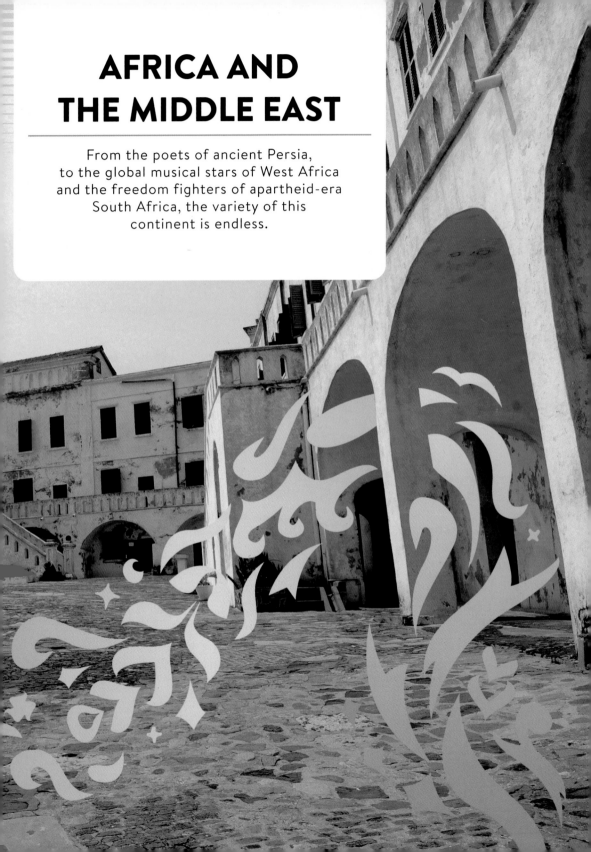

FOLLOW THE ALCHEMIST

From Spain to Egypt

Walk with: Paulo Coelho (1947–)

Route: Tarifa, Spain, to Faiyum, Egypt

Length: 2,675 miles

Essential reading: *The Alchemist* (1988)

ABOVE: Paulo Coelho, author of *The Alchemist*.

RIGHT: It's a long walk from Spain's Andalusian mountains to Egypt.

The publication of Paulo Coelho's bestselling *The Alchemist* landed the Brazilian author slapbang onto the international literary stage. The allegorical novel follows Santiago, a young Andalusian shepherd on a journey in search of treasure in the Egyptian pyramids. En route, he meets people who both help and hinder him, which leads him to discover his true self and destiny.

Coelho wrote the novel in just a fortnight, but it will take the best part of three months to walk the route that Santiago took. From the countryside of Andalusia, Santiago walks to the southern tip of Spain and the city of Tarifa, to sell his sheep's wool. Tarifa overlooks the Strait of Gibraltar, which a ferry crosses in thirty-five minutes to arrive in Tangier, Morocco. Here, Santiago has his money stolen, a setback which leads him to briefly give up on his dream. But he soon embarks once again on the journey to Egypt, on an exhausting route through the Sahara desert to Faiyum, meeting and falling in love with Fatima and being introduced to the eponymous alchemist on the way.

In the end, like all good travel stories, it transpires that the true purpose and fulfillment of Santiago's trek lies in the journey not the destination, and that the treasures life rewards you with might not be those you sought. It's a novel about the importance of pursuing a dream and the courage needed to do it. As Coelho writes: "People are capable, at any time in their lives, of doing what they dream of."

415
FROM AIR TO SEA
Tarfaya, Morocco

Antoine Marie Jean-Baptiste Roger, comte de Saint-Exupéry (1900–1944), packed a lot in to a life that at just forty-four years was barely long enough to say his full name. Saint-Exupéry was an aristocrat, but not of the idle kind. His writing included journalism, poetry, and the poignant children's novella *The Little Prince* (1943). Its narrator is a pilot who crashes in the Sahara, which is something Saint-Exupéry also did while attempting to break a world record in 1935. "I fly because it releases my mind from the tyranny of petty things," he noted. Saint-Exupéry helped to establish France's Aéropostale delivery service, managing its airfield near Tarfaya in southern Morocco. Tarfaya is now home to a museum about Saint-Exupéry, who is also commemorated with a biplane statue down on the beach; the pilot disappeared in 1944, over the Mediterranean, while on a reconnaissance mission.

416
ANDY WARHOL IN THE MOUNTAINS

Tangier, Morocco

Morocco was a favored destination for celebrities during the late 1950s and 1960s, and following in the footsteps of Yves Saint Laurent and his partner Pierre Bergé, pop artist Andy Warhol (1928–1987) regularly visited the city of Tangier. Referred to in his film *Restaurant* (1965), Tangier was a place to visit for inspiration, and to this day it is possible to discover the literary and artistic past of this magical place. Fuel yourself with mint tea and pound the winding streets laced with history, stopping at Dean's Bar and Café Hafa, which were frequented by the Warhol gang as well as the Rolling Stones.

417
WALKING THE BEAT WITH WILLIAM BURROUGHS

Tangier, Morocco

William S. Burroughs (1914–1997) moved to Tangier, Morocco, in the 1950s, after being drawn to the area by Paul Bowles' vivid descriptions of it in *The Sheltering Sky* (1949). It was here, aided by fellow Beat Generation writers Allen Ginsberg and Jack Kerouac, that Burroughs wrote *Naked Lunch* (1959). The Hotel El Muniria, where it all took shape, still stands on Rue Magellan today. It's easy to follow Burroughs and friends' footsteps around the town—the series of bars they frequented providing a clear route, from the hotel's adjoining Tanger Inn Bar to Café Central on the Petit Socco, the old medina's busy central square, via the Gran Café de Paris.

418
FIND COLOR WITH PAUL KLEE

Tunis, Tunisia

Swiss-born artist Paul Klee (1879–1940) journeyed to Tunisia with fellow artists and friends August Macke and Louis Moilliet in 1914, on a trip that is often said to have changed the course of modern art. In just two weeks, Klee produced thirty-five watercolors and thirteen drawings, and credits this time with the realization that he was an artist. He noted in his diary that: "The color possesses me. There is no need to try and grasp it. It possesses me. Here is the meaning of the happy moment: the color and I are one. I am a painter." Explore this rush of color in the first Holy City of North Africa, with a walk that takes you from the Great Mosque, to the tomb of Sidi Sahab, finishing at the impressive pools at Aghlabid Basins and the medina.

419
WALK CAIRO'S CORNICHE WITH NAGUIB MAHFOUZ

Cairo, Egypt

For Naguib Mahfouz (1911–2006), to date the only Arab to win the Nobel Prize for Literature, Cairo was often a major character—particularly in his masterpiece, the *Cairo Trilogy*. He wrote about the city with "true love," as his daughter, Om Kalthoum, once said: "He described it in granular detail. Even if he criticized it, it was still full of love." Mahfouz took frequent walks along the Corniche by the Nile, calling into his favorite cafés near Tahrir Square. Starting out from his former home on Nile Street, one can cross the Abbas Bridge to follow in the author's footsteps, searching for the Cairo found among his significant legacy of stories.

LEFT: The colorful streets of Tangier are full of inspiration for writers, artists, and musicians.

420

THE ATLAS MOUNTAINS WITH HOLST

Atlas Mountains, Algeria

Walk with: Gustav Holst (1874–1934)

Route: Djurdjura campsite to the town of Tikjda

Length: 4.5 miles

Essential listening: *Beni Mora* (1912)

TOP RIGHT: Many walkers base themselves in Bou-Saâda, well-known for its artisans.

RIGHT: Holst went to the Atlas Mountains for his health, but fell in love with the traditional music.

A keen walker, Gustav Holst went to Algeria for a holiday on doctor's orders. It was supposedly good for his asthma and depression. While in the Atlas Mountains, he discovered the culture and traditions of the belly dancers of the Ouled Naïl tribe and Berber music that so influenced his *Beni Mora* oriental suite.

Unfortunately, his Berber-inspired score was not received well by the largely conservative London audience, some of whom hissed at him during the concert—even though now it is often seen as the beginning of minimalism in music.

The Atlas Mountains stretch for more than 1,550 miles through Algeria, Morocco, and Tunisia, and by accessing it through Algeria, Holst would have visited the Saharan, Tell, and Aurès ranges. The oasis town of Bou-Saâda is a great base for walkers.

Today, many parts of Algeria are off limits to hikers. However, a walk in the Djurdjura National Park will give a sense of what Holst experienced. This part of the Atlas is lush green in summer and white with snow in winter; filled with dense forests, deep gorges, and plenty of birdlife, it often isn't the image of Algeria visitors expect. Various unmarked walking trails lead from the campsite of the national park and can go as far as the mountain peaks of Djurdjura or the nearby town of Tikjda.

DJURDJURA NATIONAL PARK

Djurdjura campsite

Tikjda

421
INSPIRATION IN ALGIERS
Algiers, Algeria

In Patti Smith's (1946–) song "Broken Flag," she sings of marching toward Algiers, and so begins her long-distance appreciation for the country. Smith was heavily inspired by a number of Algerian artists, including the rebellious French-Algerian writer Albertine Sarrazin, whose book *Astragal* guided her through her youth. Another source of inspiration was novelist Albert Camus (1913–1960), whose life in Algiers set the scene for *The Stranger* (1942), *The Plague* (1947), and *The First Man* (1995). A walk from Hotel El-Djazair, formerly known as the Hotel Saint-George, to other landmarks of Camus' Belcourt years, including cafés on Rue Mohamed Belouizdad, and finishing at Les Sablettes, will take you to the pages of his novels.

422

NIGERIA'S INTELLECTUAL HEARTLAND

Nsukka, Nigeria

Chimamanda Ngozie Adichie (1977–) grew up in the universtiy town of Nsukka, where her father was a professor, and she started off studying medicine and pharmacy. At one time, her family lived in the same house as another great Nigerian author—one of Adichie's main writing influences—Chinua Achebe, who had also worked at the university. Nsukka plays an important part in Adichie's first two novels *Purple Hibiscus* (2003) and *Half of a Yellow Sun* (2006). A wander around the university campus and streets of houses nearby gives a great sense of the intellectual energy inherent in her books.

423

HEAR THE DRUMS AT OLUMO ROCK

Abeokuta, Nigeria

Nigerian writer Wole Soyinka (1934–) was the first African to be awarded the Nobel Prize for Literature, in 1986. Born in the city of Abeokuta, in Nigeria, he is still very much involved in the community and political movements of the region. In recent years, he has organized Drumming Festivals at the town's significant Olumo Rock, which lies slightly north of Abeokuta. Take a walk from the rock to the nearby St. Peter's Primary School, where Soyinka began his formal education, then simply stroll around the village of Aké to discover the setting of Soyinka's memoir *Aké: The Years of Childhood* (1981).

424

CASTLES AND CONTRASTS IN CAPE COAST

Cape Coast Castle, Ghana

Yaa Gyasi's (1989–) novel *Homegoing* (2016) is a tale of historical fiction, following two branches of the same family line: one sister sold into slavery, the other becoming a slave trader's wife, in eighteenth-century Africa. Gyasi was inspired to write her novel after visiting Cape Coast Castle in Ghana, and being struck by the contrast between the colonialists who had lived in luxury there and the misery of the slaves kept in the dungeons below. Today the castle houses a museum, where the brutality of its history contrasts with the beauty of the surrounding Cape Coast, as can be seen on a walk along the beachfront.

425

NEGA MEZLEKIA'S LOST ETHIOPIA

Bale Mountains National Park, Ethiopia

Nega Mezlekia's (1958–) writing about Ethiopia carries echoes of homesickness for a time and a place he can never recapture. The author fled Ethiopia in the 1980s after becoming embroiled in the armed struggle for the nation's future, and has never returned. His second novel, *The Unfortunate Marriage of Azeb Yitades* (2006), spans three decades in a small Ethiopian village as the modern world threatens its idyllic identity. For a flavor of that beautiful isolation, head for the country's Bale Mountains National Park; particularly the Harenna Forest, which hugs the southern slopes of the Sanetti Plateau ("the rooftop of Africa"). Mezlekia describes his novel as "memory undermined by twenty-year-old nostalgia;" he may not be able to go to Ethiopia, but the rest of the world should take the chance.

LEFT: Cape Coast Castle with its historic connections to the slave trade, features in Yaa Gyasi's novel *Homegoing*.

426

THE LEGEND OF FELA KUTI: MUSIC FOR THE MASSES

Lagos, Nigeria

Walk with: Fela Kuti (1938–1997)

Route: Around Lagos

Length: 1.8 miles

Essential listening: *Live!* by Fela Ransome-Kuti and The Africa '70 with Ginger Baker (1971); *Zombie* by Fela Kuti and Africa '70 (1976).

ABOVE: Fela Kuti's music has had a global influence.

TOP RIGHT AND RIGHT: Kuti's hometown of Lagos is Africa's most populous place, and has the energy to match.

Fela Kuti (1938–1997) was a force of nature and a mass of contradictions. The multi-instrumentalist and musical adventurer pioneered Afrobeat, an Atlantic-spanning upbeat fusion of West African highlife with jazz, funk, and calypso, then wrote lyrics blasting inequality: "Through happy music I tell them about the sadness of others, using my music as a weapon." A forthright anticolonialist who wrote in pidgin English to maximize exposure, he publicly spurned a collaboration approach by Paul McCartney (whom he accused of "coming to steal the black man's music"), but met and got on well with the ex-Beatle anyway. The son of an Anglican minister and union leader and a feminist activist, Kuti married twenty-seven "queens" in one ceremony and insisted it was to emancipate them with civil liberties unavailable to single women. This was a complicated man, but a popular one—when he was laid in state, a million people turned up to pay tribute.

The Kalakuta Republic Museum, situated on Gbemisola Street in Ikeja, Lagos is Kuti's final resting place—ever the showman, he's buried beneath a large marble plinth at the entrance—but also the home of two of Kuti's children, not to mention a bar, hotel, and souvenir shop.

Kuti created the original Kalakuta as a commune and a recording studio, and declared it as an independent republic, which didn't play well with the Nigerian military junta. The original site was farther south at Agege Motor Road, but it burned to the ground in 1977, after a police raid.

The other great congregational place for Kuti fans is the Afrika Shrine venue; Fela played in the original venue for two decades before it, too, was torched by the military. In 2000, his son Femi Kuti, also a popular and respected musician, set up the New Afrika Shrine on NERDC Road in Agidingbi, about two miles north of Kalakuta. His father, who wrote that "music is the weapon of the progressives," would be pleased to know that his legacy lives on.

427
YOUSSOU N'DOUR'S DAKAR
Dakar, Senegal

Like the city in which he was born and still lives, Youssou N'Dour (1959–) is a fascinating combination of influences and styles that adds up to more than the sum of its parts. N'Dour was raised in Medina, a culturally vibrant area that has retained its old-fashioned feel. A walk around the gridded streets—horse-drawn carts, makeshift stalls, open stoves—helps bring to life the background N'Dour has so often described. In his twenties, N'Dour bought a nightclub called Le Thiossane—on Rue 10, the continuation of Boulevard Dial Diop—and he still performs there every Saturday night from around 2 a.m.: "I finish playing at around 4.30 a.m. I then usually try to round up some friends and go to one of my favorite bakeries, the Patisserie Medina, for breakfast. Then I go home to bed." You could do worse than follow his footsteps.

LOOK FOR THE REAL LIFE IN BINYAVANGA WAINAINA'S COUNTRY

Nakuru, Rift Valley, Kenya

Walk with: Binyavanga Wainaina (1971–2019)

Route: Rift Valley

Length: Various

Essential reading: *One Day I Will Write about This Place: A Memoir* (2011)

One of *Time* magazine's Top 100 "Most Influential People in the World" in 2014, Binyavanga Wainaina's stories and writings have had a profound affect on African writing. For many, he is best known for his satirical essay published in *Granta* in 2005, "How to write about Africa," its opening line: "Always use the word 'Africa' or 'Darkness' or 'Safari' in your title." Through humor, he laid down the gauntlet to recognize the common humanity of people everywhere: "Taboo subjects: ordinary domestic scenes, love between Africans (unless a death is involved), references to African writers or intellectuals, mention of school-going children."

Wainaina's only full-length work is his memoir, *One Day I Will Write about This Place*. In it, he tells of his struggle to find a place, between Kenya, Uganda (where his mother was from), and South Africa, where he found his literary path. And the "place" of the title is this metaphorical gap rather than a geographical place. It is a book about family, about tribes, and about nationhood.

He followed up this novel, in 2014, with what he described as a "missing chapter"—"I Am a Homosexual, Mum"; a brave move in Kenya, where homosexuality is illegal.

To understand the root of Wainaina's writing, walk around the town of his birth, Nakuru, and its hinterland. Observe the domestic scenes, the children going to school, the political debates taking place in the cafés. This is Wainaina's country, the place he wrote about.

ABOVE: Kenyan writer Binyavanga Wainaina came out as homosexual, despite it being illegal in his home country.

TOP RIGHT: Wainaina's writing urged the West to look beyond the media stereotypes of Africa.

RIGHT: A school trip visits Makalia Falls in Lake Nakuru National Park.

429

THE SONGS OF LAMU'S DUNES

Lamu, Kenya

German composer Hans Werner Henze (1926–2012) wrote his "Six Songs from the Arabian" for the singer Ian Bostridge, based on his trips to the Kenyan island of Lamu. Walk along the coast from Lamu Town to Shela, and head into the towering sand dunes behind the village for the views that inspired these songs.

430

OUT IN THE NGONG HILLS

Ngong Hills, Kenya

"The sky was rarely more than pale blue or violet... but it has blue vigor in it, and at a short distance it painted the ranges of hills and the woods a fresh deep blue." Karen Blixen's (1885–1962) lyrical memoir *Out of Africa* (1937) recounts the seventeen years she spent living in Kenya with recognizable longing. Her farm lay "at the foot of the Ngong Hills," where today a hiking trail across the seven peaks offers views of the great Rift Valley.

431

CONTEMPLATION WITH NADINE GORDIMER

Springs, South Africa

Nobel Laureate and anti-apartheid activist Nadine Gordimer (1923–2014) was born in Springs, an industrial city east of Johannesburg. She set her first novel, *The Lying Days* (1953), here, about a girl's coming-of-age and her growing realization of the racial divide and what it means to those around her. South of Springs are the Blesbokspruit wetlands, a beautiful nature reserve with an ecosystem that purifies the runoff from local industries before it enters the Blesbokspruit River, and a pleasant place for a walk. Gordimer is a writer of ideas, and here you can contemplate your own.

432

WALK IN THE VALLEY OF A THOUSAND HILLS

Ixopo, KwaZulu-Natal, South Africa

Alan Paton's (1903–1988) anti-apartheid novel *Cry, the Beloved Country* (1948) begins: "There is a lovely road that runs from Ixopo into the hills. The hills are grass-covered and rolling, and they are lovely beyond any singing of it." It is a view that can be found at the Buddhist Retreat Center in Ixopo, which overlooks the Ufafa Valley, and walking the Gavin Reilly trail. You'll pass the nesting site of the protected Blue Swallows, look upon traditional thatched homesteads in the valley below, and hear the distant echoes of cows, dogs, and children playing on the breeze.

433

DURBAN'S INDIAN QUARTER WITH AZIZ HASSIM

Durban, South Africa

Aziz Hassim (1935–2013) spent his formative years fraternizing on the streets of the Casbah, in the heart of the old Grey Street in downtown Durban. These streets are the setting for his novel *The Lotus People* (2002). Today, the Madressa Arcade, with its little shops with stairs leading to living quarters above, conjures up images of Grey Street in the 1950s: "The area had a kind of romance," with the lead character Dara's store selling, "just about anything portable, from cosmetics to cutlery, knives to nails, garden shears and stationery, axes, aromatic oils, potions, and patent medicines." As you emerge from the arcade, make your way into the quiet oasis of the Emmanuel Cathedral, then on to Victoria Street market. Around the block is the Juma mosque, "magnificent... with its minarets and many domes," as Hassim writes.

434

A WALK IN KIKUYU COUNTRY

Kamiriithu, Kenya

Author Ngũgĩ wa Thiong'o (1938–) writes mostly in Gikuyu, the language of the Kikuyu people of Kenya, as a political statement about identity. His award-winning novel *Mũrogi wa Kagogo* (*Wizard of the Crow*) (2006) is the longest known book written in Kikuyu. Take a walk about his home village Kamiriithu, where he was once arrested for his political views, to discover more about his roots and to feel the cultural influence he has had.

LEFT: Grey Street in Durban is the setting for Aziz Hassim's *The Lotus People*.

435

WALK DURBAN'S "GOLDEN MILE" BEACHFRONT WITH LEWIS NKOSI

Durban, South Africa

Walk with: Lewis Nkosi
(1936–2010)

Route: Suncoast casino
to the harbor entrance

Length: 3 miles

Essential reading: *Mating Birds*
(2006 edition)

RIGHT: Durban's golden mile
of beachfront.

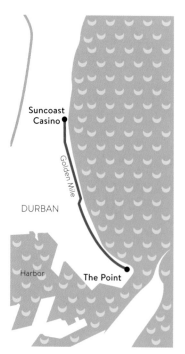

Suncoast
Casino

Golden Mile

DURBAN

Harbor · The Point

Exiled by the apartheid government for thirty years, Lewis Nkosi returned to South Africa in 2001 for a visit to Durban's "Golden Mile"—the scene of his best-known novel *Mating Birds*. An angry work, it is set largely on a beach in Durban in the 1960s, when the beaches were segregated. It is a sad tale of a black man and a white woman who fall in love and who gaze at each other over the invisible boundary line that divided their two beaches. The novel doesn't end well, as one would imagine for an apartheid-era novel, but the return of its creator had a happier ending. For a few hours, Nkosi looked at the transformation of the beaches—now racially mixed post-apartheid. He remarked presciently that although everything now looked completely altered, there were still great economic inequalities he could discern.

So, with Nkosi in mind, take one of the best city beachfront strolls in the country: start at the Suncoast Casino stretch of the promenade and head south past the novel's setting. In Nkosi's day, the stretch along the main Durban beaches was known as the "Golden Mile," after the color of the beach sand. Nowadays the beaches are less golden, given tidal movements, but the waves still attract swimmers and surfers in their droves. Piers along the length of the walk offer an opportunity to "walk out" into the sea and look back at the shore. The end is at The Point—the gateway to Africa's busiest harbor. Nkosi had his main character Ndi Sibiya wistfully watching the boats leaving South Africa for a freer world.

FATIMA MEER'S RED SQUARE
Durban, South Africa

Now a parkade in the bustling Grey Street area of Durban, traditionally settled by Indian traders, Red Square was once the gathering place for anti-apartheid rallies. As a young schoolgirl, Fatima Meer (1928–2010) attended these mass rallies addressed by Monty Naicker and other political stalwarts. Later a prominent sociologist and activist, Meer remembers an occasion in her book *Passive Resistance* (1948) when the women were encouraged to leave a rally given security fears. But the women respond: "We are in it now and we shall face it to the end … If sacrifice we must, then sacrifice we shall." Meer was a founding member of the Federation of South African Women in the 1950s.

THE REAL STORY OF LAWRENCE OF ARABIA

Wadi Rum, Jordan

Walk with: T. E. Lawrence
(1888–1935)

Route: Nabatean Temple to
Ain Salalah Spring

Length: 1 mile

Essential reading: *Seven Pillars of Wisdom* (1922)

RIGHT: A hike through T. E. Lawrence's Wadi Rum is full of stunning natural features such as the Um Fruth rock bridge.

The stories of Lawrence of Arabia by British archeologist, diplomat, and writer Thomas Edward Lawrence have grown in popularity in recent decades due to fictional portrayals from Hollywood. The iconic film *Lawrence of Arabia* was shot in Jordan in the 1960s where Lawrence also fought battles against the Ottoman Turks in the Great Arab Revolt of 1916–1918 and was based in Jordan during the First World War.

During this period, Lawrence recorded many of his experiences in the Jordanian desert in the book *Seven Pillars of Wisdom*. The autobiographical account details Lawrence's experiences from his time based in Wadi Rum, Azraq, and Amman as a member of the British Forces of North Africa. With the support of Emir Faisal and his tribesmen, Lawrence helped organize and carry out attacks on the Ottoman forces from Aqaba in the south to Damascus in the north.

Focusing on a hike through the Wadi Rum desert, start at the Nabatean Temple at the foot of the impressive cliffs of Jabal Rum. Lawrence described the area as "vast, echoing and God-like."

The walk to Ain Salalah, or Lawrence's Spring, close to Rum village, is filled with reservoirs carved in the bedrock and dams blocking small canyons, demonstrating the Nabateans' elaborate methods of harvesting and managing water. The spring was named in honor of Lawrence's evocative description: "From this rock a silver runlet issued into the sunlight. I looked in to see the spout, a little thinner than my wrist, jetting out firmly from a fissure in the roof, and falling with that clean sound into a shallow, frothing pool, behind the step which served as an entrance. The walls and roof of the crevice dripped with moisture. Thick ferns and grasses of the finest green make it a paradise just five feet square."

438
TREADING THE THIN GREEN LINE
Green Line, Jerusalem, Israel

In the summer of 2004, Mexican-based artist Francis Alÿs (1959–) walked along Jerusalem's invisible 1948 armistice border, known as the green line, while trailing a leaking can of green paint. He filmed a seventeen-minute video of his meander, showing him sauntering on road and off, along old railway lines, through towns, and past plenty of bewildered people. Alÿs used fifteen gallons of paint to mark the fifteen miles of the green line he traced, to highlight how, he says: "Sometimes doing something poetic can become political and sometimes doing something political can become poetic."

439
EAST MEETS WEST
Beirut, Lebanon

Rabih Alameddine's (1959–) *An Unnecessary Woman* (2014) is a novel about a reclusive woman who lives alone in her Beirut apartment, translating books no one reads, while musing on the past. "The Elizabeth Taylor of cities," she calls it, "insane, beautiful, tacky, falling apart, and forever drama laden." She wanders through her West Beirut neighborhood recalling how it used to be, before "the virulent cancer we call concrete spread throughout the capital, devouring every living surface." Discover the city's complex history for yourself with a walk from the Ottoman shrine and through the Beirut Souks.

A CITY OF GARDENS AND POETS

Shiraz, Iran

Walk with: Hafiz (1315–1390) and Saadi (1210–1291)

Route: Tomb of Hafiz to Tomb of Sa'di

Length: 2 miles

Essential reading: *The Rubaiyat of Hafiz* by Hafiz; *Bustan* by Saadi; *Gulistan* by Saadi

LEFT: The gardens around Hafiz's tomb are filled with flowers and cypresses.

Two of Persia's most famous and beloved poets, Hafiz and Saadi, were both born in Shiraz in south western Iran, and their tombs there now form something of a pilgrimage for readers from around the world.

During the thirteenth and fourteenth centuries, Shiraz was a center for the arts, the so-called "Athens of Persia." The two poets were among the most famous masters to emerge from this time.

A walk from the tomb of Hafiz to that of Saadi, on the city's outskirts, reveals why Shiraz is often called the city of gardens and poets. Both mausoleums are beautified by magnificent gardens filled with trees, flowers, and reflecting pools. The route itself passes through the Delgosha Garden, one of the city's oldest and most famous parks, but there are countless others, turning the city into a riot of floral colors every spring.

Wandering through the Musalla Gardens around the tomb of Hafiz, or through the flowers and cypresses that grow in abundance around Saadi's tomb, reveals the romance of Shiraz, which feeds into the work of both poets. While exploring the city, the wisdom of Saadi writing in *Gulistan (The Rose Garden)* may well come to mind: "Roam abroad in the world, and take thy fill of its enjoyments before the day shall come when thou must quit it for good."

RUSSIA AND ASIA

Stroll around the cities of epic Russian story-tellers such as Tolstoy, find peace in the hills of India with Agha Shahid Ali, and wisdom in the paintings of Katsushika Hokusai in Japan. This diverse range of cultures is a feast for the senses.

STROLL IN THE CITY THAT INSPIRED DOSTOYEVSKY

St. Petersburg, Russia

Walk with: Fyodor
Dostoyevsky (1821–1881)

Route: Sennaya Square to the
Peter and Paul Fortress

Length: 6 miles

Essential reading: *Crime and
Punishment* (1866)

Russian novelist Fyodor Dostoyevsky spent nearly thirty years living in St. Petersburg, constantly moving from apartment to apartment, never spending more than three years in each. He was particularly fond of Sennaya Square, at the time a bustling shabby neighborhood home to neglected tenements, seedy taverns, and brothels. His novel *Crime and Punishment* is largely set here. Raskolnikov, the novel's fictional protagonist, lived in an apartment that was, "more like a cupboard than a room" on Stolyarnyy Lane near Sennaya Square, while his victim lived on nearby Griboedov Embankment.

Walking south across the river is Pionerskaya Ploshchad, the site of Dostoyevsky's mock execution. In 1849, the novelist was arrested for being part of the Petrashevsky Circle, a dissident group active in St. Petersburg at the time. Just before being shot, the prisoners were told their sentence had been commuted to hard labor. Dostoyevsky would spend four years in a camp in Siberia, and many more doing compulsory military service.

Walking west along Zagorodnyy Prospekt is Trinity Cathedral, where Dostoyevsky married his wife, Anna Snitkina, while heading east is the Dostoyevsky Memorial Museum, the last apartment in which he lived, which displays a few original items from his time. Walking north along the Fontanka River is Mikhailovsky Castle, a former royal residence that today houses a branch of the Russian Museum. The castle was once an engineering school, which Dostoyevsky attended.

Across the River Neva along Troitskiy Bridge is the Peter and Paul Fortress, the very first building that Peter I erected in the city. It was soon converted into a political prison, and it was here that Dostoyevsky was imprisoned in 1849.

ABOVE: Portrait of Fyodor Dostoyevsky painted by Vasily Perov in 1872.

TOP RIGHT: Griboedov Embankment which features in Dostoyevsky's *Crime and Punishment.*

RIGHT: St. Petersburg, seen from above, with the Peter and Paul Fortress on the right.

442
WALK THE PAGES OF PUSHKIN
St. Petersburg, Russia

Widely regarded as the father of Russian literature, Aleksandr Pushkin (1799–1837) spent a large part of his adult life in St. Petersburg, attending balls, playing card games, drinking, and having affairs. He lived with his wife, Natalia, and their four children at 12 Naberezhnaya Moiki. Once home to over four thousand volumes, his study displays pages from his notebooks; it was in this room that Pushkin lay after his fateful duel with Georges D'Anthes. A short walk from the apartment is the Summer Garden, where the eponymous protagonist of his novel in verse *Eugene Onegin* (1833) strolled with his French tutor. A leisurely walk southwest past the Hermitage Museum leads to Decembrists' Square, which is dominated by The Bronze Horseman, an equestrian statue of Peter the Great that inspired Pushkin to write his eponymous narrative poem in 1833.

443

STEP INTO THE WORLD OF MIKHAIL BULGAKOV'S
THE MASTER AND MARGARITA

Patriarch's Ponds, Moscow, Russia

Walk with: Mikhail Bulgakov
(1891–1940)

Route: Patriarch's Ponds to
Sparrow Hills

Length: 9.4 miles

Essential reading: *The Master
and Margarita* (1967)

ABOVE: Author Mikhail
Bulgakov, a master of dark satire.

TOP RIGHT: Patriarch's Ponds in
Moscow is a crucial location in
The Master and Margarita.

RIGHT: Sparrow Hills is a
delightful spot to end this walk.

"At the hour of the hot spring sunset two citizens appeared at the Patriarch's Ponds," begins *The Master and Margarita*, a masterpiece of dark satire by Mikhail Bulgakov. Located in one of Moscow's most affluent areas, Patriarch's Ponds is a lovely place for a stroll, although in the novel, it is where the devil appears. Bulgakov lived nearby on Bolshaya Sadovaya Ulitsa. The house where he wrote the best-selling classic, and where he lived until his death, is now a museum.

On the northern side of Patriarch's Ponds, at the junction of Malaya Bronnaya and Yermolayevsky Lane, one of the characters gets his head cut off. After the decapitation, there's a chase through the streets (with one of the characters in his underwear, no less), to Griboedov House, which houses the Massolit Writers' Union. The building, a "two-storied, cream-colored house," is at Tverskoy Boulevard 25, from where it's a pleasant stroll south to Maly Vlasyevsky Lane, one of the locations of Margarita's house (there are more than five locations in the novel).

Walking northeast past Pashkov House on Mokhovaya Street, head to Sparrow Hills on the south bank of the Moscow River, where the mysterious foreigner in the novel, Woland, eventually leaves Moscow from. Today, it's a popular spot in winter, when children toboggan down its snowy slopes.

444
MARC CHAGALL'S NATIVE VITEBSK
Vitebsk, Belarus

Marc Chagall (1887–1985) was born in Vitebsk into a devout Jewish family. He spent his childhood and adolescence at his home on Pokrovskaya Street, today the Chagall House Museum, often frequenting the neighborhood synagogue on nearby Revolutsionnaya Street with his father (today, only the building's ruins remain). Across the Dvina River lies the Vitebsk Folk Art School, which Chagall founded after the Russian Revolution, while a short walk from here is the former home and workshop of Chagall's teacher Yehuda Pen, also known as Yuri Pen. The Marc Chagall Art Center at Putna Street 2 exhibits a number of Chagall's works.

445

RELAX IN LEO TOLSTOY'S LITERARY OASIS

Yasnaya Polyana, Moscow, Russia

Walk with: Leo Tolstoy
(1828–1910)

Route: Circular route
starting at Yasnaya Polyana
House Museum

Length: 3.1 miles

Essential reading: *War and
Peace* (1869); *Anna Karenina*
(1878)

ABOVE: Leo Tolstoy in his
later years.

RIGHT: Tolstoy's country estate
at Yasnaya Polyana.

"There was grass everywhere, birds, lungwort: no policemen, no roadway, no cab-drivers, no dirty smells, just pure delight," recounts Russian writer Leo Tolstoy, recalling the times he spent at his country estate in Yasnaya Polyana. It was here that he penned *War and Peace* and *Anna Karenina*.

Tolstoy often nipped down to the Voronka River for a refreshing swim, walking along the Bathing Path from his estate. "I would lie down in the shade on the grass and read, occasionally lifting my eyes from the book to look at the surface of the river gleaming purple in the shadow and with the first few ripples on it from the morning breeze," he recounts in his three-part autobiography.

Tolstoy would often fish here with his family too: "Those early years I remember how we used to go with him to catch pike: We would pick narrow stretches of the Voronka and he would fix the net to a stick and then I and my sister—or whoever else was there—would stir up the water and that way draw the fish into the net he was holding and he loved doing that," recounts his sister-in-law Tatyana Kuzminskaya.

From the river, the path leads back to the estate, passing through the Old Reserve Forest, which houses Tolstoy's grave.

446

RELIVE WAR AND PEACE

St. Petersburg, Russia

Leo Tolstoy chose St. Petersburg as the main setting for his masterpiece *War and Peace*, a historical novel tracing the lives of the Bolkonskys and Bezukhovs that unfolds against a backdrop of decadence, imperial drive, and aristocratic splendor. The magnificent Winter Palace, a vast ornate Baroque building that is today the site of the Hermitage Museum, was formerly the official residence of the Russian tsars. A short walk away is the elegant English Embankment, lined with sumptuous mansions, where the young countess Natasha Rostova attends her debutante ball and first dances with Prince Andrei Bolkonsky. This scene was filmed for a TV series in the mirror-lined ballroom of the Catherine Palace, built on the outskirts of the city as a summer residence of the tsars.

EXPERIENCE THE SPIRIT OF PAKISTAN WITH POET FAIZ AHMAD FAIZ

Lahore, Pakistan

Walk with: Faiz Ahmad Faiz
(1911–1984)

Route: Circular walk in
Lahore city

Length: c.2 miles

Essential reading: *Poems By
Faiz* by Faiz Ahmad Faiz (1971)

As one of Pakistan's most influential poets, Faiz Ahmad Faiz's legacy has become a symbol of the country's nationalism. Born in the era of British India in Sialkot, right on the segregation line, Faiz lived through the partition period of India and Pakistan.

Deeply affected by the conflict and difficulties of the period, his poems reflect the uncertainty and tension experienced by the Pakistan people. He had belonged to the Progressive Movement, a group of writers who exemplified the revolutionary aesthetic of the political situation during the lead up to the 1947 partition.

One of his most famous poems, "The Dawn of Freedom," written in 1947, describes the emotions that came with the situation.

*"The burning of the liver, the eyes' eagerness, the heart's grief
Remain unaffected by this cure for disunion's pain;
From where did the beloved, the morning breeze come?
Where did it go?"*

Lahore, the capital of Pakistan, is a good example of such emotional revolutionary spirits. Historical yet cosmopolitan, it is a city that embraces its heritage while progressing with modernity. Faiz had moved to Lahore in 1929, and is buried in the G Block cemetery of Model Town.

Explore Lahore starting with a walk within the walled city—don't miss the beautiful wooden facades of Haveli Nau Nihal Singh. Then, exit from either the Mori Gate or Lohari Gate and walk south toward the campus grounds of the Government College, where Faiz was a student when he first moved to Lahore. Walk through the Nasir Bagh park to reach the Lahore Museum, to learn more about the city and the partitioning of India and Pakistan. From here, you might want to take a bus to Model Town, to visit Faiz at his final resting place.

ABOVE: Influential Pakistani poet, Faiz Ahmad Faiz.

RIGHT: A walk within the walls of Lahore gives a flavor of this historic, modern city.

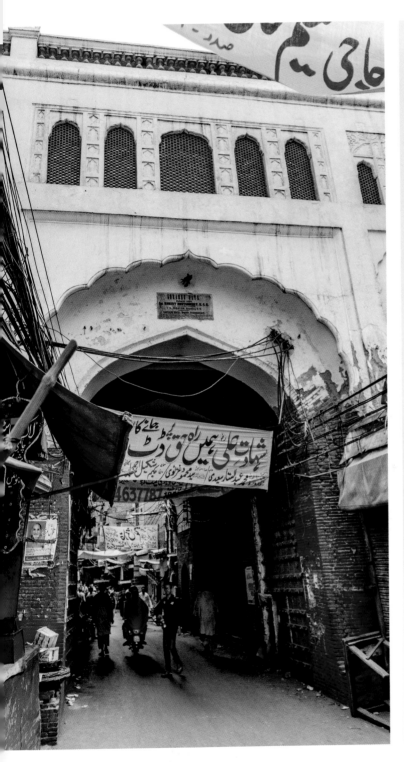

448
THE INSPIRATION FOR IQBAL BANO
Multan, Pakistan

Originally from India, Iqbal Bano (1935–2009) began her education in the classical form of vocal music in her home city of Delhi. Marriage took her to Multan in Pakistan where she made a name for herself, especially for singing the ghazals of Urdu poet Faiz Ahmed Faiz. The city itself is historically poetic, with layers of cultural traditions and architecture. Take a long walk and visit the thirteenth-century Shrine of Bahauddin Zakariya, Shahi Eidgah Mosque, Multan Ghanta Ghar, fourteenth-century Tomb of Shah Rukn-e-Alam, Shrine of Shamsuddin Sabzwari, and the blue-tiled tomb of Shah Gardez, and feel the serenity and power of Bano's singing.

449
LISTEN TO THE KING OF KINGS
Faisalabad, Pakistan

As a vocalist, Nusrat Fateh Ali Khan (1948–1997) is considered to be the "King of Kings" of Qawwali, a form of devotional Islamic music. Vibrant and cosmopolitan Faisalabad, Khan's birth city, is a great place to feel the energy of his performances. Start at the Nusrat Fathe Ali Khan Arts Council, then head to the clock tower, before walking on through the busy city center toward Jhang Road and the Qabrastan graveyard, to pay tribute to Khan at his final resting place.

TAKE A STROLL AROUND AGHA SHAHID ALI'S SRINAGAR IN KASHMIR

Srinagar, Kashmir, India

Walk with: Agha Shahid Ali (1949–2001)

Route: From Raj Bagh to Shankaracharya Temple

Length: 6.2 miles

Essential reading: *Call Me Ishmael Tonight: A Book of Ghazals* by Agha Shahid Ali (2003)

LEFT: Discover the emotions found in Agha Shahid Ali's poetry on a walk around Srinagar.

Although Agha Shahid Ali was born in New Delhi, his family is from Srinagar in the Kashmir Valley, a hillside region that has been the focus of many conflicts between India, China, and Pakistan. Often referred to as a poet in exile, Ali grew up in Kashmir but moved to the United States in his late twenties. Memories of Kashmir's beauty, struggles, and the pain of its destruction by war have influenced much of his poetry. Poems "In Memory of Begum Akhtar" and "The Country Without a Post Office" show his love and concern for the people of Kashmir during the Kashmir conflict, which began in 1947, and continues today.

Despite all this, the town of Srinagar, surrounded by hills, is a popular summer city, and is visited by locals and international tourists alike. Start a walk at the park at Raj Bagh, cross the Jhelum River on the Zero Bridge, and walk along this river that flows gently with a hint of melancholy, just like Ali's poetry.

Keep following the river until the junction that turns right onto M.A. Road. This busy artery of Srinagar, cutting through the city center with multilaned traffic, is where all life happens. Coming from the river walk, it can feel frenetic. If you want something calmer, find the almost parallel Residency Road instead, and keep going until the end, where a hill climb will take you to the Shankaracharya Temple at the top for a superb view of the city and the lake beyond.

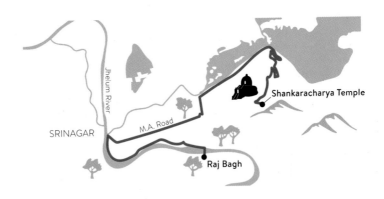

451

A TASTE OF THE RAJ IN RUDYARD KIPLING'S INDIA

Shimla, Himachal Pradesh, India

Walk with: Rudyard Kipling (1865–1936)

Route: The Mall, from Chotta Shimla to the Viceregal Lodge

Length: 3.7 miles

Essential reading: *Plain Tales from the Hills* (1888); *Kim* (1901)

RIGHT: Shimla in the Himalayan foothills is nicknamed the Queen of the Hills.

Shimla (or Simla), nicknamed the Queen of the Hills, is a cool mountain retreat, high up in the Himalayan foothills. The capital of Himachal Pradesh, it is a sprawling town with a network of bustling streets and bazaars, very different to the sleepy forest glade the British first "discovered" in the mid-nineteenth century. When Rudyard Kipling arrived in Shimla, it was a capital for the entire British Colonial government, who would decamp here—an onerous five-day journey from Kolkata—when the heat in the plains became too stifling.

In *Plain Tales from the Hills*, Kipling wrote that Shimla was a "center for power, as well as pleasure," with a reputation for "frivolity, gossip, and intrigue." Then, as now, The Mall was the center of life in Shimla, and it's here that the most remnants of Colonial architecture—in various states of romantic disrepair—are found. The Mall runs from Chotta Shimla, southeast of the center, to Scandal Point, the unofficial center of town where Indian gentlemen in tweed jackets gather to talk over the day's events, and continues west to the Viceregal Lodge (now the Indian Institute of Advanced Study). Landmarks along the way include the Victorian Gaiety Theater, which Kipling is said to have performed at, the half-timbered Town Hall, and the brightly painted cast iron and steel Railway Board Building.

In a post-Colonial world, people are divided on Nobel Prize-winning Kipling. R. K. Narayan wrote, "Kipling, the supposed expert writer on India, showed a better understanding of the animals in the jungle than the men in an Indian home or marketplace," and George Orwell considered him a "jingo Imperialist." But Kipling's book about life in the hills is a fascinating relic of intriguing times.

452
FOLLOW THE KIPLING TRAIL
Dehradun to Mussoorie, India

After a miserable schooling in England, Rudyard Kipling returned to India to work as a journalist. He was part of British Indian high society, and in the sweltering summer months, he, like the rest of the British Raj, retreated to the mountains. Mussoorie, with its familiar colonial-style buildings and cedar-tree backdrop, sits at two thousand feet and has dramatic views of Dehradun and the Doon Valley below. An old bridle path, a steep 5.6-mile trail from Rajpur, has recently been revived and renamed the Kipling Road. The trail "among the terraces of the Doon" is described in Kipling's novel *Kim*.

453

BELONG TO THE MOUNTAINS OF RUSKIN BOND

Landour, India

"It is always the same with mountains. Once you have lived with them for any length of time, you belong to them," declared Ruskin Bond (1934–) in his semi-autobiographical book of musings, *Rain in the Mountains* (1993). Bond certainly belongs to the mountains around Landour, where he has lived since the 1960s. The nature captured so lyrically in his various diaries—the deodar cedars, the "insect musicians," the "spirit-haunted" mountains—can be witnessed while following the Landour Chakkar, a circular path that loops around Landour's mountain ridge. But as Bond himself will tell you, "the best kind of walk… is the one in which you have no particular destination when you set out."

454

SEEK SOLACE IN THE HIMALAYAS

Mussoorie, India

Anita Desai (1937–) set the final, titular story in her triptych of novellas *The Artist of Disappearance* (2011) in Mussoorie, the Himalayan hill town in which she was born. Ravi, a reclusive artist, returns to the burned-down mansion of his adoptive parents, seeking solace in nature. "He needed to be at altitude, a Himalayan altitude, so he might breathe," writes Desai, as Ravi spends his time rambling in the hills around Mussoorie. Search for his echo on a trek through the nearby Bird Sanctuary to the top of Benog Hill. Try, like Ravi, to make the most of the rich natural setting; "to be silent, aware, observe, and perceive."

455

HIKE IN KHUSHWANT SINGH'S MOUNTAINS

Kasauli, India

One of India's best-known writers, Khushwant Singh (1915–2014) made his second home in the small hill town of Kasauli. Tucked into the pine forested hills of Himachal Pradesh, it's easy to see why the romantic hill station setting was so inspirational to Singh. Not only did the author do much of his writing here, but the area also features in many of his works. The Khushwant Singh Nature Trail offers a shortcut from Kasauli bazaar to the plains of Kalka town beneath, a route that was often traversed by the author himself.

456

DISCOVER AMRITA SHER-GIL IN SHIMLA

Shimla, Himachal Pradesh, India

Indian-Hungarian painter Amrita Sher-Gil (1913–1941) lived a short but vivid life. Born in Budapest, she moved to Shimla, then the summer capital of the British Raj, in 1921. This 3.2-mile walk starts at the Gaiety Theater, where Sher-Gil performed as a child. It continues west along The Mall, to Scandal Point, where the Shimla set once met for an afternoon gossip, and on past the railway station, to the Summer Hill neighborhood, location of Sher-Gil's family home, the Holme. When she returned to the house as an adult in the 1930s, Sher-Gil produced some of her best-known works, including *Hill Women* (1935).

TOP LEFT: The town of Kasauli, which Khushwant Singh made his second home.

LEFT: Start your walk in Kasauli bazaar to experience the contrast with the plains beneath.

THE RICH VEIN OF PRODUCTIVITY OF THE BOMBAY POETS

Mumbai, India

Walk with: Bombay poets of 1960s and 1970s

Route: Around the Fort area of Mumbai

Length: 2.5 miles

Essential reading: *Mumbai Modern: Arun Kolatkar and Bilingual Literary Culture* by Anjali Nerlekar (2016); *Collected Poems, 1952–1988* by Nissim Ezekiel (1989)

RIGHT: The Jetha Fountain in the inspirational and artistically vibrant Fort area of Mumbai.

The 1960s and 1970s were something of a boom time for poets in Mumbai. Two of Indian literature's greatest writers in the English language, Nissim Ezekiel and Dom Moraes, both called the city home. Around them others flocked: Kamala Das, Adil Jussawalla, Arvind Krishna Mehrota, Gieve Patel, and Arun Kolatkar, creating a community of poets who met regularly to read their poems and exchange ideas. Several of them even established their own publishing houses for poetry books.

In truth, their legacy is in their words, but their inspirations can be found on the streets and in the special energy that is Mumbai.

The poets would meet at the house of Keralan poet Kamala Das, on Marine Drive in the Fort area of Mumbai. From here, head east to the leafy grounds of the Sir J. J. Institute of Applied Art, where several of the poets trained as artists before they became poets.

Following Dr. Dadabhai Naoroji Road south will bring you to the Kala Ghoda area where there is the Jehangir Art Gallery (which used to have a café, the Samovar, that was popular with poets) and a vibrant Artists Center. In the 1980s, a new generation of poets established Mumbai's Poetry Circle, which initially used the Artists Center as its base. For its opening event, Dom Moraes came out of a seventeen-year poetic hibernation to do a reading.

458
INDIA'S "PICASSO"
Mumbai, India

Dubbed the "Picasso of India," M. F. Husain (1915–2011) studied at Mumbai's Sir J. J. School of Art. From here, head to Joy Shoes in the Taj Mahal Palace Hotel, where Husain designed the shop's interior and left behind his own "golden footprint." A stroll away is the Olympia Coffee House, one of the artist's favorite haunts.

459
A WALK WITH RUSHDIE
Mumbai, India

His hometown of Mumbai permeates many of Salman Rushdie's (1947–) novels, particularly *Midnight's Children* (1981). The narrator, Saleem, provides a route through his, and Rushdie's, old stomping ground. "Past the great houses on Malabar Hill," where Rushdie himself grew up, "round Kemp's Corner giddily along the sea… down my very own Warden Road." Follow the route "right up to the huge Mahalaxmi Temple and the old Willingdon Club."

460
HARRISON'S AWAKENING
Mumbai, India

In 1966, George Harrison (1943–2001) traveled to Mumbai to take sitar lessons with Ravi Shankar. This and subsequent trips had a huge influence on Harrison. Start your own enlightenment tour at the Taj Mahal Hotel, where he stayed, then walk down Marine Drive to the temples of Malabar Hill.

461

DISCOVERING E. M. FORSTER'S INDIA

Dewas, Madhya Pradesh, India

English author Edward Morgan Forster (1879–1970) made two visits to the town of Dewas, in the west-central part of Madhya Pradesh, India. From October 1912 until April 1913, and then later in 1921, he acted as private secretary to the Maharajah of Dewas. Forster wrote his novel *A Passage to India* (1924) between the two visits and a memoir, *The Hill of Devi*, was published in 1953. At the center of Dewas is the hill of the Devi, a site of Hindu pilgrimage to two temples. Take the sloping road uphill to the temples, where a stunning panorama of Dewas and beyond adds to the spiritual journey.

462

AYMANAM WITH ARUNDHATI ROY

Aymanam, Kerala, India

The minute village of Aymanam has served as a source of inspiration for many authors, and especially for Indian author Suzanna Arundhati Roy (1961–) in her Man Booker Prize-winning novel, *The God of Small Things* (1997). Within the novel, Arundhati Roy describes the Ayemenem House and History House of Kari Saippu, which, while both based on a combination of real buildings, are not actual places. Instead, soak up inspiration from this picturesque town with a walk from Kottayam railway station, along the Meenachil River, and through the ubiquitous rice fields.

463

SETTING SAIL FOR AMITAV GHOSH'S KOLKATA

Kolkata, India

Throughout the *Sea of Poppies* (2008), Amitav Ghosh (1956–) compares the Ganges to the River Nile, both lifelines to the civilizations they nourish. The Ganges is equally central to the plot of the novel, although by the time it reaches Ghosh's native Kolkata, the river is in fact the Hooghly, an arm of the sacred river. It is from Kolkata that the *Ibis*, a former slave ship, sets sail laden with opium destined for China, along with its jumbled set of disparate passengers. Walking the banks of the Hooghly through the center of Kolkata offers a glimpse of how essential this river is to life in the city—and how much the city has changed since the days of the poppy trade.

464

"I SOMETIMES IMAGINE MYSELF A FOREIGNER"

Kolkata, India

"So in the streets of Calcutta I sometimes imagine myself a foreigner, and only then do I discover how much is to be seen… It is the hunger to really see which drives people to travel to strange places," wrote Nobel Prize-winning poet, author, musician, and artist Rabindranath Tagore (1861–1941). This 1.2-mile walk starts in the Jorasanko Thakur Bari, the former Tagore family mansion in north Kolkata. Now a museum, this is where Tagore was born, grew up, and later died. The route continues southeast to College Street, famous for its book stalls, and finishes at the Indian Coffee House, one of Tagore's regular haunts. Experience how much there is to see when you imagine yourself a foreigner.

LEFT: There's always plenty to see in the streets of Kolkata, says Rabindranath Tagore.

THE REBEL POET: KAZI NAZRUL ISLAM

Dhaka, Bangladesh

Walk with: Kazi Nazrul Islam (1899–1976)

Route: A trek through Dhaka city

Length: c.7 miles

Essential reading: *Kazi Nazrul Islam: Freedom's Poet* by Sumanta Sen (2003)

TOP RIGHT: Ramna Park, with its plethora of walking trails.

RIGHT: The poetic ideal of a moonlit lakeside walk by Dhanmondi Lake.

As an anticolonial revolutionary and activist for political and social justice, Bangladesh's national poet Kazi Nazrul Islam is also known as the "Rebel Poet." Nazrul's works often include themes of religious devotion and rebellion against oppression. He criticized the British Raj in poems such as "Bidrohi" ("The Rebel") and "Bhangar Gaan" ("The Song of Destruction"), which led to many periods of imprisonment by the British authorities.

A walk around the monuments and sites of Bangladesh's capital city is the best way to experience the nationalism expressed by Nazrul. Today's Dhaka is progressive and modern, and the independence which Nazrul fought for is very much celebrated.

Start with the Liberation War Museum to learn about the liberation of Bangladesh and how Nazrul was a voice and inspiration during the Bangladesh Liberation War. From here, it's a short walk to the National Library of Bangladesh, where works of Nazrul can be found as well as books referencing his influence to Bengali people. Walk through the university grounds to admire the modern architecture of the Parliament House, a symbol of Nazrul's nationalist ideals, then on to the Kazi Nazrul Islam Institute by the picturesque Dhanmondi Lake. Enjoy the poetic surrounds of the lakeside walk, before getting back into the chaos of Dhaka traffic through Panthapath, to reach Kazi Nazrul Islam Avenue. Head south to reach a complex of parks including Ramna Park, with great walking trails. Nearby is a cluster of landmarks, including the Independence Tower, the Museum of Independence, and the Bangladesh National Museum, while across the road is the Mausoleum of Kazi Nazrul Islam, the great poet's final resting place.

466
THE PEASANTS OF
S. M. SULTAN
Narail, Bangladesh

Sheikh Mohammed Sultan (1923–1994), also known as S. M. Sultan, painted a series of works based on rural life in Bangladesh, featuring muscular peasants working the fields, and the villages and rivers. Sultan was from the former Jessore District (now Narail District), where the main agricultural produce was rice. Outside the city of Narail, a walk around the rice fields and along the Chitra River, to watch farmers at work, is one way to see the scenes that inspired Sultan's paintings. End the walk back in Narail's gallery at the S. M. Sultan Memorial to view a collection of his paintings.

467

WALK INTO THE FRAME WITH ZHANG ZEDUAN

Kaifeng, China

Walk with: Zhang Zeduan (1085–1145)

Route: Around Millennium City Park

Length: As long as you've got

Essential viewing: *Along the River During the Qingming Festival*

RIGHT: The riverside in Kaifeng, China's former ancient capital, is beautifully lit up at night.

BELOW: Millennium City Park is a theme park based on Zhang Zeduan's 16 ft scroll painting.

In his sixteen-foot scroll painting *Along the River During the Qingming Festival*, Chinese painter Zhang Zeduan captured the daily life of people and the landscape of China's former ancient capital, Kaifeng, during the Northern Song. The painting, also known by its Chinese name as the *Qingming Shanghe Tu*, is one of the most renowned works in China with each house, boat, store, and food stall depicted in vivid detail.

The painting celebrates the festive spirit of the festival with people from all levels of society, as well as in rural and urban settings.

Zeduan's original landscape has long since disappeared, but today you can almost literally walk through the painting at the somewhat surreal Millennium City Park—a life-sized theme park depicting the scenes from the scroll painting.

Within the one hundred acres of the park, there are fifty ancient decorated boats, more than four hundred buildings reproduced in the style of the time, and beautiful old timber bridges—not to mention performances in traditional dress and the chance to take part in marriage ceremonies and imperial exams. It's as close as you'll get to time travel— with a souvenir store!

468
ADMIRE NATURE WITH QI BAISHI
Beijing, China

A wander through Beijing's "hutongs" can feel like a wander through history. These narrow alleys contain shops, temples, and homes. In Yu'er Hutong in north Dongcheng, you'll find the memorial hall of artist Qi Baishi (1864–1967), famous for his delicate depictions of nature—especially the smaller details, such as a gathering of shrimps or dragonflies.

469
IN THE FOOTSTEPS OF LOST LOVE
Great Wall of China, China

In 1988, artists Marina Abramović (1946–) and Ulay (1943–) stood at either end of the Great Wall of China and began to walk toward each other. *The Lovers* was originally conceived as a "performative marriage," but by the time the walk went ahead, the artists' relationship was almost over. Upon meeting, rather than marry, they broke up. Experience their emotion along the Great Wall.

470
FOR THE LOVE OF NATURE
Paozilun Hiking Trail, New Taipei City, China

As a poet and nature writer, Liu Kexiang (1957–) has wandered along many of the Taiwan province of China's ancient trails. After it was damaged by a tropical storm in 2004, he helped to repair Paozilun Hiking Trail outside Taipei, which meanders through hills and villages, rice terraces, forests, and waterfalls.

471

FEEL THE INSPIRATION
OF LAND AND SEA

Tongyeong City, South Korea

Isang Yun (1917–1995) is undoubtedly Korea's most influential composer, famed for creating music that mixed western avant-garde with a distinctly Korean sound—most famously, his breakthrough orchestral piece *Réak* in 1966. He was born and brought up in what is now South Korea, and although he lived in Germany for almost all of his adult life, it is his hometown of Tongyeong (which he moved to at the age of three), at the southern tip of South Korea, that has embraced him as its son. Surrounded by sea and mountains, it is a beautiful spot, and Yun acknowledged the inspiration that the place had on his music. He wrote:

The calm sea
and its blue color.
Sometimes the waves hit,
it sounded like music to me.
The gentle breeze
softly passing by the grass
sounded like music to me.

There is the Isangyun Memorial at the site where Yun once lived, complete with a replica of his house in Germany and his car, but it is to the Tongyeong Concert Hall where you should head, for a walk around its grounds with its views of the sea and the mountains, as that is where Yun found his inspiration.

RIGHT: The sea around Tongyeong had a great influence on Isang Yun's work.

KOREA IN TEN VOLUMES

Taebaek Sanmaek, Korean Peninsula

Few writers have written such epic explorations of their country's histories as Jo Jung-rae (1943–). His trilogy of novels, *Taebaek Mountain Range* (1989), *Arirang* (1995), and *Han River* (2002), stretch to more than ten volumes each and have sold over ten million copies in Korea alone. They look at the divisions in Korean society and their historical roots. To attempt to get a feeling for this, head to Seoraksan National Park in the Taebaek Mountains and explore both urban and rural Korea with a hike from Outer Seorak up to the range's highest peak, Daecheongbong Peak.

473

WALK DOWN ART STREET

Jeju Island, South Korea

Occasionally one person can influence the development of a whole area. In the town of Seogwipo, on South Korea's Jeju Island, this has happened around Lee Jung-Seob's Art Street. The Korean artist Lee Jung-seob (1916–1956) lived on this street for a short but happy period of his life and produced many of his great works here. The street was renamed in his honor in 1996, and has since become a cultural center for art in the area. Walk the length of the street, looking out for engravings of Jung-seob's work—and especially the white bulls for which he is most famous—etched into the pavement.

474

ASCEND MOUNT FUJI WITH KATSUSHIKA HOKUSAI

Mount Fuji, Chubu Region, Japan

Walk with: Katsushika Hokusai (1760–1849)

Route: Yoshida Trail

Length: 9.5 miles

Essential viewing: *Thirty-Six Views of Mount Fuji*

TOP RIGHT: The unmistakable symmetrical form of Mount Fuji.

RIGHT: One of the best-known paintings from Katsushika Hokusai's series, *Thirty-Six Views of Mount Fuji.*

"At one hundred I will surely have reached a phenomenal level and when I'm one hundred and ten, everything I do, be it a dot or a line, will be alive," wrote Katsushika Hokusai.

Sadly, Japan's most influential artist died at the age of eighty-nine but despite not reaching his target, left behind a remarkable body of work.

Between 1830 and 1832, Hokusai produced his most famous collection, *Thirty-Six Views of Mount Fuji.* This series of *ukiyo-e* woodblock prints depict Japan's tallest peak from a range of different perspectives: reflected in a lake, blanketed by snow, fringed by cherry blossom.

Although it's an active volcano, Mount Fuji last erupted in 1707, and it's climbed by around 300,000 people each year. It is a 9.5-mile hike up (and down), with spectacular views, including of the Fuji Five Lakes at its base.

Once you have climbed Mt. Fuji, it is wise to bear in mind a well-known Japanese proverb: "A wise man climbs Mt. Fuji once, only a fool climbs it twice."

Mt Fuji Summit

Descent Path

Ascent Path

Fuji Five Lakes

Fuji Subaru Line 5th Station

475
HOKUSAI'S OBUSE
Obuse, Japan

In his eighties, when most people are slowing down, Katsushika Hokusai moved to the elegant town of Obuse, 134 miles northwest of Edo (now Tokyo). Here the "Old Man Crazy to Paint"—one of the nicknames he adopted over a long career—produced some of his most noted works. This 1.4-mile walk starts at the edge of town at the Ganshōin Temple, home to Hokusai's remarkable mural of a phoenix, a symbol of eternal life. It then winds through the town center along chestnut-wood pavements, passing immaculate gardens and homes, to the Hokusai Museum, which contains several *Waves* and a series of *One Hundred Views of Mount Fuji* sketches.

476

FOLLOW THE PATH
YOU FOLLOW

Kyoto, Japan

Nishida Kitarō (1870–1945) took daily walks to relieve his mind, and preferred to walk alone. Kitarō's biographer wrote, "taking a daily walk helped him to switch his mood. He therefore began a daily routine." The path he took is now The Path of Philosophy, which runs along a tranquil canal in the northern Higashiyama area of Kyoto. Kitarō took solace on his walks, and his feelings are perfectly described in his poem, which is written on a stone along the walk:

People are people,
and I will be myself.
Regardless,
the path I follow
I will follow on…

477

A LOVE AFFAIR IN KYOTO
WITH MIYAMOTO

Kyoto, Japan

Kinshu: Autumn Brocade (2005) was Teru Miyamoto's (1947–) first published book in the U.S.A. The word *Kinshu* has a multitude of meanings: brocade, poetic writing, the brilliance of fall leaves; and so works well for a story that is complex and dramatic. Take a walk from the train station, into temple complexes, to the tranquil and rather melancholic gardens, to the traditional wooden framed ryokans (inns) of the city, to inhabit the world of the novel's two central characters. Visit in fall to be surrounded by the flaming red leaves of maple trees, making the entire city a living brocade.

478

MURAKAMI IN TOKYO

Jingu-Gaien, Tokyo, Japan

For most of his life, Haruki Murakami (1949–) has lived in Tokyo, and it's possible to find his inspirations almost anywhere in the city. Murakami is a keen runner and he talks of the beautiful park area around Jingu-Gaien as his favorite place to run and tune out. Walk around the Meiji Jingu-Gaien and the nearby Shinjuku Gyoen National Garden to feel the tranquil surrounds of Murakami's runs. This is also a chance to visit the Jingu Stadium, where, at a baseball game in 1978, he was hit with the notion that he could write a novel, and his literary future began.

479

A WALK DOWN MEMORY LANE

Kobe, Japan

In his essay published in *Granta* in 2013, Haruki Murakami describes a walk he took two years after the Hanshin Earthquake, from Nishinomiya to Sannomiya in downtown Kobe. Murakami had grown up around the Kobe area and saw this particular 9.3-mile route as his "home," which he had not really visited as an adult. To follow his footsteps, start from the railway station in Nishinomiya and roughly follow the line westward toward Kobe. For Murakami, there was an element of self-discovery to the journey, and he wrote: "There had to be at least some connection, I felt, with who I am now."

LEFT: Who wouldn't fall in love with the city of Kyoto and its atmospheric old streets lined with wooden-framed ryokans?

IN BETWEEN THE LINES OF MARGUERITE DURAS' SEMI-AUTOBIOGRAPHICAL WORK

Sa Đéc, Vietnam

Walk with: Marguerite Duras (1914–1996)

Route: Around the town of Sa Đéc

Length: 1 mile

Essential Reading: *The Sea Wall* (1950); *The Lover* (1984)

RIGHT: The villa of Huynh Thuy Le in Sa Đéc brings readers close to the reality of Marguerite Duras' semi-autobiographical novel.

Born in 1914, in what was then Indochina, Marguerite Duras didn't have the happiest childhood. Her parents had moved there to teach as part of a French government campaign, but her father contracted dysentery, returned to France, and died. Her mother stayed on with her three children. She bought a plot of land to farm (near Prey Nob, in what is now Cambodia) but the land she was assigned was a salt marsh, flooded by the sea for half the year and therefore useless for farming. She had sunk twenty years of savings into the land, and was left in relative poverty and a deep depression.

This event was the basis for Duras' semi-autobiographical novel, *The Sea Wall*, but her time in southeast Asia is better known for her later novel of *The Lover*, which charts the semi-autobiographical relationship between a poor fifteen-year-old French child and a twenty-seven-year-old rich Chinese man.

Duras met the older Chinese man, Huynh Thuy Le, on a ferry crossing of the Mekong while traveling from her family home in Sa Đéc to her boarding school in Saigon. His family was also from Sa Đéc, and their home, described in the book as "a big villa" with "blue balustrades" and "tiers of terraces overlooking the Mekong," is now open to the public and contains photos of "The Lover" and his family, as well as some of Duras. From here, it is a short walk to the Trung Vuong primary school, which is most likely the one in which Duras' mother taught, and on to the buddhist temple of Chua Hurong, which has a shrine to Huynh Thuy Le.

481
OPEN-AIR
ART
Naoshima Island, Japan

The Lee Ufan Museum opened on the "art island" of Naoshima, Japan, in 2010, showcasing the work of Korean-born painter and sculptor Lee Ufan (1936–). Wander among his large stone, concrete, and iron installations and paintings, housed in the geometric building designed by Japanese architect Ando Tadao. Tadao designed two other museums on the island—Benesse House and Chichu Art Museum—each a ten-minute walk or so in opposite directions from here. The island is littered with outdoor artworks—there are nearly twenty on the lawns and beaches around Benesse House alone.

482
SEARCH FOR
LOVE
Ubud, Bali, Indonesia

Elizabeth Gilbert's (1969–) novel *Eat, Pray, Love* (2006) has put the town of Ubud in Bali firmly on the map as the place where she found "love" again. It is a town of beautiful architecture surrounded by breathtaking rice terraces, and the air is fragrant with incense. Unlike the beaches of Bali, life is slow and steady here. Walk between the houses, and on to the paths of the rice fields and those that lead to the temple gates.

NOT IN TRANSLATION: THAILAND'S MOST FAMOUS POETRY

Klaeng District, Rayong, Thailand

Walk with: Sunthorn Phu (1786–1855)

Route: Around Sunthorn Phu Memorial

Length: 0.3 miles

Essential reading: *Phra Aphai Mani* (1844)—in Thai

RIGHT: The Sunthorn Phu Memorial park in Klaeng has a statue of the poet.

Astonishingly, the works of Sunthorn Phu, Thailand's much-loved royal poet, have never been officially translated. So while his epic poetry remains ever popular in his country today—and can be recited by thousands of Thai schoolchildren—he remains virtually unknown outside of Thailand.

Sunthorn Phu was appointed court poet by King Rama I, but his penchant for ladies and alcohol saw him ousted from court and jailed for fighting. It was while he was in prison that he began writing his *Phra Aphat Mani* opus, a 48,700-line saga about a fictitious prince's romantic adventures in ancient Thailand. His poem was so well received by King Rama II that it led to his pardon, and all went well until Sunthorn Phu publicly corrected one of the next king's—King Rama III's—own poems, and was promptly stripped of all his titles, whereupon he became a monk. Finally, to complete the circle, King Rama IV's daughter read Sunthorn Phu's unfinished poem and asked him to complete it two decades after it had begun, earning him a royal title again, before his death in 1855.

There are statues and shrines to Sunthorn Phu all over Thailand, but the Sunthorn Phu Memorial in Klaeng, Rayong Province, is particularly special, being in his family hometown. This monument takes the form of a park, opened in 1970, and centered around a small hillock, on which there is a life-sized bronze statue of the poet. In the surrounding gardens, ponds, and fountains are further bronze statues depicting some of the mythical characters from his famous works.

484
KUNG CHANG KHUN PHAEN
Suphan Buri, Thailand

The Kung Chang Khun Phaen legend is one of Thailand's oldest and best known stories, passed down for years from generation to generation. It brings together love, war, and tragedy in a tale of Kung Chang, a king in Suphan Buri; a warrior, Khun Phaen; and a beautiful woman, Wanthong. Visit Wat Khae temple in Suphan Buri, which is mentioned in the epic tale, and the tamarind tree in its grounds, which is believed to have given Khun Phaen magic powers. From here, it is a short walk to Khum Khun Phaen, a recreation of the style of house that Khum Phaen would have lived in.

AUSTRALASIA

The rich colors of the outback and stunning scenery of New Zealand have inspired many artists. Follow their paths to experience the scale of an Albert Namatjira scene, or to stumble upon the exact lonely building painted by Rita Angus.

485

EXPLORE ANCIENT INDIGENOUS CULTURE WITH ALBERT NAMATJIRA

Northern Territory, Australia

Walk with: Albert Namatjira (1902–1959)

Route: The Larapinta Trail

Length: 139 miles

Essential viewing: *Mount Sonder, MacDonnell Ranges* (c.1957–1959)

Albert Namatjira was born in Ntaria, in Australia's Northern Terrritory. Until the age of thirteen, he was educated in the Lutheran Mission, but then returned to his Arrernte community.

He never received any formal art-school training, but employed a style of contemporary Indigenous Australian art that borrowed from Western landscape painting, making it his own, with deeper, brighter colors. He is best known for his vivid watercolor landscapes of Central Australia's "Red Center," where he worked as a camel driver, and, in particular, the West MacDonnell Ranges, with their dramatic gorges, chasms, ghost gum trees, and dry creek beds.

The Larapinta Trail is a long-distance track that cuts through this remote land along the spine of the ocher-red West MacDonnell Ranges. Most people hiking the full trail do so east to west, in order to end on a figurative and literal high on Rwetyepme (Mount Sonder) at 4,527 feet.

In his painting, *Mount Sonder, MacDonnell Ranges*, Namatjira perfectly captures the texture of the scrubland and the huge scale of the mountain.

ABOVE: Australian artist Albert Namatjira never received any formal art training.

TOP RIGHT: Namatjira painted many pictures of the West MacDonnell Ranges, with their vivid red rocks and canyons.

RIGHT: Ormiston Gorge in the West MacDonnell range.

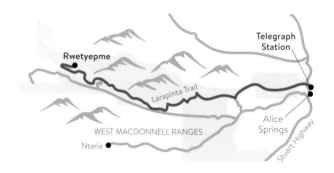

486
NAMATJIRA'S PALM VALLEY
Northern Territory, Australia

South of the Indigenous community of Ntaria, where Albert Namatjira was born, is Finke Gorge National Park and Palm Valley, his mother's country. In the 1940s, Namatjira painted many landscapes with the valley's famous red cabbage palms towering in a vast, red desert. The park is about a two-hour drive west of Alice Springs, and it's possible to visit and walk a couple of short trails in a day. The Arankaia Walk (1.5 miles) and the longer Mpulungkinya Walk (three miles) meander through a lush oasis of slender palms.

487

A TOWN LIKE ALICE

Alice Springs, Northern Territory, Australia

Nevil Shute's (1899–1960) *A Town Like Alice* (1950) describes the romantic plight of Jean Paget, who moves to Australia to be with Joe, a fellow prisoner of war during the Second World War. With her inherited fortune, she sets out to turn her small outback community into "a town like Alice," referring to Alice Springs. A walking tour around the town reveals both the Indigenous and colonial histories, as well as the difference in lifestyle in this harsh environment compared to cities on the coasts, just as Jean and Joe would have had to endure.

488

BRUCE CHATWIN'S OUTBACK

Northern Territory, Australia

In his book *The Songlines* (1987), travel writer Bruce Chatwin (1940–1989) goes on a walkabout for three days in "the outback" with the purpose of learning about Aboriginal songs in Australia. He based himself in the Northern Territory and took time visiting communities and their surroundings for inspiration. Today, many marked trails allow visitors to experience the incredible nature and the Indigenous culture in the territory's many National Parks. Take a walk on the cliffs of Kings Canyon, the varied landscape of Ruby Gap National Park, or the circular path around Uluru.

489

ARTHUR STREETON'S GOLDEN FLEECE LANDSCAPE

Grampians National Park, Victoria, Australia

Arthur Streeton (1867–1943) is one of Australia's beloved landscape painters and leader of Australian Impressionism. His paintings depict the vast expanses of the Grampians and Western regions of Victoria. There are many day walks in the Grampians National Park, in particular the four miles of Mud-Dadjug (Mount Abrupt) trail, which offers a scenic rocky route and an awe-inspiring panoramic view of the surrounds at the peak. It is easy to see why Streeton was inspired to produce his painting *The Grampians (Mount Abrupt)* in 1921.

490

THE ICONIC SYDNEY TRAIL WITH MARGARET PRESTON

Sydney, New South Wales, Australia

Margaret Preston (1875–1963) is one of the first non-Indigenous Australian artists to use Aboriginal motifs in her work; she is also an icon of modernist art and the style of "Australian national art." Her works feature local scenery and flora and fauna, scenes of which can be experienced by walking the new fifty-mile Bondi to Manly coastal walk. This urban walking route hugs the outer harbor as it passes through the most stunning lookouts, with prime vistas of two of Sydney's most iconic landmarks—the Sydney Harbour Bridge and the Opera House—from various angles. Stop by the Art Gallery of New South Wales on the way, where Preston's works are on permanent display.

TOP RIGHT: The fifty-mile coastal walk from Bondi Beach to Manly offers fabulous views of Sydney's landmarks.

RIGHT: The route passes by the Art Gallery of New South Wales, where Margaret Preston's distinctive work is on permanent display.

491

SEEK OUT SIDNEY NOLAN'S INSPIRATION

Fraser Island, Queensland, Australia

Walk with: Sidney Nolan (1917–1992)

Route: From Dilli Village to Happy Valley

Length: 56 miles

Essential viewing: *Mrs. Fraser* (originally titled *Woongoolbver Creek*)

RIGHT: The colors and wild landscape of Fraser Island enraptured Nolan.

K'gari (Fraser Island), the world's largest sand island, sits off Australia's eastern Queensland coast. It's an exotic place of rainforests growing up from shifting sand dunes, dark tannin-stained lakes, strikingly colored sand cliffs, and intense, bright light. The island was originally known to Europeans as Great Sandy Island, but was renamed Fraser Island in the wake of tales about *Stirling Castle* shipwreck survivor Eliza Fraser, a Scottish woman who washed up here in 1836. Whether she was rescued or enslaved by the Butchulla people has caused centuries of controversy.

Artist Sidney Nolan arrived on the island in 1947, interested in the myth that had become Mrs. Fraser. He was so inspired by the vivid landscape and the idea of an outsider set against a hostile environment that he painted a series of twelve large paintings, one of which was *Woongoolbver Creek* (renamed *Mrs. Fraser* in 1958). Wanggoolba Creek (as it is now spelled) is a crystal-clear freshwater creek running through piccabeen palm forest near the center of the island. The fifty-six-mile K'gari Great Walk follows a boardwalk beside the famous creek on the section from Central Station to Lake McKenzie, via Basin Lake, which often has turtles at the water's edge, or via Pile Valley and the cool, shady rainforest.

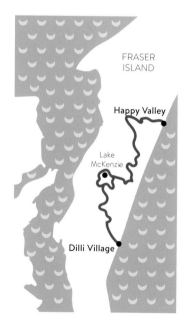

FRASER ISLAND

Happy Valley

Lake McKenzie

Dilli Village

492
ST. KILDA FORESHORE TRAIL
Melbourne, Australia

Sidney Nolan's family moved to the St. Kilda neighborhood, Melbourne's beachside playground, when he was a young child. In the 1940s, the artist painted a St. Kilda series based on memories of freedom from his boyhood, including St. Kilda's funfair, Luna Park, and its pier and sea baths. The short St. Kilda section of the seven-mile Foreshore Trail passes all of these sights.

493
WARBY RANGES TRACK
Victoria, Australia

Another series of paintings for which Sidney Nolan is well known depict outlaw Ned Kelly. Kelly and his gang of bushrangers shot dead three policemen in Victoria and were on the run for nearly two years, before their last stand in the small town of Glenrowan. Nolan painted the Australian folk hero in the outback of Victoria in which he survived, which has since become known as "Kelly Country." Here, the seven-mile Mount Glenrowan hike has views over the township below and the plains and Alps in the distance.

RITA ANGUS AND THE
SOUTHERN ALPS SCENERY

Canterbury, New Zealand

Walk with: Rita Angus
(1908–1970)

Route: Begins and ends on
State Highway 73 (not a
loop track)

Length: 21 miles

Essential viewing: *Cass* (1936);
Mountains, Cass (1936)

Feminist, pacifist, and pioneer of modern painting in New Zealand, Rita
Angus is most revered for her bold Canterbury landscapes, with their
clarity and repetitions of form and line. In the summer of 1936, Angus
spent ten days on a sketching holiday near the small settlement of
Cass, a couple of hours west of Christchurch, with fellow artist Louise
Henderson. Two of her greatest landscape paintings were inspired here,
in the foothills of the Southern Alps; watercolors *Cass* and *Mountains,
Cass* depict the scale and magnificence of the mountain range as it dwarfs
man-made structures.

It's possible to tramp for two to three days through the Canterbury High
Country that so galvanized Angus. The trailhead for the Cass-Lagoon
Saddle Track is not far from the iconic timber-framed lean-to railway
station she painted on Settlement Road at Cass—the track begins from
the signposted car park at the east end of the Cass road bridge. The
twenty-one-mile unmarked trail through Craigieburn Forest crosses
riverbeds and rivers, ascends and descends forest tracks, and crosses two
alpine saddles. In the right conditions, Harper River offers swimming
holes for a dip.

ABOVE: Rita Angus at work.

TOP RIGHT: Rita Angus' work
evocatively depicts the scale
of nature.

RIGHT: The iconic timber railway
station that features in Angus'
work *Cass*.

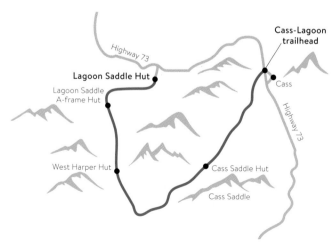

495
THE VIEWS OF ISLAND BAY
Wellington, New Zealand

In 1955, Rita Angus moved to Wellington, and some of her artwork from this time were seascapes of Island Bay, a beachside suburb to the south of Wellington. It's here that *Boats, Island Bay* (1968) was painted. Picture-postcard perfect Island Bay can be reached from Oriental Parade on Wellington Harbour on the winding 6.5-mile (one-way) Southern Walkway. This urban trail passes through parks and woodland, and is steep in parts as it follows a ridge of hills. The panoramic views of the south shore are unbeatable.

496
THE LIGHT OF THE CENTER
Central Otago, New Zealand

Rita Angus spent two weeks traveling through Central Otago in 1953, and later worked on a composite landscape called *Central Otago* (1954–1956/1969), an amalgam of scenes bathed in the golden light for which the region is famous. Tracks and walkways crisscross Naseby, Arrowtown, the shores of Lake Wakatipu, and the Remarkables mountain range, all of which feature in the painting. The Queenstown Hill Walkway is easily accessed from central Queenstown and is a steep 1,640-feet hike to the summit of Te Tapu-nui ("mountain of intense sacredness"), with sensational views over Lake Wakatipu and the Remarkables.

COLIN McCAHON'S MODERNISM

Titirangi, Auckland, New Zealand

Walk with: Colin McCahon
(1919–1987)

Route: Opou Reservation to
McCahon House

Length: 1.3 miles

Essential viewing: *French Bay*
series of paintings (1956)

LEFT: Huge kauri trees featured
in McCahon's work to highlight
their deforestation.

Colin McCahon was New Zealand's foremost artist of the twentieth century, introducing concepts of late modernism to his paintings, which explored themes of religion and spirituality. In the 1950s, he visited the U.S.A. to study the work of contemporaries such as Mark Rothko—a trip that had a profound influence on him, both spiritually and aesthetically.

This walk begins at the Opou Reserve, a small conservation area heavily planted with huge kauri trees, which are often found in McCahon's landscapes. His reason for their inclusion is not simply aesthetic, but—as with much of his painting—political, highlighting the massive deforestation of the trees. The tree is also considered sacred to the Maori. From here, the walk continues along Otitori Bay Road to French Bay, painted several times by McCahon from several viewpoints across the Manukau Harbour. His painting *French Bay* (1954) is redolent of landscapes painted by Paul Cézanne.

Back on Otitori Bay Road, the walk heads north uphill for about a third of a mile to reach The McCahon House, the artist's studio and residence between 1953 and 1959. The house, which is now a museum dedicated to his work, is surrounded by kauri trees. McCahon moved from here to Auckland in 1959, and began absorbing and incorporating American Abstract Expressionism in his work, traveling extensively throughout the North Island. This influence is most notable in his *Kaipara Flats* series in 1971, of which landscape he remarked: "This is a shockingly beautiful area, empty and utterly beautiful. This is, after all, the coast the Maori souls pass over on their way from life to death. The light and sunsets here are appropriately magnificent."

498

RALPH HOTERE, HOMAGE TO A MAORI ARTIST

Port Chalmers, Dunedin, New Zealand

Up at the top of the Flagstaff Lookout Point in Port Chalmers, Dunedin is a charming sculpture garden created on the wishes of abstract artist, Ralph Hotere (1931–2013). His work, *Black Phoenix II,* is here, made from the timber of a burned fishing boat. The garden is a peaceful spot to enjoy spectacular views over the bay. A walk down the steep Constitution Street will bring you to St. Joseph's Cathedral on Magnetic Street, which was filled to overflowing for Hotere's funeral service in 2013. "This was his place for over thirty-five years," his widow Mary McFarlane said. "Most of his creative output originated in this village. He could have worked anywhere in the world—Italy, France, Germany, or the UK or U.S.A.—but he felt most at home here."

499

CHANNEL YOUR INNER MICHAEL NYMAN

Karekare Beach, near Auckland, New Zealand

Karekare Beach, near Auckland, was the backdrop of Jane Campion's 1993 film *The Piano.* The film won three Oscars, but it was Michael Nyman's (1944–) soundtrack that truly soared. The roar of the waves combined with the music of the piano to create an unforgettable atmosphere. Visitors can walk down to the black-sand beach—which they will often have all to themselves—and then tackle the 4.9-mile scenic walk to the equally stunning Kitekite Falls.

RIGHT: Listen to the inspiration for Michael Nyman's soundtrack on Karekare Beach.

FAR RIGHT: Five miles from the beach, you can hear the roar of Kitekite Falls.

500

INHALE GAUGUIN'S TAHITI

Mataiea, Tahiti, French Polynesia

Walk with: Paul Gauguin (1848–1903)

Route: Coastal road

Length: 2 miles

Essential viewing: *Woman with a Flower* (1891); *The Seed of the Areoi* (1892)

When Paul Gauguin first went to Tahiti in 1891, he claimed that it was to pursue a more simple existence than European life offered and to escape "everything that is artificial and conventional." Others would suggest that it was because his art wasn't selling in Europe and he wanted to create a more exotic story for himself and his painting. He is a controversial figure who beat his wife, abandoned his family, and took child brides during his time in Polynesia.

His first visit to Tahiti lasted two years, most of which he spent living in a small hut in Mataiea. He painted scenes from Tahitian life, influenced by the color and light around him. In 1893, he took these paintings to Europe to sell, but was not welcomed back either by his friends or the art world, and in 1895, he returned to Tahiti forever.

A forty-minute walk along the southern coastal road of Tahiti is all it takes to experience some of the sensations experienced by the artist in the 1890s. Begin at the Water Gardens Vaipahi in Ataiti, a peaceful setting next to the ocean, and continue east to the Harrison Smith Botanical Garden to see examples of the flora that Gauguin used in many of his paintings. Between the two locations is the Gauguin Museum, dedicated to the artist and his work.

ABOVE: The controversial Paul Gauguin.

RIGHT: The lush vegetation of Tahiti inspired many of Paul Gauguin's best known paintings.

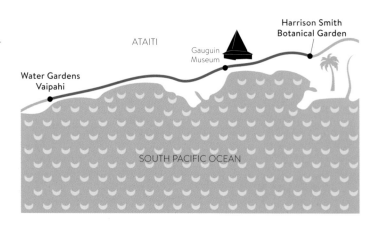

ATAITI

Gauguin Museum

Harrison Smith Botanical Garden

Water Gardens Vaipahi

SOUTH PACIFIC OCEAN

INDEX

CONTRIBUTORS

MICHAELA BUSHELL

Michaela Bushell is a writer and editor with a love of literature and travel. She co-authored the *Rough Guide to Cult Fiction*, and helped write *The Bucket List: 1,000 Adventures*. Her work has taken her driving across the Saharan desert, hunting the Loch Ness monster in Scotland, and celebrating the cherry blossom in Japan.

KIKI DEERE

Brought up bilingually in London and northern Italy, Kiki Deere has written dozens of travel guidebooks and articles for magazines and UK broadsheets on destinations from the remotest province of the Philippines to glamorous Lake Como. You'll find her enjoying the great outdoors, whether trekking in the Brazilian Amazon or enjoying a Sunday afternoon stroll in the British countryside.

EMILY LUXTON

Emily Luxton is a Hampshire-based writer and travel blogger. She has worked as a contributing author on two travel books, and written for a range of online publications including *Lonely Planet* and *The Telegraph*. Emily's passion for hiking has taken her on adventures around the world, including climbing Mount Fuji at sunrise, and coming face-to-face with a black bear while hiking solo in Canada.

AMY McPHERSON

Amy McPherson is a travel writer based in London. Her features have been published in Australian and UK publications covering outdoors active travel from hiking, to cycling, and scuba diving. Preferring nature over concrete jungles, Amy is always on the move in the great outdoors.

SHAFIK MEGHJI

Shafik Meghji is an award-winning travel writer, journalist, and author based in South London. He has worked on all seven continents, co-authoring more than thirty-five Rough Guides and DK Eyewitness Guides to destinations across Latin America, Asia, Australasia, North Africa, and Europe. He also writes for BBC Travel, Wanderlust, and Adventure.com, and talks about travel on TV, radio, and podcasts. www.shafikmeghji.com; @ShafikMeghji.

RACHEL MILLS

Rachel Mills lives by the seaside and works as a freelance travel writer, specializing in sustainable and responsible tourism in the UK, India, Canada, and New Zealand. She writes guidebooks for Rough Guides and DK Travel, as well as print and online articles for *The Telegraph*, *AFAR*, *Culture Trip*, and loveEXPLORING.com. @rachmillstravel.

NICK MOORE

Nick Moore is a freelance writer based on the Isle of Skye. He has worked as a music, sport, and lifestyle journalist for twenty years, covering events from the World Cup and Olympic Games, to Glastonbury festival, for publications such as *FourFourTwo, Q, Evening Standard,* and *The Independent.*

ROSALIND ORMISTON

Rosalind Ormiston is an historian of art, architecture, and design, working as a freelance arts and travel writer. Based in London, she is a member of the British Guild of Travel Writers contributing regular features for global, national, and regional media. Contributing to *500 Inspiring Walks* defines her insatiable interest in the cultural locations of artists, composers, and writers.

EMMA JANE PALIN

Emma Jane Palin is a multi-award-winning blogger and writer with a focus on creativity, travel, and culture. Based in Margate, Emma champions a lifestyle that involves taking note of the little things and exploring the world around her. From the Kent coastline to the streets of Morocco, she believes there is always something to be found via walking.

GARY PARKINSON

Gary Parkinson is a writer, editor, and walker whose work has appeared in *The Daily Telegraph, Daily Mail, Metro, FourFourTwo, The Athletic,* and *SportBible.* He is fascinated by people and place, and how the two interconnect; he recently wrote about a 75 mile circumnavigation of London that he did for charity. garyparkinsonmedia.com.

MICHAEL ROBINSON

Michael Robinson is a freelance writer and professional tourist guide. He has written extensively on the history of art and authored several travel titles. As a tourist guide, he has walked the length and breadth of England. His latest walking ventures include *The Thames Path* and *In the Footsteps of the Impressionists.*

KATH STATHERS

Kath Stathers is a London-based editor and writer, lead author of *The Bucket List* and author of *The Bucket List: Wild.* She has written travel articles for UK magazines and newspapers on subjects ranging from snowmobiles in Iceland, to treehouses in Spain and woodlands in Kent.

LINDY STIEBEL

Lindy Stiebel lives outside Durban, South Africa. She heads KZN Literary Tourism research project (www.literarytourism.co.za) in KwaZulu-Natal, her home province. She's a keen hiker having ticked Kilimanjaro, and the base camps of Mt. Everest and Annapurna off her bucket list. Now she prefers local walks which link writers and place for her tourism project, and 'slack packing' South African wilderness trails.

IMAGE CREDITS

Alamy: Andre Jenny 23 top; Arcaid Images 275; Barnabas Davoti 219 bottom; Bernard Philpot 165 bottom; BIOSPHOTO 256; Blaine Harrington III 49; Bob Jenkin 12; Carol Barrington 71; Carol Di Rienzo Cornwell 66 bottom; Claude Thibault 226 Bottom; Danita Delimont 23 bottom left, 93; David R. Frazier Photolibrary, Inc 57; Derry Robinson 162 top; Don Johnston_WC 16 bottom; Don Smetzer 61 bottom; Gary Benson 101; Gary Cook 326 bottom; GAUTIER Stephanie/SAGAPHOTO.COM 255 top, 255 bottom; Geofff Marshall 350; Gillian Pullinger 159 top; Greg Balfour Evans 181 top, 191 bottom; Grethe Ulgjell 321; Harry Harrison 188 bottom; Hemis 251 top and bottom; HP Canada 18; Ian Dagnall 236–237; Image Professionals GmbH 166 top, 296; imageBROKER 221 top, 338; itanistock 219 top; James Wheeler 13; Joe Mamer Photography 61 top; John D. Ivanko 45; Jon Arnold Images Ltd 118, 383 top; Keith Fergus 213 top and bottom; Lebrecht Music & Arts 171; Luca Barbieri 27; Luke Peters 233 bottom; M. Sobreira 106–107; Majority World CIC 125 bottom; mauritius images GmbH 119, 126; Michael Kemp 315 bottom; Nature Photographers Ltd 191 top; Neilson Abeel Jr 83 top; parkerphotography 166 bottom; Pat & Chuck Blackley 99; Peter Cripps 208; Peter Eastland 317; Peter Horree 80; Petr Bonek 308; Phillip Scalla 85 top left; Photononstop 28; Randy Duchaine 86; RayArt Graphics 175; Realimage 183 top; Renato Granieri 129 top; Richard Ellis 58 top right; Richard Levine 79; robertharding 184, 252, 332; S. Forster 371; Sajjad Nayan 361 top; Samantha Ohlsen 4–5; Sergi Reberedo 77; Sergio Nogueira 234; Simon Burt 145 top; Simon Dack 165 top; SPK 195; Stephen Saks Photography 23 bottom right; Stuart Pearce 113; TAO Images Limited 362; Unlisted Images, Inc. 331 top; Westend61 GmbH 221 bottom; Will Perrett 307 bottom; Wilmar Photography 331 bottom; yannick luthy 307 top; yvo 302–303; ZUMA Press, Inc. 63; Zvonimir Atletic 358.

Flickr: Jason Pratt 2.0 Generic (CC BY 2.0) 53.

Getty: © Kamrul Hasan 2010 361 bottom; AGF 117; ANDREAS SOLARO/AFP via Getty Images 293; cesarhgv 31; Chris Hill 143; Daniel Bendjy 41; David Corio/Redferns 328; David Schweitzer 16 top left; Design Pics/The Irish Image Collection 136 top; Education Images 51; Emilia Doer/EyeEm 299; Glen Allison 389; Heritage Images 22; Hulton Archive/Stringer 182; James Leynse 83 bottom; michaeljung 335; mstroz 58 bottom; Peeter Viisima 108; PIUS UTOMI EKPEI/AFP via Getty Images 318–319; PIUS UTOMI EKPEI/AFP via Getty Images 326 top; Popperfoto 206; Rune Hellestad - Corbis 100; Simon Casetta/EyeEm 286–287; STF/AFP via Getty Images 123; Sven Creutzmann/Mambo Photo 125 top; Thomas Slatin/500px 85 bottom; Tony Evans/Timelapse Library Ltd 216; Westend61 384.

Library of Congress: 138, 228, 294.

Public Domain: 32, 44, 48, 52, 70, 76, 104, 124, 128, 132, 137, 151, 158, 160, 164, 167, 192, 198, 201, 220, 223 bottom, 224, 238–239, 241 bottom, 254, 259 top, 262, 273, 298, 304, 342, 344, 346, 352, 367 bottom, 376, 388.

Shutterstock: AK-Media 231 top; Alastair Wallace 200 bottom; Alejo Miranda 114; Alex McIver Aerial 187 top; Alexandr Medvedkov 343 bottom; AlexelA 349; Andrew Mayovskyy 289 top; Andrey Bayda 8–9; Anourbi 161 bottom; Anton_Ivanov 105 top and bottom; ARTOUSS 325 bottom; Artur Bogacki 311; asiastock 176; ATGImages 211 bottom; Baylor de los Reyes 42; Boris Stroujko 284–285; Boris-B 277 top; Brian Blades 211 top; Caron Badkin 188 top; cge2010 313 top; Chanachai Saenghirun 373; ChandraSekhar 387; Charlesy 153; chrisdorney 205; Chrislofotos 193 top; Claudio Divizia 193 bottom; Colin D. Young 89; Colin Woods 20; Cortyn 325 top; cwales 149 top; db79 203 top; Deatonphotos 179 top; DeBusk Photography 58 top left; Deekshant Yadav 354 top; Diego Grandi 120 top; DmitrySerbin 386; dvlcom 140–141; E.J. Johnson Photography 102; Engel Ching 35; EQRoy 379 bottom; eugeniusro 263; Eva Bocek 130–131, 277 bottom; f11photo 122 top, 340–341, 368; Fotomicar 149 bottom; Frank Fell Media 15; Gary C. Tognoni 39; Gena Melendrez 226 top; Giusparta 363; gvictoria 129 bottom; Hamdan Yoshiba 337; Heather Pereira 84, 69 bottom; Helen Hotson 217 bottom; Horst Lieber 259 bottom, 272; Ian Crocker 374–375, 377 bottom; ian woolcock 181 bottom; ianmitchinson 136 bottom; Ivan Mateev 243 bottom; James Elkington 199; James Kirkikis 95; Javen 379 top; Jelle Tijsse Klasen 381; JeremyRichards 122 bottom; Jess Kraft 110–111; Joe Dunckley 161 top, 200 top; Jon Bilous 66 top, 94; Jonathan A. Mauer 55 top; kan_khampanya 278; Karin Bredenberg 315 top; Karin Jaehne 264; Kathryn Sullivan 322; Keith 316, 146; Ken Wolter 85 top right; Kevin Standage 156; LaMiaFotografia 267 top, 283; LesPalenik 19; LorenzoPeg 281 top; maria_t 98; marinafromvladimir 215; mark stephens photography 103; Martin Kemp 217 top; Mathias Berlin 133; Mauro Carli 291; Maykova Galina 343 top; Milosz Maslanka 223 top; MISHELLA 73 bottom; Mistervlad 271 top; MOdAMO 329 bottom; Mr Nai 207 top; Nadiia_foto 249 bottom; navarro raphael 260; Nicholas Floyd 24; Nikolay Sachkov 345 top; ninapavisic 305 bottom; onemu 367 top; Oscar Johns 155; Oxie99 267 bottom; Panwasin seemala 364–365; Patryk Kosmider 135; Paul Nash 145 bottom; Pete Stuart 203 bottom; Petr Kovalenkov 243 top, 245, 249 top; Phillip Roberts 169; PhotoFires 159 bottom; pisaphotography 289 bottom; pxl.store 75, 207 bottom; r.nagy 173, 231 bottom; Radomir Rezny 196; Rahul D'silva 357; Rhys Hafod 183 bottom; Rolf_52 69 top; rontav 214; Rosemarie Mosteller 97; Roy Harris 139; salajean 313 bottom; Sean Xu 10–11, 46–47; sebastianosecondi 246; Sergey Fedoskin 300–301; Sergey Rybin 345 bottom; sergioboccardo 6–7; Sheryl Watson 383 bottom; sixtyeightwest 33; skyfish 229 top; Songquan Deng 73 top; Stefano_Valeri 233 top; Stephen William Robinson 150; Steve Heap 162 bottom; steved_np3 187 bottom; Tayvay 329 top; timsimages.uk 377 top; Toniflap 121 bottom, 229 bottom; Travelbee Photography 268 bottom; travelview 36–37, 65; TTstudio 271 bottom; Vaclav Volrab 305 top; Val Thoermer 268 top; Valdis Skudre 179 bottom; Vishal_Thakur 353; Vladimir Grablev 55 bottom; Vladimir Mucibabic 295; Wangkun Jia 90 top and bottom; Yogesh_biebz 354 bottom; Yury Dmitrenko 225; zebra0209 241 top.

Wikimedia Commons: Agência Brasil CC BY 3.0 br 320; Alexander Williamson CC BY 2.0 202; Blaues Sofa CC BY 2.0 310; Bpldxb CC BY-SA 3.0 348; celest.ru CC BY-SA 3.0 347; German Federal Archives CC BY-SA 3.0 de 266; Joop van Bilsen/Anefo CC0 148; Nightscream CC BY 3.0 330;; Syrio CC BY-SA 3.0 281 bottom; [u:Eddaido] CC BY-SA 2.5 382.

While every effort has been made to credit photographers, The Bright Press would like to apologize should there have been any omissions or errors, and would be pleased to make the appropriate correction for future editions of the book.